MULTICULTURAL EDUCATION SERIES

James A. Banks, Series Editor

Frogs into Princes:
Writings on School Reform
LARRY CUBAN

Educating Citizens in a Multicultural Society,
SECOND EDITION
JAMES A. BANKS

Culture, Literacy, and Learning:
Taking Bloom in the Midst of the Whirlwind
CAROL D. LEE

Facing Accountability in Education:
Democracy and Equity at Risk
CHRISTINE E. SLEETER, ED.

Talkin Black Talk:
Language, Education, and Social Change
H. SAMY ALIM AND JOHN BAUGH, EDS.

Improving Access to Mathematics:
Diversity and Equity in the Classroom
NA'ILAH SUAD NASIR AND PAUL COBB, EDS.

"To Remain an Indian":
Lessons in Democracy from a Century of
Native American Education
K. TSIANINA LOMAWAIMA AND TERESA L. MCCARTY

Education Research in the Public Interest:
Social Justice, Action, and Policy
GLORIA LADSON-BILLINGS AND WILLIAM F. TATE, EDS.

Multicultural Strategies for Education and
Social Change: Carriers of the Torch in the
United States and South Africa
ARNETHA F. BALL

We Can't Teach What We Don't Know: White
Teachers, Multiracial Schools, SECOND EDITION
GARY R. HOWARD

Un-Standardizing Curriculum: Multicultural
Teaching in the Standards-Based Classroom
CHRISTINE E. SLEETER

Beyond the Big House: African American
Educators on Teacher Education
GLORIA LADSON-BILLINGS

Teaching and Learning in Two Languages:
Bilingualism and Schooling in the
United States
EUGENE E. GARCÍA

Improving Multicultural Education: Lessons
from the Intergroup Education Movement
CHERRY A. MCGEE BANKS

Education Programs for Improving Intergroup
Relations: Theory, Research, and Practice
WALTER G. STEPHAN AND W. PAUL VOGT, EDS.

Walking the Road: Race, Diversity, and Social
Justice in Teacher Education
MARILYN COCHRAN-SMITH

City Schools and the American Dream:
Reclaiming the Promise of Public Education
PEDRO A. NOGUERA

Thriving in the Multicultural Classroom:
Principles and Practices for Effective Teaching
MARY DILG

Educating Teachers for Diversity: Seeing with
a Cultural Eye
JACQUELINE JORDAN IRVINE

Teaching Democracy: Unity and Diversity in
Public Life
WALTER C. PARKER

The Making—and Remaking—of a
Multiculturalist
CARLOS E. CORTÉS

Transforming the Multicultural Education of
Teachers: Theory, Research, and Practice
MICHAEL VAVRUS

Learning to Teach for Social Justice
LINDA DARLING-HAMMOND, JENNIFER FRENCH, AND
SILVIA PALOMA GARCIA-LOPEZ, EDS.

Culture, Difference, and Power
CHRISTINE E. SLEETER

Learning and Not Learning English:
Latino Students in American Schools
GUADALUPE VALDÉS

Culturally Responsive Teaching: Theory,
Research, and Practice
GENEVA GAY

The Children Are Watching: How the Media
Teach About Diversity
CARLOS E. CORTÉS

continued

MULTICULTURAL EDUCATION SERIES, *continued*

Race and Culture in the Classroom:
Teaching and Learning Through
Multicultural Education

MARY DILG

The Light in Their Eyes: Creating
Multicultural Learning Communities

SONIA NIETO

Reducing Prejudice and Stereotyping in
Schools

WALTER STEPHAN

Multicultural Education, Transformative
Knowledge, and Action: Historical and
Contemporary Perspectives

JAMES A. BANKS, ED.

Frogs into Princes

Writings on School Reform

LARRY CUBAN

TEACHERS COLLEGE PRESS

Teachers College, Columbia University
New York and London

Permissions for Selections:
Chapter 1: "Teaching at Glenville," Presentation at the National Council for the Social Studies, Philadelphia, September 1962.
Chapter 2: Larry Cuban, "Teacher and Community," *Harvard Educational Review, 39*:2 (Spring 1969), pp. 253–272. Copyright © by the President and Fellows of Harvard College. All rights reserved.
Chapter 3: Larry Cuban, "Transforming the Frog into a Prince: Effective Schools Research, Policy, and Practice at the District Level," *Harvard Educational Review, 54*:2 (May 1984), pp. 129–151. Copyright © by the President and Fellows of Harvard College. All rights reserved.
Chapter 4: "The 'At-Risk' Label and the Problem of Urban School Reform," *Phi Delta Kappan,* June 1989, pp. 780–784, 799–801.
Chapter 5: "Reforming Again, Again, and Again," *Educational Researcher, 19*(1), 1990, pp. 3–13.
Chapter 6: "Urban School Leadership: Different in Kind and Degree," Institute for Educational Leadership, September 2001, p. 7.
Chapter 7: "Introduction," *How Teachers Taught* (New York: Teachers College Press, 1993).
Chapter 8: "Reflections on Two Decades of New Technologies in Classrooms" (Talk given at American Education Research Association, San Francisco, April 2006).
Chapter 9: "Hugging the Middle: Teaching in an Era of Testing and Accountability," *Education Policy Analysis Archives, 15*(1), from http://epaa.asu.edu/epaa/v15n1.

Published by Teachers College Press, 1234 Amsterdam Avenue, New York, NY 10027

Copyright © 2008 by Teachers College, Columbia University

Library of Congress Cataloging-in-Publication Data

Cuban, Larry.
    Frogs into princes : writings on school reform / Larry Cuban.
  p. cm. – (Multicultural education series)
    Includes bibliographical references and index.
    ISBN 978-0-8077-4859-6 (pbk. : alk. paper) –
    ISBN 978-0-8077-4860-2 (cloth : alk. paper)
    1. Educational change–United States. 2. Education and state–United States. 3. Education, Urban–United States. 4. Public schools–United States. I. Title. II. Series.
  LA217.C83 2008
  370.973–dc22   2007045678

ISBN 978-0-8077-4859-6 (paper)
ISBN 978-0-8077-4860-2 (cloth)

Printed on acid-free paper
Manufactured in the United States of America

15 14 13 12 11 10 09 08   8 7 6 5 4 3 2 1

Contents

Series Foreword *by James A. Banks*   vii

Acknowledgments   xi

Introduction   1

    Lessons Learned   5

    Selected Writings and Speeches   7

PART I: TEACHER AS REFORMER: AN INSIDER'S PERSPECTIVE

1. 1962—Teaching at Glenville   13

2. 1969—Teacher and Community   20

    Necessary Revisions in Teacher Education   23

    A Role Problem: Teacher or Social Worker?   32

    An Assessment of the Proposed Training Model   35

PART II: MOVING FROM AN INSIDER TO AN OUTSIDER PERSPECTIVE

3 1984—Transforming the Frog into a Prince: Effective Schools Research, Policy, and Practice at the District Level   41

    District Policies   45

    Implementation Strategies   50

    Unanticipated Consequences   61

4. 1989—The "At-Risk" Label and the Problem of Urban School Reform   70

    Framing the Problem   72

    The Case Against the Graded School   75

    Past Efforts to Redesign Schools   76

    The Difficulty of Redesign   77

    Incremental Change   79

5. 1990—Reforming Again, Again, and Again   85
    Classrooms: Teacher-Centered Instruction   86
    Curriculum: The Academic and the Practical   87
    Centralizing and Decentralizing Authority   89
    Why Do Reforms Appear Again and Again?   91
    A Rational Explanation for Recurring Reforms   91
    Value Conflicts: A Political Perspective   97
    Institutional Perspective   102
    Concluding Comments   105

6. 2001—Leadership for Student Learning:
    Urban School Leadership—Different in Kind and Degree   111
    Nationalizing Education Reform   111
    Learning from the Past   113
    Reforming Schools—The Current Agenda   115
    Dispelling Some Urban Myths   118
    An Initial Agenda for Action   122

    PART III: MERGED PERSPECTIVES
    IN REFORMING CLASSROOM PRACTICE

7. 1993—Introduction to *How Teachers Taught*   127
    Reforming Schools and Classrooms   129
    Explanations for Constancy and Change   140

8. 2006—Reflections on
    Two Decades of Computers in Classrooms   148
    Introduction   148
    1:1 Computing   149
    A Final Word   157

9. 2007—Hugging the Middle:
    Teaching in an Era of Testing and Accountability   159
    How Have Teachers Taught?   160
    How Are Teachers Teaching?   164
    A Follow-Up Study of *How Teachers Taught*   165
    Making Sense of Conflicting Evidence   180

10. Reflections on Urban School Reform   188

Index   197

About the Author   204

Series Foreword

The nation's deepening ethnic texture, interracial tension and conflict, and the increasing percentage of students who speak a first language other than English make multicultural education imperative in the 21st century. The U.S. Census (2007) estimates that people of color made up 28% of the nation's population in 2000, and predicts that they will make up 38% in 2025 and 50% in 2050.

American classrooms are experiencing the largest influx of immigrant students since the beginning of the 20th century. About a million immigrants are making the United States their home each year (Martin & Midgley, 2006). Almost four million legal immigrants settled in the United States between 2000 and 2004. Only 15% came from nations in Europe. Most (66%) came from Mexico or from nations in Asia, Latin America, Central America, and the Caribbean (U.S. Department of Homeland Security, 2004). A large but undetermined number of undocumented immigrants also enter the United States each year. In 2007, *The New York Times* estimated that there were 12 million illegal immigrants in the United States (*New York Times,* June 4, 2007, p. A22). The influence of an increasingly ethnically diverse population on U.S. schools, colleges, and universities is, and will continue to be, enormous.

Schools in the United States are characterized by rich ethnic, cultural, language, and religious diversity. U.S. schools are more diverse today than they have been since the early 1900s, when a flood of immigrants entered the United States from southern, central, and eastern Europe. In the 30-year period between 1973 and 2004, the percentage of students of color in U.S. public schools increased from 22% to 43%. If current trends continue, students of color might equal or exceed the percentage of White students in U.S. public schools within 1 or 2 decades. Students of color already exceed the number of White students in six states: California, Hawaii, Louisiana, Mississippi, New Mexico, and Texas (Dillon, 2006).

Language and religious diversity is also increasing among the U.S. student population. In 2000, about 20% of the school-aged population spoke a language at home other than English (U.S. Census Bureau, 2007). Harvard professor Diana L. Eck (2001) calls the United States the "most religiously diverse nation on earth" (p. 4). Islam is now the fastest-growing religion in the United States, as well as in several European nations, such as France and the United Kingdom (Cesari, 2004). Most teachers currently in the classroom and in teacher education programs are likely to have students from diverse ethnic, racial, language, and religious groups in their classrooms during their careers. This is true for both inner-city and suburban teachers.

An important goal of multicultural education is to improve race relations and to help all students acquire the knowledge, attitudes, and skills needed to participate in cross-cultural interactions and in personal, social, and civic action that will help make our nation more democratic and just. Consequently, multicultural education is as important for middle-class White suburban students as it is for students of color who live in the inner city. Multicultural education fosters the public good and the overarching goals of the commonwealth.

The major purpose of the *Multicultural Education Series* is to provide preservice educators, practicing educators, graduate students, scholars, and policymakers with an interrelated and comprehensive set of books that summarize and analyze important research, theory, and practice related to the education of ethnic, racial, cultural, and language groups in the United States, and the education of mainstream students about diversity. The books in the *Series* provide research, and theoretical and practical knowledge, about the behaviors and learning characteristics of students of color, language minority students, and low-income students. They also provide knowledge about ways to improve academic achievement and race relations in educational settings.

The definition of multicultural education in the *Handbook of Research on Multicultural Education* (Banks & Banks, 2004) is used in the *Series:* Multicultural education is "a field of study designed to increase educational equity for all students that incorporates, for this purpose, content, concepts, principles, theories, and paradigms from history, the social and behavioral sciences, and particularly from ethnic studies and women's studies" (p. xii). In the *Series,* as in the *Handbook,* multicultural education is considered a "metadiscipline."

The dimensions of multicultural education, developed by Banks (2004) and described in the *Handbook of Research on Multicultural Education,* provide the conceptual framework for the development of the publications in the *Series.* They are: *content integration, the knowledge construction process, prejudice reduction, an equity pedagogy,* and *an empowering school culture and social structure.* To implement multicultural education effectively, teachers and administrators must attend to each of these five dimensions of multicultural education. They should use content from diverse groups when teaching concepts and skills, help students to understand how knowledge in the various disciplines is constructed, help students to develop positive intergroup attitudes and behaviors, and modify their teaching strategies so that students from different racial, cultural, language, and social-class groups will experience equal educational opportunities. The total environment and culture of the school must also be transformed so that students from diverse groups will experience equal status in the culture and life of the school.

Although the five dimensions of multicultural education are highly interrelated, each requires deliberate attention and focus. Each publication in the *Series* focuses on one or more of the dimensions, although each book deals with all of them to some extent because of the highly interrelated characteristics of the dimensions.

In this engaging, incisive, and significant collection of studies and essays, Larry Cuban brings wisdom and insights gained from nearly 5 decades of thinking about and working in schools and in a distinguished school of education. His deep and contagious compassion for students, teachers, and administrators—and his commitment to educational equality for all of our nation's children, including its most neglected children and youth—is evident on every page of this skillfully crafted and compelling book. Cuban speaks truth to power and truth about the powerless. He describes how the current standards and accountability movement, which has been propelled by the No Child Left Behind Act, views schools as peas in a pod, obscures the tremendous diversity between middle-class suburban schools and low-income city schools, and pursues policies and practices that are detrimental to both.

Cuban argues convincingly that schools are deeply embedded within the contexts and cultures of their communities, and that the problems of inner-city schools cannot be solved without comprehensive reform strategies involving major efforts to eliminate poverty and racism within the larger society. Cuban points out that it is much more politically expedient and acceptable for leaders to blame schools for the nation's serious social and economic problems than it is to mobilize the political will and resources needed to bring about needed structural changes within society. In making this astute observation, Cuban makes it clear that schools and professional educators have an essential role to play in structural change, but that it is unrealistic and counterproductive to expect them to make these changes alone or to accept an undue share of the responsibility for change.

The apt title of this book, *Frogs into Princes: Writings on School Reform,* conveys its central message, that—unlike in *The Frog Prince,* in which the frog is magically transformed into a prince—school reform requires hard work, vision, money and resources, a grasp of its complexity, and a long-term commitment by district leaders to stay the course. Cuban marshals compelling evidence to support his arguments, maintains a "tempered optimism" that urban school reform can succeed after 45 years of involvement in educational reform, and offers empirically based and practical wisdom about ways to maximize the possibilities for successful school reform. Cuban provides important questions that school leaders should ask when engaged in school reform, and blends "an optimistic heart with a skeptical mind to cut through reformers' all too common pattern of overselling solutions . . . while under-estimating the influence of deeply embedded social, economic, political, and organizational structures" (p. 189, this volume).

This is a needed and timely book. Cuban, with the eye of a gifted anthropologist, a rich sociological imagination, and the skills of a seasoned historian, describes the harm that is done to students, teachers, administrators, and our democracy when reform designed to improve schools confuses standards with standardization, ignores the enormous diversity among schools, denies history, and perpetuates myths and lies that harm children. If heeded, Cuban's clarion call for school reform that is rooted in history, wisdom of practice, empirical data, and common sense will help our nation move closer to the ideals of justice and equality that it loudly proclaims around the world.

–James A. Banks

REFERENCES

Banks, J. A. (2004). Multicultural education: Historical development, dimensions, and practice. In J. A. Banks & C. A. M. Banks (Eds.), *Handbook of research on multicultural education* (2nd ed., pp. 3–29). San Francisco: Jossey-Bass.

Banks, J. A., & Banks, C. A. M. (Eds.). (2004). *Handbook of research on multicultural education* (2nd ed.). San Francisco: Jossey-Bass.

Cesari, J. (2004). *When Islam and democracy meet: Muslims in Europe and the United States.* New York: Pelgrave Macmillan.

Dillon, S. (2006, August 27). In schools across U.S., the melting pot overflows. *The New York Times*, pp. A7, A16.

Eck, D. L. (2001). *A new religious America: How a "Christian country" has become the world's most religiously diverse nation.* New York: HarperSanFrancisco.

Martin, P., & Midgley, E. (1999). Immigration to the United States. *Population Bulletin, 54*(2), 1–44. Washington, DC: Population Reference Bureau.

New York Times. (2007, June 4). Immigration sabotage [editorial], p. A22. Retrieved October 21, 2007, from http://www.nytimes.com/2007/06/04/opinion/04mon1.html?emc=etal

United States Census Bureau. (2007). *Statistical abstract of the United States* (126th ed.). Washington, DC: U. S. Government Printing Office.

United States Department of Homeland Security. (2004). *Yearbook of immigration statistics, 2004.* Washington, DC: Office of Immigration Statistics, Author. Retrieved September 6, 2006, from www.uscis.gov/graphics/shared/statistics/yearbook/Yearbook2004.pdf

Acknowledgments

No book is written alone. I had help from many friends and family.

Jim Banks asked me if I were interested in collecting my writings on urban school reform for a series that he edited. I was both flattered and touched by the request. It came, however, as I was finishing a book with a colleague. I felt all "booked out," so I asked for a few months to think about it. Once planted, of course, the seed of the book sprouted in my mind and I began thinking of the overall questions and framework I would use were I to gather selections I had written during nearly 50 years of work in schools. And this book slowly evolved in my mind.

By the time I had chosen the selections included here and written the Introduction and Reflections, I knew that I was too close to the manuscript and needed tough, fair-minded readers whom I trusted to tell me what needed to be done to improve the manuscript. After many years of writing, I know that to have friends and colleagues who can say what needs to be said is a precious gift more rare than rubies. I asked Gary Lichtenstein, Jane David, Herb Ware, Joel Westheimer, and Sondra Cuban to give the manuscript a careful reading. They did not disappoint me. While I winced at times as I read their comments, I knew that their suggestions were on the mark. So I thank them and relieve them of any responsibility for errors that appear in the pages ahead.

Finally, I want to acknowledge the debt I owe to my students, beginning in 1955, whom I taught at McKeesport Technical High School, Glenville High School, Cardozo High School, Roosevelt High School, Los Altos High School, Menlo-Atherton High School, and Stanford University School of Education. They have inspired me to keep learning and teaching. Thank you.

–Larry Cuban, August 2007

Introduction

Why write about reform?[1] A half-century ago when I began teaching history in a largely Black high school, my answer would have been anger toward top district administrators and national policymakers. My anger at these well-intentioned decisionmakers who promoted better teaching, innovative curriculum, school-wide cultural programs, and fancy equipment to lift minority students out of poverty came from the stark gap between what they said was supposed to happen in schools like mine, and what I experienced in my high school classroom.

I was a politically naive teacher in my early 20s, eager to push my unvarnished passion for teaching history onto urban students bored with traditional lectures and note-taking. As a classroom-bred reformer in Cleveland's Glenville High School, I invented new lessons and materials in what was then called Negro history. I thought then that the problem of disaffected students could be solved through delivering fascinating lessons that would hook them into learning. My success in engaging many students in studying the past emboldened me to think that the gap between what policymakers say and what teachers do could be closed by sharp, energetic teachers (yes, like me) creating and using new curriculum materials. Even though in 7 years of teaching at Glenville, I came to realize that I could not motivate all students and others were beyond my reach as a teacher, my solution to the problem of disengaged students was still creating "can't miss" history lessons.

After teaching at Glenville, I took a job as a master teacher in history in a federally funded project located in Cardozo High School in Washington, D.C. to train returned Peace Corps volunteers to teach in schools then euphemistically called "inner-city." I was eager to join those who wanted to reshape not only the classroom but also the school while helping the community. My initial anger at the disconnect between what policymakers claim and what happens in classrooms had moved me from a classroom-based curriculum reformer into a reform-minded teacher–educator helping novice teachers do what I did in creating new materials for supposedly unmotivated poor youth while working in the community. Now, the project funders framed the problem of urban students doing poorly in schools as not having enough well-trained and determined teachers who did more than just create engaging lessons. The solution to the problem was to have master teachers train recruits and have them learn the community's culture. Once trained, these Peace Corps returnees would become crackerjack teachers who could hook listless students through both creative lessons drawing from their knowledge of neighborhoods and personal relationships with students and their families. Thus, here was a teacher-driven, neighborhood-centered solution to the problem of low-performing students.

Yet teaching at Cardozo High School, and eventually directing the project that spanned four District of Columbia schools, opened my eyes about how politically and bureaucratically complicated it is to engage students and raise academic achievement in just one school. The intersection between a school and its community became concrete to me and other teachers as we worked in Cardozo neighborhoods. But it took 4 long years to convince the D.C. superintendent and school board that this program for recruiting and training returned Peace Corps men and women was not only a good idea but also a decided benefit to the entire system. The superintendent and board finally agreed to take over the program, re-naming it the Urban Teacher Corps, expanding it from recruiting and training 50 new teachers a year to over 100 annually.[2]

After this exhilarating but exhausting experience with a federally funded program, I returned to teaching history in another D.C. high school and to write about these experiences. After 2 years at Roosevelt High School, a top official in the district office invited me to head a new department aimed at revitalizing the district's teaching corps. I reported to the deputy superintendent of schools. I was again a reformer but now was located in district headquarters from which I worked closely with the superintendent and, through him, met frequently with school board members.

In coming to this post, the school board and superintendent had defined the problem of poor schools and low-performing students as one where teachers' capacity to learn content and skills was underdeveloped. The organizational solution, I convinced myself, was for the system to provide rigorous staff development for the entire teaching corps in the district. But school reform from that perch looked very different than when I was teaching in Cleveland, working at Cardozo High School with Peace Corps returnees, and teaching history in District of Columbia high school classrooms.[3]

After 2 years in the district office, however, I grew weary of seeing aggressive policies pushing system-wide changes get shot down time and again by headquarters' staff or get strangled in the fierce racial politics that governed the newly elected school board, mayor, and city council. I voluntarily returned to the classroom, "demoted without prejudice" my transfer notice read. Here I was, in my mid-30s, again a high school history teacher after serving in school and district administrative posts, again disappointed with–but not yet cynical about–a reform process that zigzagged erratically from the board of education to schools and, in some cases, even wandered into classrooms.

For nearly a decade, then, I had seen up close how the District of Columbia schools eagerly embraced reform after reform and proceeded to bury each one in bureaucratic channels or alter the policies so much as to become unrecognizable when they appeared at the classroom door. That smoldering anger I had felt toward policymakers and top administrators over the disconnect between reforms they endorsed publicly with rich rhetoric, the actions they took, and what happened in classrooms, arose again.

I had gone from being a youthful teacher whose concept of reform began and ended within the four walls of a classroom—change the teacher's pedagogy and content and students will learn—to a teacher–educator believing that the cure for the ills of urban schooling was a school-based teacher education program aimed at recruiting and training nontraditional novices to create sparkling lessons and work in the community. Yet that youthful teacher had come to learn that all of his efforts within a classroom still could not reach some students and, further, that even an innovative teacher education program in the District of Columbia can get entangled in system politics and bureaucracy or be dumped by one of the turnstile superintendents that went through its swinging doors. After nearly a decade in D.C. schools, classrooms, and the central office, my experiences had convinced me that system-wide problems needed system-wide solutions unimpeded by racial politics and bureaucrats protecting their turf. Maybe, I thought, I might be able to supply those solutions as a superintendent.

To become an urban superintendent, however, I had to get a Ph.D. So after returning to a university as a middle-aged graduate student with family in tow, I got a doctorate. After being turned down by 50 school boards—I had no experience as a superintendent—a reform-minded (and risk-taking) school board appointed me school chief in Arlington, a city of around 160,000 people at that time, just across the Potomac from Washington, D.C.

For 7 years I worked within a district becoming culturally diverse and smaller at the same time as test scores declined. The school board and I had defined the central problem as the public's loss of confidence in the district, never reversing the downward spiral in academic achievement as minority enrollments rose. Drawing from a strong tax base to operate schools and with close superintendent oversight of each school's performance toward five basic school board goals, we believed that steady pressure on schools wedded to ample support of teachers and principals would lift achievement and renew community confidence in its schools. That did happen for the elementary schools but less so for secondary schools.

Heading a complicated organization with multiple stakeholders inside and outside the system where political and organizational tradeoffs between prized values were standard procedure proved to be a powerful learning experience for me as a reformer. School board and superintendent policy initiatives aimed at making incremental changes in both school practices and the culture of the system stirred up fierce political struggles and volatile conflicts, particularly during two economic recessions. After a newly elected school board eager to reduce school spending wanted a school chief more in sync with their values than I was, I completed my contract and, after 7 years, departed for Stanford to teach and do research.

In those 7 years as superintendent, I learned that school reform didn't mean driving constantly in first gear if I and the school board wanted improved academic achievement for all students; I had to shift to fourth gear to consolidate earlier policy changes. Moreover, I learned the difference between problems that can be solved and unsolvable dilemmas that have to be well managed (more about these distinctions later).

In Arlington, I found out that reforms needed jump-starting in a system, but once initiated had to be prodded, elaborated, massaged, and adapted as they entered schools and were put into classroom practice. Yes, I did learn that problems of low achievement were intricately connected to what teachers did in their classrooms, how principals worked in their schools, what families and students brought with them to schools, how amply student services were funded, and how boards and superintendents finessed (or fouled up) the intersecting political, social, and economic interests of various stakeholders inside and outside the schools. Most of all, in leaving the superintendency and moving to academia, I became allergic to those who offered me fairy-tale solutions—kissing a frog to get a prince—to the problem of low-performing schools.

As a university professor for 2 decades, I have sought through my teaching and writing to improve schooling. I was a veteran practitioner who had framed and reframed the problem of disengaged students, tired teachers, and lousy academic achievement and sought, at first, classroom, then school, and finally system-wide solutions without ever losing sight of the importance of the teacher. I wanted deep changes in a district (and a community) but saw that byte-sized increments over time were necessary to achieve gigabyte reforms both inside and outside schools. This chastened reformer also saw that snappy reforms—particularly those applicable to schools and classrooms—were so highly contingent on savvy leadership and certain conditions being in place—particularly adequate funding—that when either shifted or were absent, a reform had a short, happy life and, poof, disappeared.

So I speak from direct experience as a practitioner–scholar who has tried to pin down the problems of poor schooling, convert policies into classroom practices, and fallen on his face numerous times in seeing reforms shrivel and disappear. I have thought and written about these experiences over nearly 5 decades. So after many stumbles, small victories, and outright failures, what have I learned generally about reform?

LESSONS LEARNED

The first thing I learned is the importance of framing the problem. I realized that how problems are framed and analyzed, especially in organizations, is often negotiated with others and is highly subjective.[4]

I discovered that organizations have two kinds of problems: tame and wicked. Tame problems are familiar situations facing both policymakers and practitioners, and for which they have a large repertoire of solutions. Tame problems often involve procedures (e.g., too much classroom time taken in collecting lunch money) and relationships (e.g., dropping a high school student because of too many absences). In most districts, policy manuals lay out step-by-step ways of dealing with routine problems. Seldom, however, do those policy manuals or repertoires deal with wicked problems.[5]

Wicked problems are ill-defined, ambiguous, and entangled situations packed with potential conflict. For policymakers, wicked problems arise when people compete for limited resources (e.g., since we cannot fund both the new phonics program and smaller class sizes for K–3, we will have to choose) and hold conflicting values (e.g., the superintendent believes that project-based and inquiry-driven ways of teaching will eventually lead to higher test scores, but the school board demands immediate results that require teachers to spend more instructional time preparing students for tests).

Unlike tame problems, wicked problems cannot be solved; they can only be managed. For this reason, I call them dilemmas. Dilemmas require anguished choices between competing, highly prized values that cannot be simultaneously or fully satisfied.

Consider the options facing small high school champions in districts with large comprehensive high schools. Decisionmakers have to wrestle with several competing values. How, for instance, do you break up a big high school into small autonomous learning communities and give parents choices of where to send their children, and still provide efficient school-wide services and retain traditional norms of behavior (e.g., sports, clubs, food service, disciplinary procedures, counselors)? Or consider the abiding dilemma over student test results: How do you raise state test scores high enough and soon enough to satisfy both supporters and critics of small high schools when growing such innovations is a long-term process yielding a variety of difficult-to-measure student outcomes going well beyond test scores?

Surely, tame problems can involve some degree of conflict. But dilemmas are far messier, less structured, and often intractable to routine solutions.

They are dilemmas rather than tame problems because, I discovered, organizational constraints make it impossible for any prized value to triumph. Every person, every organization operates under constraints of time, money, laws, cultural norms, and political assumptions that limit action at any one point in time. Faced with conflicting but highly desirable options, as a policymaker and practitioner I often constructed compromises—"good-enough bargains"—rather than neat, all-encompassing solutions.[6]

Think of a mouse negotiating a maze in search of Gouda and settling for cheddar. That is, when we cannot get the best, good enough is okay. I learned to "satisfice" in coping with dilemmas—that is, to satisfy, I had to sacrifice.[7] These good-enough bargains, however, to my surprise time and again, had to be renegotiated repeatedly as circumstances and people changed. That is why, more often than not, as a high school teacher, superintendent, and professor I ended up managing recurring dilemmas, not solving problems.

Yet it remains rare for policymakers, practitioners, researchers, and taxpayers to consider this simple distinction between problems and dilemmas. Too often the notion of intractable dilemmas is anathema to reform-minded policymakers and practitioners because the idea seemingly erodes hope and curtails efforts to improve schooling. Not for me. I came to accept the realities of unrelenting conflicts in reforming districts, schools, and classrooms without succumbing to despair or losing hope that better schooling of poor and minority children could happen.

I also learned an important lesson that, at the core of every school reform, is a solution (or compromise) hiding an idea, a belief, or a value. Many decisionmakers latch on to a reform, say, mayoral takeovers of big city districts, parental choice, one-to-one laptops in classrooms, or reorganizing middle schools into K–8 elementary schools. These buzz-creating, media-hyped reforms are policy shells that have buried within them a pearl of an idea (posing as a belief or value), fashioned to solve a perennial problem. Ideas, then (camouflaged as solutions), do matter when policymakers launch reforms and mobilize taxpayers, parents, and other constituencies to embrace the belief and value buried within the reforms.

If ideas matter, so does putting those ideas into practice. Even well-planned policy implementation trips over the unanticipated. Most policymakers, I also learned, see implementation as a technical process best handled by subordinates who can work out the details, write the regulations, and fix problems that arise. As a result, then, policymakers either fail to anticipate or ignore the practical, emotional, and political realities that sabotage an artfully crafted policy on its journey into the school and classroom. It is as if policymakers scramble to find glasses they think they lost without realizing that the "lost" glasses are perched on their noses.

If some reform-driven policies are ill conceived, that is one thing–after all, some reforms are simply bad ideas (e.g., paying teachers solely on the basis of their students' standardized achievement test scores). Other reform-driven policies, however, contain a few good ideas (e.g., No Child Left Behind), but decisionmakers fail to anticipate the inevitable value clashes and practical logistics that will occur when those policies enter schools. Of course, educational policymakers are not alone in underestimating the power or importance of considering the details of implementing policies–think of what occurred in Iraq between 2003 and 2008 or getting aid to Hurricane Katrina survivors in New Orleans. This myopia about on-the-ground implementation, I have learned, is what repeatedly (and shamefully) drives policymakers to grasp at fairy-tale solutions like kissing frogs to get princes.

So here is the story of a classroom-bred reformer defining and redefining the problem of student disengagement and low academic achievement in urban schools as he moves back and forth from the classroom to teacher education to administration and, finally, to academia. In short, my career in figuring out what goes on in urban schools and unraveling problems and dilemmas has moved from an insider–classroom teacher–to an outsider perspective–dispassionate, analytic observer who uses history to frame school reform policies–and finally to a friendly critic of urban school reform who merges both perspectives. Thus, the following selections begin and end in the classroom, for that is the crucible where any attempted national, state, and district reform of urban schools is tested by fire.

SELECTED WRITINGS AND SPEECHES

The nine selections capture both insider and outsider perspectives. Although tempted to update the language in these talks and articles, I resisted. Except for corrections in spelling and grammar, they appear in their original form. The two pieces in Part I, written in 1962 and 1969, both reveal and recast what occurred in schools where I worked. They reflect the passions of the insider railing at the stereotypes of urban schools and teaching, yet neither the talk nor the published article is despairing. Both offer hope to those who seek to repair and rebuild urban schools. In Part II, the 1984 and 1989 articles display the transition from insider to outsider perspective on urban school reform. In these pieces my voice is no longer that of the outraged teacher but that of an older, seasoned teacher and administrator who has come to understand the frustrations of that younger self after experiencing how district policymakers adopted policies, and who has seen these policies get mired in the political and organizational realities of community constituencies and bureaucratic layers. In these pieces, I arrive at a more systemic view of reform—systemic within the organizational framework of a district and systemic in the sense of the district being connected to larger social, political, and economic structures within a state and the larger nation. The policy-driven articles in Part II, written in 1990 and 2001, are less passionate, more rational, measured, and historical. The systemic outsider point of view is obvious.

The last three articles in Part III return the reader to the classroom. Here I embrace again the insider perspective of the experienced classroom teacher, but now the passions are tempered by considering the broader framework of school district and community—each shaped in part by state and national influences and functioning as political and organizational systems massaging reform as it works its way into or bypasses classrooms.

As I have reflected on my classroom, school, and district experiences, my thinking about urban school reform has gone from solely insider to solely outsider to a blend of the two in these final selections. Yet I have never lost sight of the hard-core realities of teachers being the infantry of reform regardless of what the generals pronounce. It is the classroom—independent of policy, rhetoric, and fairy-tale hype—where reform is played out between teachers and students. We must never lose sight of that.

NOTES

1. Rather than go through an extensive history of the concept of "reform" and its many uses in America over the past 4 centuries—recall that 17th-century immigrants to the east coast of North America were religious reformers—I offer a definition of reform anchored in institutions. Policy elites, social movement leaders, and individuals frame reforms as solutions to problems; these solutions (aka reforms) are deliberate, planned interventions to solve problems within and across religious, political, social, economic, and educational institutions.

2. In 1966, the U.S. Congress authorized the National Teacher Corps, basing it on the model we created at the Cardozo High School. I served on the advisory board for the National Teacher Corps. In 1981, President Ronald Reagan ended federal funding for the Teacher Corps. There is a similar punch line to the success story of the Urban Teacher Corps in the District of Columbia. In 1971, after 4 years of recruiting and training teachers in this school-based program, a new superintendent abolished the program.

3. I described and analyzed these District of Columbia experiences, particularly in the Cardozo project, in *To Make a Difference: Teaching in Inner City Schools* (New York: Free Press, 1970). Those experiences at Cardozo, in the District of Columbia bureaucracy, and as superintendent in Arlington are also described in *The Managerial Imperative: The Practice of Leadership* (Albany: State University of New York Press, 1988).

4. Much of this section on problems and dilemmas comes from my experience in the classroom and superintendency. I created materials for workshops enrolling teachers, administrators, and district policymakers when I was on the faculty at Stanford. See *How Do I Fix It? Finding Solutions and Managing Dilemmas, An Educator's Roadmap* (New York: Teachers College Press, 2001).

5. Richard Mason and Ian Mitroff distinguish between tame and wicked problems. See *Changing Strategic Planning Assumptions: Theory, Cases, and Techniques* (New York: John Wiley & Sons, 1981, pp. 10–13).

6. For constructing this view of dilemmas, I have used the following sources: Ann Berlak and Harold Berlak, *Dilemmas of Schooling* (London: Methuen, 1981); Michael Billig, Susan Condor, Derek Edwards, Mike Gane, David Middleton, and Alan Radley, *Ideological Dilemmas: A Social Psychology of Everyday Thinking* (Newbury Park, CA: Sage, 1988); Peter Elbow, "Embracing Contraries in the Teaching Process," *College English, 45*(4), 1983, pp. 327–339; Seymour Sarason, *The Culture of the School and the Problem of Change* (Englewood Cliffs, NJ: Prentice Hall, 1971); Magdalene Lampert, "How Do Teachers Manage to Teach? Perspectives on Problems in Practice," *Harvard Educational Review, 55*(2), 1985, pp. 178–194.

7. Herbert Simon coined the word *satisfice*. See *Models of Man* (New York: John Wiley, 1957, pp. 204–205).

PART I

TEACHER AS REFORMER: AN INSIDER'S PERSPECTIVE

CHAPTER 1

1962—Teaching at Glenville

Let me begin by giving you a brief profile of the high school I teach in:

It is 56 years old.
There are 1,500 students of which 99% are Negro.
The faculty is 60% White with an annual turnover of 20%–30%.
The median I.Q. of the school is 91.5.
As far as absenteeism, last year our school had the highest rate.
Our dropout rate, in the last school year, was 14% of the student
    body.

Possibly from this sketchy description one would categorize my school as "culturally deprived," a "slum school," or just plain "disadvantaged." To be fair, however, I should complete the profile.

About 35% of our student body is in a college preparatory course and approximately 80% of those go on to college. From the June, 1961, graduating class, our school had the highest percentage attending college from all Cleveland schools. The director of the National Scholarship Service and Fund for Negro Students cited our school for producing more capable college students for that organization than any other school in the country.

The point I'm driving at should be clear. We have become too bogged down in a pseudoscientific jargon where pat labels substitute for thinking and stereotypes cripple effective teaching, in short, a semantic rigor mortis. My school is *not* culturally deprived, culturally disadvantaged, or any other euphemism. It *is* overcrowded, understaffed, and decrepit, however. It is also a complex school having a whole range of problems, some of which are peculiar to its environs and others, problems common to all schools. So enough of stereotyping by ethnic group, neighborhood, or other crude measuring sticks. Instead, let's try to cut through the maze of ambiguous and fuzzy phraseology and reach the core of the issue: the individual student.

However, immediately we are confronted by another label: culturally deprived. Unfortunately, here is a class-biased word that has a snobbish ring to it implying that all that is good in life is of the middle class. It conjures up the picture of a school attempting an Operation Bootstrap of museum trips, operas, plays, etc. Also inferred is that the lower-class value structure has nothing to offer. I prefer to substitute for this label a phrase that is far more precise and, I feel, strikes at the root of the problem facing all of us: educationally disadvantaged. It is more exact for it encompasses the children who come from a blighted home and community environment and the able students who have suffered from overcrowded, understaffed schools and substandard teaching. Opportunities, in short, have passed them by. To anyone acquainted with the current literature upon this subject, a profile of an educationally disadvantaged child is all too familiar.

a. He may be an immigrant.
b. He is often from an unstable home environment.
c. His neighborhood is in various stages of decay.
d. He brings to the school half-learned skills of reading and writing.
e. Most probably, he has a negative attitude toward education.

Now what can be done for such an individual? The answer, I would suggest, lies in the realm of the function of the school and the quality of the teacher. Not original, I agree, but I care not for gimmicks or tricks of the trade. I'm interested not in the superficial, but the fundamental.

First, let's turn to the job of the school. The school must assume some of the responsibilities usually left to the parents. It must offer social services as part of the educational program. Finally, and most important, it must offer a quality education program geared to the needs and capacities of the students—a difficult combination, indeed.

In Cleveland, as part of the Great Cities Improvement Project (GCIP), the Ford Foundation had allocated $300,000 to the Board of Education to discover techniques that are operable for the educationally disadvantaged. Thus far, the Hough Project has been limited to one junior high and six elementary schools. After 3 years, according to the directors of the program, the following techniques have been used and found successful in Addison Junior High School.

1. Home Visitor Program—Ten teachers who are not social workers or truant officers, but human links between the school and home. Seeking out parents to explain the educational program, they are also trained to spot cases of deprivation and poor relations between parents and children.
2. School-within-a-school—There is a guidance counselor each for the 7th, 8th, and 9th grades. There is also an assistant principal at each level. Two home visitors complete the personnel for each year. The idea is that the pupils will more readily identify

with the administration of each grade, thereby creating a greater stability within the grade.

3. Concept of readiness for the junior high—It has been found that some entering 7th graders cannot make the adjustment from the rigid, self-contained atmosphere of the elementary school. For these students, the self-contained class on the junior high level is retained with some modifications, thereby affording a transitional period of adjustment.
4. Remedial and Developmental Reading Program.
5. Saturday morning cultural trips.
6. Group guidance in study halls—With character building as the motif, movies and lectures by well-known personalities emphasize such traits as courtesy, ambition, and how to get a job.
7. Broader health program.
8. Orientation of faculty—Week-long contact by new teachers with the Hough community, its churches, homes, and streets. Experienced teachers are brought in to acquaint beginners with some of the problems they will probably confront. These, then, are the contributions of the Hough Project. Much as efforts in other cities have demonstrated, the Project points to one of the approaches that must be employed to deal with the educationally disadvantaged child.

Now, let us turn to the other point that I wish to make; that is, the quality of the teacher. First, permit me to be candid. My underlying assumption is that, at present, the teacher in an urban school which is predominately Negro or any disadvantaged minority has—by and large—educationally short-changed his students. Of course, this should not be construed as a blanket condemnation of teachers in urban schools. There are many dedicated, committed teachers who form the core of some faculties in urban schools. The point is that it is only a core and not anywhere near the number needed to cope with the problems at hand.

I would argue that teachers, in schools of the type we are discussing, are captives of the very stereotypes and misconceptions that befog the intelligence of the public when it comes to urban schools. Such stereotypes as "urban schools are places where little teaching takes place; all is discipline and one must always be on his guard." Or the stereotype that "the teaching that does take place is abysmally elementary, seldom intellectually stimulating." Or "the Negro student cannot achieve as well as the White student" (I heard this one from one of my former colleagues at lunch). And finally, the misconception that the home and community surroundings are so impoverished that the school can do little to surmount these environmental conditions. Some teachers believe all to be true; others accept only portions. Unfortunately, this forms the intellectual baggage of too many teachers, and their methods reflect these underlying beliefs.

What happens next is known to many as the self-fulfilling prophecy. Briefly, this is viewing a life situation inaccurately, then acting upon these inaccurate assumptions, thereby making the falsely defined situation come true. Examples are legion. A "run" on a bank in the 1930s was a classic case. The initial assumption, eventually disproved, was that the banks were unstable—ready to fold—and the depositors' money would be lost. Acting upon this incorrect belief, thousands of depositors panicked, besieged the banks, and demanded their savings. This behavior led to the collapse of the bank and the initial false belief became an actuality. Or, more appropriately to our day, two countries believe that war is inevitable, arm themselves, and thereby create the conditions necessary for war, and the explosion takes place.

Applied to the school situation, the self-fulfilling prophecy operates in a similar manner.

A teacher, our stereotyper—if you will—might reason like this.

> Why challenge the students with a stimulating assignment if they won't be able to do the work? Why spend extra time in preparing lessons if they won't appreciate it? Why read their papers and write comments on them? They're either copied or have nothing to say. Might as well have them read from the book in class; that will take up some time. Maybe I'll have them do the questions at the end of the chapter—that should keep them busy. No sense in starting a discussion; whatever they have to say isn't worth much anyway.

Is it any wonder that given these "methods" (step into some classes in city schools and it will be seen that this is no caricature), the responses of the students would be less than brilliant. If treated as a dull student, why not act dull. Students who are unmotivated, uninspired, and underestimated respond by being apathetic or by provoking trouble in and out of class. As a result, the students who are stereotyped as to behavior and ability, are taught by methods that conform to those stereotypes, and the logical outcome—though inaccurate—substantiates the original premises in the mind of the teacher. The self-fulfilling prophecy has come full circle.

The teachers who fall prey to this, more often than not, are the ones who couldn't adjust to the change in school population from White middle class to Negro lower-middle and lower class. Other teachers, fresh from college, are full of idealism compounded from courses that look upon American education as suburban education.

Both types of teachers are woefully unprepared for the situation that confronts them. The idealism of one ferments into apathetic disillusionment while the maladjustment of the other is converted into griping and a counting of days toward transfer or retirement. As a result, these teachers march into the classroom with the stereotypes mentioned previously, compounded by hearsay, sensational newspaper exposés of schools, and visions of *Blackboard Jungle*. It is not difficult to predict that their methods will reflect these premises.

Yet, in all honesty, everyone should realize that we do have a large share of undereducated students who bring to their classes half-learned rudimentary skills, a negative attitude toward learning, and a huge reservoir of frustrations built upon demotions, repeated grades, and failing marks. Something must be done about these students, since the high number of dropouts are recruited from their ranks. James Conant's *Slums and Suburbs* has alerted the public to the explosive quality of this problem. But there is a significantly large portion of average and above-average students in these urban schools who are being cheated of an education by a vicious, pessimistic determinism and stereotyped, narrow-minded thinking on the part of teachers and administrators.

This is the burden of my paper. The educationally disadvantaged have been deprived of opportunities that should have been given to them, and a measure of responsibility for this rests squarely on the shoulders of the classroom teacher.

A question should be raised. What proof is there that schools which are predominately Negro, for instance, have students capable of achieving academic excellence? Ample proof is there. My own school, mentioned earlier, is only one example of many. The Cleveland Board of Education has recognized this fact by stipulating that every high school must institute an academically talented program for its capable students. The Higher Horizons Program has unquestionably demonstrated that the talent is there. It is only a matter of developing it. But–and this is an important but–even if the evidence is scanty (and it is not!), what justification is there to label groups as dull, prone to cause trouble, inferior, etc.? Do teachers merely give lip service to the fundamental concept in American education of treating the student as an individual? These very same teachers would complain vociferously if their own children were not treated as individuals with different capacities and personalities by other teachers. Yet, in their own classes, they show a singular lack of perception and concern for the individual student. Harsh words? Possibly. But harsh words are needed to pull administrators and teachers out of the paralyzing torpor which annually squelches the potential of tens of thousands of students across the country.

I hope the point I'm driving at has emerged. The teacher himself—his assumptions and training—determines the course he offers. He can elevate or depress aspirations; broaden or narrow the horizons of his students.

A few words of my few efforts to break free from the clichés and stereotypes that victimize our profession. At Glenville High School, in my American and world history classes, two objectives underlie my teaching: to present to the best of my ability a quality course, and to integrate into the study of history the important part that minority groups have played in the past—in particular the role of the Negro.

Take for example my American History course. Rather than the "Columbus to Korean War gotta finish the text" approach, I'll begin with a unit on colonial civilization and the class will treat in depth such topics as the colonial economy, society, and religion. One of the topics is the origin of slavery. Here, such relevant subjects as west African civilizations, the slave trade, and the origin of racial prejudice are discussed, much to the interest of the students. But neither the text nor I are the only sources of information. Therefore, reading lists for each unit are drawn up with a heavy reliance upon selected primary and secondary sources. Student comments testify to their broadened knowledge. Many are surprised to discover that all Negroes were not slaves or that the stigma of slavery was not attached to the Negro until the end of the 17th century. Discussions revolve around the fundamental question of why the Negro was enslaved. Was racial prejudice brought to the New World by settlers or was it a product of the continued interaction between Negroes and Whites?

Such questions inevitably provoke interesting and relevant discussions. And so on through the course, as each unit is dealt with, the role of the Negro in that particular period is not only mentioned but discussed.

In world history class, the two fundamental objectives mentioned before still remain foremost. The first half of the semester is spent on the ancient civilizations. Here again, selected readings are used. Herodotus, Thucydides, Plutarch, and Plato become familiar names. The readings are carefully chosen beforehand, and certainly some of the students have a difficult time with some of the selections; nevertheless, they are read and discussed. In fact, one of the better class discussions grew out of one of Plato's Dialogues, the "Apology." To many of the students, Socrates then became a flesh and blood figure. The two classes which are under this reading plan, after being given the choice of returning to a text, overwhelmingly chose to continue the readings.

I'd like to think that this is a step in the right direction toward broadening the intellectual horizons of my students and offering to them a quality course that will stand up under criticism.

How shall I end? With a ringing declamation calling all people with a social conscience to heed the message? No, since eloquent rhetoric to date has not been as effective as one would wish it to be. Instead, I'll end on a note of hopefulness tinged with some pessimism. Pessimism because of the immensity of the problem confronting us now, of the intellectual and environmental curtains that remain to be pierced. With the current trend of urban areas becoming increasingly non-White, the number of educationally disadvantaged will multiply even further. Here is a human resource that needs development as assuredly as our finest Peace Corps endeavors overseas. Finally, my hopefulness stems from the growing sensitivity in many areas of the country to the needs of a group that must receive the same kind of education that others receive—an education that teaches them how to learn, and that gives them the intellectual discipline and depth of understanding that will enable them to meet new conditions as they arise. Let's sincerely hope that this will be achieved.

CHAPTER 2

1969—Teacher and Community

Waves of protest and change dash against the schoolhouse door. Decentralization, community schools, experimental programs, boycotts, and freedom schools testify to the buffeting that teachers and administrators have received over the past few years. Indignantly, they ask: Who do the schools belong to? And the question, just as indignantly, is hurled back: Yes, who *do* the schools belong to?

Although the specific issues of control and power have recently emerged in low-income areas, voicelessness and a general lack of participation sum up the inner-city community's traditional role in the affairs of the school. Unsurprisingly, relationships between the poor and their schools have been hostile and abrasive. Mistaken perceptions help explain such imperfect relationships. Inside the school, too many teachers and principals see the community and its inhabitants as deprived and depraved. Outside the school, any teacher or principal who has taken the time to meet and to speak with parents knows that the poor have high aspirations (although sociologists would remind us that these hopes are unrealistic) and a strong but eroding faith in the dollars and mobility that public education promises.

We have, then, on the one hand, parents who are serious about the education of their children and, on the other hand, schoolmen who believe that parents and community are hostile to their efforts. As others have pointed out, the gap between community and school may be the result of class, color, or value conflicts. No doubt such explanations have validity, and evidence can be marshaled to support each of them. But none of these explanations attacks the myth of professionalism, one of the deeper problems that has become both a cause and effect of that distance between home and school.

By myth I mean the belief that schoolmen know precisely how kids must be taught, how they should learn, and what their "true" nature is. Certainty, not inquiry, defines that belief. According to one popular analogy, teachers and principals know so much more than parents about instruction, curriculum, and scheduling that to expect intelligent questions and helpful suggestions from parents would be as unprofessional as for a doctor to ask a cancer patient for his opinion on whether chemotherapy or cobalt treatment should be used. The analogy, of course, is ridiculous. Information is not wisdom. And any teacher who has maintained his honesty will tell you how much he doesn't know. The helplessness and frustration of teachers in answering questions about motivation, the learning process, and behavior are well known to informed observers. Diagnosis and prescription in inner-city schools remain, at best, a seat-of-the-pants operation.

Frantically trying to establish professionalism and to prevent parental interference, educators have let loose a smoke screen of scientific jargon which obscures rather than clarifies issues. Only in the past decade, thanks to the civil rights and Black movements, has the smoke screen lifted to reveal schoolmen trying to cover up their professional nakedness by blaming parents for low reading and achievement scores. Thus, "professionalism" has been a code word for keeping parents at arm's length, for resisting the development of any meaningful face-to-face contact between school and parent and between teacher and community. Because schoolmen react negatively to inquiries about performance of youngsters, teachers, or the school, no personal relationships with the broad spectrum of the community can materialize.

More face-to-face and sustained contacts between school staff and community in dealing with children could bring a humaneness to community relations that is obviously missing. Bringing community people into the schools as paid aides is one possibility. Another is hiring community workers as part of the faculty. Joint planning between community leaders and schoolmen is yet another possibility. None of these, however, deal with the greater need to expand the vision of teachers to see that their role requires active involvement with parents and participation in community life. Unless that is done, the simple infusion of paraprofessionals and community coordinators will result only in more intramural squabbling.

Even if the current intense movement for local control and community participation succeeds in establishing autonomous fiefdoms, it will still have to confront the same problem of how to get school people interested and concerned about the children. Hiring dedicated people and firing hacks will help, but ultimately, even a locally controlled board will discover that despite all its autonomy and power, teachers may not be willing to look outward toward the community—teachers may not believe that it is their job to be concerned about how parents feel about the schools. This is possible, and my guess is that it is probable. The thrust for local control springs both from dissatisfaction with school performance (although grassroots polls have yet to uncover a majority of local residents in favor of community-run schools) and from a strong desire for political control of a very vulnerable institution. But unless these motives for control are accompanied by a commitment to restructure the role of teachers and increase the time available to them for work in the community, there will be no guarantee that professionals in community-operated schools will be more responsive to parents and community than they are in conventionally operated schools.

And time is essential. Currently, teachers don't have time to do anything well. About 90% of a teacher's day is spent in giving out, explaining, and summarizing information for groups of students. In most public schools there are five to seven contact periods with kids each day. Visit a school between 2 and 3 o'clock if you want to see a tableau of pooped teachers and exhausted kids clock-watching together. In addition to the impossible instructional load, there are the familiar money-collecting chores, extracurricular activities, record-keeping, and other clerical trivia.

If teachers are to become effective, they must be given time to play three extremely important roles: instructor, curriculum material developer, and liaison with the community. This tripartite role recognizes the fact that a teacher makes three crucial kinds of decisions every day: in the classroom, he decides what to teach and how to teach it, and in the community, he decides how a variety of influences can help his students benefit from education.

Consider instructional decisions first. If the class load were reduced to one-third or one-half of what it is now, teachers—with additional training—could expand instruction as never before. With more time available, more experiments with class groupings could be performed—more analysis of teacher and student talk, and more individual diagnosis and prescription for students could take place. Instruction need not be exclusively explaining, telling, and summarizing. In the area of curriculum decisions, the teacher is now either preempted by district- or school-wide course, text, and test prescriptions, or forced to scrounge bits of time in the summer or after school to improvise his own materials. In the teaching model proposed here, however, the teacher would have a third of his time free to create diverse materials for each of his classes. Without such a restructuring, the piety of individualizing instruction will remain just that. Reams of curriculum materials are essential for individualizing classroom work, and the teacher who knows his students and their communities firsthand would be the logical person to produce these materials. Of great importance to both instructional and curriculum decisions is the fact that teachers with a reduced class load would have time to read and think. They could learn how to see themselves, their students, and the act of teaching in ways that encourage inquiry and analysis and personal growth, ways that the traditional instructional role foreclosed.

Time also must be made for the teacher to familiarize himself with the individual student and the community—the third facet of his tripartite role. Because this facet is both complicated and controversial, the remainder of this paper will deal with the teacher and the community. Simply stated, effective teaching is intimately related to how well a teacher knows his charges and the nature of their surroundings. To be effective, teachers must get out of their fortresses and into the neighborhood. They must work with youngsters in nonauthoritarian settings. They must get to know people in the community. Even though teaching is more than instruction, contact with kids and community must be made if for no other reason (and there are others) than to improve the quality of instruction.

Improving instruction begins with the perceptions of a teacher before he sets foot in the classroom. If a teacher does not have realistic and humane relationships with parents and children outside of school, his perceptions will continue to be shaped by TV, newspapers, social science formulas, and fear. And if the media do not get him, the school will. The teacher culture of a school socializes new members with folk beliefs and attitudes toward students, the system, and one's self as well as any tribal group.

Thus the relationships that a teacher can establish with students and parents inside and outside the school setting, more than any abstract sociological data, will create that personal base of information from which a teacher can make critical decisions about instruction and curriculum. More important is what such information and experience can do to perceptions. Except for the bigot, a teacher who knows the community through individuals can sort out assumptions and attitudes about the poor and test them against flesh-and-blood evidence. For some, initial beliefs may be confirmed; face-to-face contact might even produce a negative reaction. My hunch, however, is that most teachers, given a comprehensive and supervised experience in learning about themselves and the community, will come to see the poor as they are: a diverse group of human beings who have learned to survive on a marginal income. I don't think teachers, Black or White, who profess interest in working with the "disadvantaged" can understand this unless they can sit down comfortably and have a beer with a man who is trying to raise five kids on the wages of a short-order cook. For "professional" reasons, then, it is imperative that teachers reexamine fundamental assumptions about the poor, assumptions that have been proved to influence the achievement of children—and reexamine them through individual contacts.

NECESSARY REVISIONS IN TEACHER EDUCATION

Imagining a better relationship between teacher and community, where gaps in lifestyles can be transcended by a sensitivity to differences and a common concern for better education, is one thing; bringing it about is another. Teachers are trained by institutions that all too often sharpen differences and build calluses rather than sensitivities. Where the need is greatest—preparing teachers equipped with the knowledge and skills to work with students in low-income communities—the response from universities has been the weakest.

Some institutions have tried to meet such criticism by creating 5th-year or master of arts in teaching programs. Other universities, after putting their fingers to the wind, have set up small experimental programs under ambitious assistant professors and waited until federal funds expired. The easiest way to check out these efforts is to compare the style and content of these programs with conventional undergraduate teacher-training efforts. Many urban universities that participate at the graduate level in innovative programs for preparation of inner-city teachers continue to offer undergraduate students traditional courses in methods and content divorced from any meaningful and sustained involvement in the public schools which are, in some cases, only a few blocks away.

The federal government, unfortunately, hasn't gone far enough in unlocking universities from their middle-class, suburban bias. The National Defense Education Act Title XI (now under the Education Professions Development Act) poured millions of dollars into higher education, subsidizing MAT programs, undergraduate tuition for prospective teachers, and summer institutes for tens of thousands of experienced teachers. To put it crudely, the federal government has given money to many of the very institutions, and in some cases to the same faculties, that have failed to prepare teachers adequately in the first place. I see nothing wrong with colleges getting a second crack at trying to improve themselves, but after 4 years of evaluating proposals submitted to the Office of Education for funds, I see little progress in teacher-education institutions from their traditional position toward a firm commitment to preparing teachers for schools where the need is greatest.

There is no doubt in my mind that universities must fundamentally change their teacher-education programs, because the problem is much deeper than merely cranking out more teachers for urban schools; numbers are of less importance than the quality of the training. The question, as always, is change toward what?

Basically, I see a teacher-education model that is firmly rooted in day-to-day human experiences in inner-city schools and communities, enriched by university support. Let me hasten to add that the general model I have in mind has many variations. The thrust, however, is to shift the center of gravity from the university to the classroom and community.

The model contains four basic components. First, an enormous body of knowledge on child growth, the learning process, urban sociology, ethnic history, race relations, and languages of the city must be assimilated. Second, the process of reevaluation of personal attitudes and the development of increased self-awareness must begin. Third, classroom and community must be the crucible of training where this knowledge, skill, and self-awareness have an opportunity to be applied, modified, and further created. Last, competent supervision from practitioners, academicians, and community residents who are involved in schools must be always accessible to trainees.

Baldly stated, the model appears on paper no different from what many educators would point to in their programs. However, a comparison of a number of basic elements in both kinds of training will demonstrate that there are fundamental differences (see Table 2.1). The comparison, by the way, was made by a professor of education, former dean of a large midwestern school of education, and sympathetic critic of teacher training.

This comparison is not with a straw man, either. Ask teachers about their training; other than salary, no issue is more guaranteed to anger inner-city teachers than the irrelevant professional education courses they took. Educators will point out to angry teachers that changes are afoot in the university; the model described here is being implemented on a growing scale, many would say. Perhaps the forms are, but seldom the substance.

Our model tries to narrow the gap between word and deed, to mesh the rhetoric of teacher-education programs with the reality. Consider what some well-intentioned people and programs say and do. When the importance of children's discovering concepts for themselves is stressed repeatedly through lectures, there is an obvious inconsistency. When the importance of knowing your students well so that wise instructional decisions can be made is matched against the professor's office hours of 2:00 to 3:00 on Friday, there is another inconsistency. When professors talk of the importance of getting involved in the community and knowing its dynamics, yet members of the community are never seen on the campus and students take only occasional "field trips," again there is an inconsistency. And when the great value of public school teaching is continually verbalized by people who never teach kids, future teachers correctly sense deep hypocrisy.

These inconsistencies are forms of nonverbal communication, and, as in any classroom, they tell undergraduates and graduates much more about the integrity of the professor and the particular program than lecture-hall pieties or professorial publications ever can. Action and behavior carry far more weight than words. The model suggested here does not guarantee that hypocrisy will disappear from teacher education. But emphasis upon experience and performance, and concern for effective classroom instruction, supervision, and community involvement, make it at least *possible* that a wholeness of word and deed can occur. And that is critical to the success of any program.

Another advantage to this model is its elasticity. To have validity for teacher education, a model must have application to all training experiences from a 2-year course at a junior college leading to an associate of arts degree for teacher assistants, to 5th-year MAT programs, and to systematic staff-development programs for career teachers. From pre-service to inservice, the model should be both flexible and effective. But like any model it will be effective only if the people who execute it are committed to an

TABLE 2.1. Comparing Models of Teacher Preparation

	Proposed Model	**Traditional Teacher-Education Programs**
Control	Centered in school system with cooperation of university.	Centered in colleges with cooperation from school system.
Location	Primarily in inner-city schools with commuting to universities.	Primarily on campus with students commuting to local schools.
Approach	Practical, inductive, and inquiring–with trainees relating theory to teaching as they work with youngsters in classrooms and community.	Academic, deductive, and didactic– with prospective teachers first learning about teaching vicariously through listening to lectures, reading books, and observing others teach.
Orientation	Specifically to prepare teachers for work with inner-city students and schools.	Generally to teach pedagogical theory and prepare teachers for work in White, middle-class, suburban schools.
Sequence	Professional and academic content is related to clinical experience through group and individual study and personal investigation.	Professional content is treated in formal courses such as history and philosophy of education, educational psychology, methods of teaching–prior to actual clinical experience.
Clinical Experience		
a. Responsibility	Real–trainees can have responsibility for individuals, small groups, and classes.	Artificial–relationship is that of a viewing observer and assisting teacher throughout.
b. Supervision	From competent teachers, academicians who also teach, and community residents.	From college staff members who may be years out of touch with actual teaching in elementary or secondary schools and who may never have taught inner-city students.
c. Instructional Materials	After training, materials prepared by trainees for inner-city students.	Usually selected by supervising teacher from commercial products.
d. Methods of Teaching	Trained in inductive and deductive approaches in line with the needs and interests of students.	Modeled after those employed by supervising teacher or prescribed by college supervisor–with patterns often in conflict.

From Lindley Stiles et al., "Cardozo Project in Urban Teaching: Evaluation and Recommendations," February, 1967, pp. 13–15 (Mimeographed).

experience-based approach. Such commitment implies a redefinition of what course work is, what expertise is, and a conscious recognition that insights produced by involvement in the classroom are as valid and have as much integrity as those produced by scholarly investigation.

The model of training suggested here—not a new one by any means—will not only prepare teachers for the tripartite role laid out earlier, but will also immerse a teacher in the community in such a way that his experiences will inevitably help shape his decisionmaking roles in instruction and in the development of curriculum materials.

At this point it is well to ask what community activities teachers could engage in, provided they have the time and training. Again, the available guidelines come from scattered programs such as the Teacher Corps, a handful of specially funded university efforts, and occasional Title I and III programs. The following excerpts come from reports submitted to me from 1965 to 1967 when I directed the Cardozo Project in Urban Teaching (presently the Urban Teacher Corps, funded entirely by the District of Columbia schools). The selections are meant to be illustrative, not definitive or prescriptive.

Intern teachers had been introduced to the neighborhoods of the three schools where they taught by spending one afternoon a week for 3 months in local centers of the city's antipoverty program. (Remember that teachers were also teaching half of each day and were expected to create lessons and units for their classes.) A staff member at each neighborhood center was responsible for orienting the teachers to the particular activities and services of the center and filling them in generally on the anatomy and dynamics of the community as they understood it. Employment, social services, housing, and youth work became familiar—at least at the intellectual level—to the teachers. Each teacher developed a fund of information that ultimately proved useful in making referrals and suggestions to parents. After 3 months of this, the teachers were asked to develop some community involvement of their own choice. Individually or in teams, the teachers spent the rest of the school year and the following summer working on what interested them.

Performance was uneven. Besides all the difficulties encountered in beginning something without guidelines to follow, there were problems of personality, attitude, and purpose. I discovered, for example, that those teachers who were having a rough time with their classes were reticent about contacting students or families. When classroom success increased, the desire to meet with students rose correspondingly. Also, some teachers felt most strongly that visits with students and their families smacked of social work and this, they felt, was to be avoided. Others wanted to make these contacts but simply could not find the emotional energy or master the skills to cross the barriers of race and class that, in their minds, loomed ominously.

These reasons may explain why some of the teachers did not immediately plunge into the lives of their students, but other interns found fewer obstacles and did actively and systematically commit themselves to a program of contacts with students and community. Let me quote some excerpts from their reports:

Elementary intern: female, White

I met Gregory's father in the lot behind Florida Avenue Church after work. Mainly I was looking into Gregory's complaint that his brother ran home before him and ate the lunch their father had prepared for them before he went to work. We had to laugh when his brother appeared, as he was smaller and Gregory said that the tale wasn't true. Then his father got angry and told Gregory that there would be no more of this. He also asked me if I knew why the boys' names hadn't appeared on the lunch list, for he had signed at the beginning of school. All we could do for this was wait it out and give him an extra lunch whenever there was one. His name and his brother's are now on the lunch list.

Renaldo and his mother had not come to receive his report card, and as she was at home and not working, I went to see her with her son. Their apartment, although in a run-down building, was furnished well with separate beds for each child, and was clean and warm. The mother has three small children, and as such couldn't come to school. We talked about Renaldo's marks which included a few "no progresses" and the rest "some progresses." The mother was very upset about the minuses in self-control and independence and cooperation. She said that because Renaldo was almost 9 years old they would try talking to him about things that needed improvement, but that if this didn't work she would have to turn to a spanking, and she told him that she would give him one after school for the disobedience he had been showing. Renaldo accepted this seriously, not as something that was handed out daily, which is not the case with other children's parents I visited. He then read for his mother and I showed her how to help him sound out words or get them by other clues. She reads well and wants definite direction in working with this at home. As none of the schoolbooks can be taken home, I have been borrowing some from the library and letting some children use them. But I need to check up on the bookmobile service, as I don't know of a library close to the homes of most of my children; in fact, I know there isn't one.

In the meantime I took two books out of the Mount Pleasant branch for Renaldo, and will have him take them home with beginning book report pages to work on. He definitely needs to do all the reading he can, and it's great that he's got definite help at home, and a family that is interested in what he's doing.

High school intern: female, White

Mary is one of my 11th grade students with very low reading ability. After noticing the great trouble she was having with reading and any written work, I spoke to her after school. The next day I went with her to see the counselor. We arranged her program to include a reading class second period. This "extra attention" seems to have helped her to be more interested in the class. Her attendance has improved.

Sylvia is a 20-year-old 11th grade student. She is married and has a baby. We have become quite friendly after a few long talks. She is having internal troubles and has been going to the clinic regularly. The doctor is suggesting a serious operation which will make her unable to have children. She does not seem to understand the trouble completely nor is she aware of the alternatives. I spoke with her before her last visit, encouraging her to bring her husband again to the *clinic* and get all the information possible.

Sylvia is constantly asking me for extra work. I have given her a long-term assignment on children's literature. She will be analyzing children's books and learning (from a text on children's literature of mine) the importance of reading for children.

She is also interested in part-time work. I suggested that she fill out an application from Mr. _____. She tried to get a job here at the project office, but her typing is not yet good enough. I suggested she go to the large department stores (in person rather than phoning) to inquire about "Christmas rush" jobs.

I have met three times with my 11th grade girls. They have decided that our discussion group can do a variety of things. Therefore, they would like it to be a "club." The girls are now thinking of a name for the group. We meet at Roger's apartment after school. I have found that this informal setting (drinking Cokes, sitting on the floor) is a great aid in helping the girls speak more freely. We have discussed sex at some length. From these talks, I am now more aware of their fear of sex, their sense of shame, and their curiosity. I hope to bring in a speaker to discuss birth control with the group. This is the area in which the girls show the most interest and naiveté. Although eager to talk about the subject, none of the girls connects birth control with their lives, present or future!

We have also discussed "boy–girl" problems and social life at Cardozo. I was interested to learn that social life for these girls does not revolve around school. The boys they date are from their neighborhood or church group. They feel the social life at Cardozo is greatly lacking and the boys are immature.

High school intern: male, White

Took student to "walk through" application forms and red tape at public library central office. National Youth Corps student felt overwhelmed by bureaucracy. Asked me to drive him down to office and help him fill out forms. Only took 3 hours.

Worked with consumer education office of a neighborhood poverty project. Planned section of unit with civics class on "where to shop—how to shop?" Planning field trip and class visit for lecture.

Working with Neighborhood Legal Service to prepare material for unit on criminal law. Planning to coordinate material with law reform and education unit. Also had speaker, young lawyer, talk to class about credit law. Also explained Neighborhood Legal Service to student.

Officer from No. 13 visited class. Students were well-prepared with questions based on personal "brushes" with law. Criticized No. 10 community relations. Police officer visibly upset. After bell, students surrounded visitor with many questions. Asked him to return. Officer replied he would enjoy to make return visit.

High school intern: male, White

Recently a teacher from a neighboring suburban school called the office to inquire into the possibilities of doing some sort of combined class in history. The school was Walt Whitman High School located in an all White middle-class community. We felt that our aim was to have students communicate on a level of understanding that they are not able to do as adults because of many deeply rooted feelings. In short, as these students worded it, "We want to learn more about each other."

In the early stages, four of my students and four from Walt Whitman met for some planning sessions. We went to their school to observe other history classes, and also for the discussion about what we were going to do together. At first, the air was thick with tension, but it soon dissipated into profound discussion about the project's possibilities. As was stated, the kids set as their theme, "To Learn More About Each Other," which we think is a good one.

After two of these sessions, we agreed that a subtle approach to civil rights would be of interest to both schools. It was felt that many of the White students would be expecting a discussion of civil rights and would automatically reject it. Instead, we chose to take a historical approach, and really get to the root of the problem, beginning with a unit on slavery.

The slavery unit would last approximately 2 weeks, and we would meet twice; one time at Cardozo and one time at Whitman. The students, particularly those from Cardozo, felt that the first session should be held here at Cardozo, since "The Negroes are always coming to the Whites with their problems, and it might be better for the Whites to feel a bit of the responsibility and obligation, by finding themselves in a minority situation." The conclusion of the unit on slavery would be made at Whitman with both classes meeting together to summarize what had been discussed in the unit, or what had been learned in the unit.

The most interesting lesson for me came when we were returning home from school in my car, and one of my students mentioned what a surprise it was to her, "to find that teachers were human." It was also mentioned how little we knew about each other, and I confess that this was true for me.

Elementary intern: female, Black

I visited the home of Jacqueline where she lives with her parents and seven brothers and sisters. I went there early in the afternoon; and found her mother washing with a wringer washer in the kitchen. One of the boys was on the dilapidated couch in the living room, covered with a blanket. He was unable to attend school that day because he had torn his pants, and his mother had misplaced her needle. There was a preschool child present and a baby of a neighbor, whom the mother watched during the day.

The mother was pleased that I visited her, and explained that she never went out because she was nervous. The house was a two-story frame row house and was crumbling with decay. There were clothes lying about in every room. It was a cool day, but the small kerosene stove warmed the living room. She explained that she had been living there 4 years and her only complaint was its lack of closets.

I spoke to her about Jacqueline, who is an attractive and responsive child. She was pleased and said that she wished that all of her children would always be so. She said, however, that she was worried because her 14-year-old son had been missing for 3 weeks, and that neither the police nor school officials could find him. She seemed, though uneducated, to be intelligent in her conversation about her children and her hopes for them. The visit ended pleasantly as we talked about the latest episode of one TV soap opera. I told her that if I could be of assistance to her to let me know through Jacqueline.

How nice it would have been to record success stories, happy endings, and startling results. There were a few, but only of a minor variety. These teachers were inexperienced, forced to play their roles by ear, constantly keeping their fingers crossed. But they did get out of the classroom with students and meet parents and neighbors on a face-to-face basis. In doing so, they discovered the diversity of poor people, reexamined many of their basic assumptions about race and class, and probably realized the complexity of teaching in inner-city schools. They began to see the meaning of ghetto life more clearly than they ever could using only textbooks or lectures. The process of seeing kids as individuals improved so that a name in a class took on a face, parents, friends, and a home. The myriad decisions about instruction and curriculum materials and the simple conversational give-and-take that is so important to youngsters began to take on a deeper meaning. In other words, teachers' personal knowledge of children, their neighborhoods, and their parents spilled over to affect how teachers began to relate to students informally, and how they decided what should be taught and how it should be taught. The community can be an effective teacher.

A ROLE PROBLEM: TEACHER OR SOCIAL WORKER?

With community involvement, teachers are confronted with the serious question of identity: Am I a teacher or a social worker? This question has paralyzed and frustrated earlier efforts at cracking the narrowly conceived role of the teacher. Unresolved, the question of identity numbs activity and shrinks imagination. Is the teacher supposed to be a teacher first, who gets involved in the community through students and parents; that is, should involvement be an extension of the classroom? Or should the teacher see himself as a high-powered social worker who hangs his hat in the classroom, but spends his energies and time in the streets?

Over this question, a sort of schizophrenia split apart our intern teachers continually. It wasn't enough to caution them that a double vision was necessary—one eye on the classroom, the other on the neighborhood. Such advice was worthless, often resulting in myopia toward one or the other.

It took me some time to figure out what the real issue is. Basically, it is the question: Do the roles of teacher and community worker conflict? Can the demand that teachers work closely with parents and children in the community through home visits and involvement in neighborhood action centers turn them into a new breed of social workers, perhaps subverting their function as teachers? More specifically, if a teacher organizes a rent strike in a neighborhood tenement, does he compromise his role as a classroom teacher? The answer to all three questions, I feel, is yes.

I see the role of the teacher in the community as analogous to that of the public health worker whose ticket into the home is health care. The worker has a service to deliver. Most of it is delivered in the clinic or school; some of it is delivered in the home. These sites must reinforce one another. His chief concern, however, is to improve the health of individuals and the family. He should not see his job as one where he organizes community action on political issues, nor should he encourage adjustment to unhealthy conditions.

Similarly, the teacher has a service to deliver—the craftsmanship of learning, unperfected but still useful. His clients are students. Most of the delivery occurs in the school, but a significant portion must be extended into the homes and community if the service is to be effective. It is necessary for the parent to see the teacher as someone who does, indeed, have some skills to offer and is not just another well-intentioned individual who is bent on "organizing" the community. Activities such as establishing a study center in someone's home and helping a parent run it, or giving concrete skills and suggestions to the parents of James and Deborah to help them improve in school, can be of great benefit to individuals and community.

As the teacher functions as a middleman linking up people with services and building relationships with individuals, confidence in that teacher will grow. As long as the community involvement is seen as an extension of the classroom with the kids as the focus of all activities, then there should be little danger of a conflict of roles. On the other hand, if a teacher organizes a rent strike or urges students to boycott a school, he seriously undercuts his role as a classroom teacher. In the classroom, where critical thinking and inquiry are supposed to develop and be practiced, advocacy is counterproductive. Parents must have confidence in their teachers not to manipulate their children for certain ends, no matter how socially desirable those ends appear at the moment. The classroom is where questioning, skepticism, and analysis properly belong; advocacy generates a thrust toward dogmatism and indoctrination. Parental and even student confidence will erode if teachers behave as doctrinaire militants rather than open-minded inquirers.

The distinction I draw between the roles of social reformer and effective teacher in and out of the classroom should not be construed as meaning that the teacher mindlessly protects the status quo or sits idly by as events flit past. Teachers should protest when they feel that their rights, as well as students' rights, are abused. Teachers should, if they choose, march and demonstrate. The distinction is between a teacher's seeing his prime responsibility as organizing and agitating or as developing the intellects and emotions of students. The two are not mutually exclusive, but I feel that responsibility to kids is stretched beyond meaning when teachers spend most of their time and energy "organizing" the community and reforming institutions. That job has to be done, but not by teachers operating as activists in the classroom.

Protest and effective teaching are not entirely separate categories, however. A teacher I know proved that well. He taught in an all-Black high school. At the peak of the peace movement in the winter of 1967, his students (labeled "slow learners" by the administration) wanted to know more about the issues in Vietnam. For the most part, as a poll of students and the neighboring community indicated, President Johnson's policies received wide support; nevertheless, there was a large number of dissatisfied responses.

The class began a study of Vietnam. Other students, on their lunch period, occasionally stopped in to listen, especially when the disagreement got vigorous. Some of these drop-ins asked for an after-school discussion for those students interested in exploring the topic further. One of these drop-ins, a member of a militant Black Students Union, offered to get a friend who was active in the National Black Anti-Draft Union. The teacher agreed and invited the chairman of the social studies department to present the government position, a position which he wholeheartedly supported.

Since all outside speakers have to be finally cleared by the main office, the teacher went to the principal with the required information on the activist. The principal, upon hearing the name of the student who had suggested the speaker, reading the biography of the proposed speaker, and seeing the format of the program, refused to let the teacher invite the speaker on the ground that he might provoke violence among the students. Two weeks earlier, there had been an anti-Vietnam rally outside another school and the police had been called. The teacher explained patiently that it was to be a debate, not a rally, that both points of view were to be presented, and that the meeting would be in a classroom holding about 40 people, not in the auditorium or stadium. No, again. When the teacher asked if the principal had always had such little faith in students, there was only a scowl and a curt dismissal.

The teacher and the student got together and considered the risks if they held the meeting in the face of the principal's refusal. The teacher was without tenure and the student was a senior; retaliation could be simple and swift, but they agreed to continue their plans. The teacher arranged another meeting with the principal, wrote out a summary of the first session, and indicated that this meeting was the first step in the union grievance procedure. He informed the principal that she had deprived him of the right to invite a speaker who, in his judgment, would help students interested in discussing a crucial issue clarify different points of view. Her reply was that he could not do what he wanted.

The grievance was filed. The principal and her assistant harassed the student by calling in his parents and speaking to teachers about his classroom performance. The social studies chairman was asked not to participate in the debate, but he refused. The teacher received cold stares, but nothing happened to him. The union representative in the school arranged another meeting between the teacher and the administrator, at which he urged the principal to reconsider her decision on the speaker because he felt that the teacher had a good case and the grievance would definitely result in a hearing. After a great deal of talk, she finally agreed to withdraw her objections.

The after-school meeting drew about 60 kids, 15 teachers, and 2 parents. It was held in a crowded and stuffy room. The positions presented by the anti-war speaker and the chairman of the social studies department produced a noisy exchange of opinion lasting well over 2 hours. Afterwards, the teacher discovered that the principal had assigned a teacher to take photos of all teachers in attendance and that she had gotten the precinct captain to assign two patrolmen outside the doors of the classroom.

This incident illustrates the distinction I am trying to make between the roles of social reformer and effective teacher. The source of the teacher's protest was an intrinsic part of the teaching act; what the teacher stood for was inquiry, not mindless avoidance of controversy. While the incident was school-based, similar situations arise in the community. Teachers must judge whether their efforts to make changes will or will not compromise their effectiveness in the classroom.

Some distinctions can be made, some cannot. There remains a fuzzy area of teaching and community involvement that awaits a more precise clarification. Nevertheless, unless the teacher sees his community participation as an extension of what he does in the classroom, he will increasingly view the school and community as isolates bearing little relationship to one another.

AN ASSESSMENT OF THE PROPOSED TRAINING MODEL

In conclusion, a rough estimate of the benefits and costs of training teachers for a tripartite role including community involvement might be helpful in furthering discussion about the implications of such training for pre- and in-service education both on campus and in the school. I hasten to add that I use no standard deviations or regression analyses in reaching my conclusions; at the same time, I hope there is nothing anti-intellectual in my posture. If there is a "gee whiz" ring to my comments, it is because I simply have a strong faith in the validity of insights derived from experiences in classrooms. With that caveat, let me lay out what I feel were some of the important byproducts of this model.

Such training experiences quickly stripped away the romanticism that some teachers had about poor children, about their freedom as professionals, and about being instant agents of change. Others were successfully persuaded that training for the tripartite role in an inner-city school prepares an individual with the skills to teach in any situation. We also found that training teachers through total immersion under close supervision functioned as a rigorous deselection process, thereby lessening the number of teachers who drift and settle into the classroom. The training model produced a high percentage of effective teachers. Aside from all of these considerations, there were other substantial benefits.

First, because time was made available to teachers, the model captured the intellectual stimulation inherent in the teaching act and married it to an active, continuing, personal involvement with adults and children. The mindless sterility and mechanical operations common to most teaching were missing, according to most observers and participants. Intellectual isolation and random superficial contacts with students and adults have dehumanized teachers; perhaps this model caught a glimpse of a future that excited teachers. As important as money is, unless intellectual growth and meaningful personal interaction are structural components of teaching, all the talk about making teaching an attractive career will remain, in Eliza Doolittle's phrase, just words, words, words. The training model readily brought candidates into teaching; how much more might the pull be to keep people in teaching if the training model were the expected way that teachers operated?

A second benefit is that the model stipulated teacher involvement in the community where none existed before. Once his identity as a teacher was established, an intern could learn from the community how 18 hours of each student's day were spent outside the classroom. This knowledge could only enrich instruction and curriculum. In return, the teacher could establish relationships with significant people in his student's life and could, if called upon, render certain services. The abyss between school and community will hardly be bridged by threats or the creation of petty bureaucracies; it could be bridged by a network of humane relationships created by teachers reaching out beyond the classroom door. I saw it happen many times.

The third benefit came as the center of gravity in teacher training shifted from the university to the Washington school system. The dimensions of the training program were established by the schools, and universities accredited the training offered in those schools. In short, the needs of the teachers and the thrust of the training model set the priorities, not the universities. I count this as a benefit and a demonstration of the growing awareness among schoolmen that universities are not far enough ahead in formulating and attacking educational problems to justify their training monopoly. Many people are reevaluating the colonial relationship that has developed over the years between academe and schoolhouse. The public schools are beginning to see that training of teachers is properly a school responsibility, yet the university is needed if imaginative and resourceful training is to take place. Some school systems have gone so far as to train BA graduates lacking certification; some want university assistance and have negotiated guidelines within which the schools and colleges cooperate in joint appointments, investment of resources, training centers, and the like. The training model can help to shove universities, many of which want to move but don't know how, off dead center.

There were costs as well as benefits. Probably the most severe and frustrating was what happened to those trained in the model after they moved into conventional teacher roles. Exceedingly high percentages (80%–90%) of the trainees moved into the classroom after completing the internship. Within a year or two, after carrying a full load of classes, being required to complete much clerical trivia, and being assigned extra duties, the teachers inevitably built up an explosive frustration which forced some to leave the classroom. The head of steam resulted, understandably, because the new teachers didn't have the schedule flexibility, political maneuverability, freedom, and resources to do what they had been trained to do. Most former interns taught 2 to 3 years and, like an incandescent bulb, burned out. While the majority has stayed in the field of education, moving into leadership positions, only a minority has remained in the classroom for 5 years.

University educators can point eagerly to such a retention record and argue that a training program which performs no better than the notorious conventional teacher-training institutions can hardly be held up as an effective model. Superficially, they are correct. The teachers now coming from schools of education are not trained for the reality of the classroom, especially that of the inner city. They exit like lemmings. And, from appearances, the products of the tripartite training model seem no better. The major difference, however, is that the university-trained people couldn't survive in the classroom because they weren't prepared for the teaching reality; our interns not only mastered the survival skills, but transcended mere survival to become creative teachers. They opted for other jobs dealing with inner-city schools because the structural reality of the school kept them from performing in a way consistent with their training.

It would be a great mistake to tally cost only in classroom teachers lost because that would ignore the many individuals who moved into training and administrative positions, those that started curriculum-reform programs, and the few who completed graduate work to return in leadership positions in urban school systems. Also, it would ignore the momentum for change that subtly builds up in those school systems that have employed similar training models. Often, entry training in this model leads to pressure for more services for experienced teachers; closed doors are wedged open for the first time when teachers and administrators demand "staff development" like "those interns" are getting. In a word, if cost is totaled up only on a body-count basis, then much of value in the final reckoning of a model's worth may be lost.

This discussion leaves ample room for criticism: no hard data, too much passionate pushing, uncritical acceptance of first-hand experiences, selective omission of evidence. I don't doubt that such criticisms have merit, but before any eager critics plunge too deeply into such a task, they should ask themselves what their own alternatives are. To deal with the Biafra of bitterness unleashed by the struggle over community control, and to upgrade instruction and curriculum, can we do less than reform the teacher's role? Educational reform, at least meaningful and sustained reform, must involve such a role change. Anything short of that is arguing about angels on the head of a pin. And I, for one, am tired of medieval debates.

PART II

MOVING FROM AN INSIDER TO AN OUTSIDER PERSPECTIVE

1984—Transforming the Frog into a Prince: Effective Schools Research, Policy, and Practice at the District Level

The current California superintendent of public instruction, who campaigned on a platform celebrating a Norman Rockwell view of schooling, appointed as his deputy a savvy school superintendent who had developed one of the few systematic efforts in the state to implement the findings drawn from the effective schools research. In 1981 Alaska Governor Jay Hammond appointed the Task Force on Effective Schools that recommended practices drawn from the same body of research for all of the state's schools. According to a recent report from the Education Commission of the States, eight other states have established specific projects anchored in this literature. New York City, Seattle, Pittsburgh, Milwaukee, Atlanta, and a score of other cities across the country have installed programs to improve the academic performance of students. *Consumer Reports, Parents* magazine, and other popular journals feature articles entitled "How Effective Are Your Schools?" or "What Makes a Good School?" Television programs portray "miracle worker" Marva Collins in her private preparatory school in Chicago as an exemplar of a first-rate teacher who has established an effective school. Finally, in the surest test of popularity, the vocabulary of effective schools research has entered the daily language of school administrators: high expectations, instructional leadership, an orderly environment, a positive climate, and consensus over academic goals echo a trendy jargon.[1]

The initial impulse behind the study of effective schools was to improve student academic performance in low-income, largely minority schools. Researchers in the mid- and late-1970s reacted sharply to the 1966 Coleman Report and its progeny, which suggested that teachers and administrators could have little effect on student achievement. One line of research was based on the linkage between teaching practices and improved test scores—the coin of the realm à la Coleman; another utilized investigations of schools which, given their ethnic and socioeconomic mix of students, produced unexpectedly high test score gains. Both strands of research identified teacher behaviors and school practices that intersected neatly with practitioner wisdom on what schools should do to become academically productive. Like the Coleman Report, these studies measured productivity in terms of performance on standardized tests in math and reading.[2]

Practitioners seldom wait for researchers to signal that school improvement can move forward. Nor have the substantial methodological problems in the research findings on effective schools halted policymakers from converting them into programs. With a quick look over their shoulders at a skeptical public, many school boards and superintendents, believing that tightly coupled organizations can affect children's academic performance, have moved quickly to implement the growing body of research on effective schools. I do not suggest that policies anchored more in faith than in statistical significance are misguided. On the contrary, I suggest that policies are forged in a crucible that mixes political realities, practitioner wisdom, technical expertise, and whatever can be extracted from research. The task is difficult because the empirical research seldom reveals clear causal links to policy, and yet practitioners, who must make decisions every day, are anxious to locate those decisions in a technical rationality.

When I served as superintendent of schools in Arlington, Virginia, I initiated, with the school board's blessing, a six-school improvement project. These schools contained predominantly minority children, many of them from low-income families, who scored in the bottom quartile of the district's elementary schools. Lacking designs drawn from research or a tested formula that had worked elsewhere, we invited leading advocates of effective schools to speak to teachers and administrators. Resources, modest to be sure, were set aside to purchase staff time and materials for the six schools. Enthusiasm ran high, and my successor continues to support the project. Standardized test scores in the six schools have risen. The school board has identified the improvement of elementary schools as a top priority for 1983–1984 and has expanded the mission of the district team of specialists to encompass all elementary schools in the county.

My own experience and that of other superintendents and school boards who have converted research findings into mandates for improvement informs the following policy discussion. I will concentrate on those policy issues with which local boards and superintendents must wrestle when transforming research findings into different administrative and teaching behaviors. Unlike the way things happen in fairy tales, school reform requires more than a kiss to convert a frog into a stunning prince. Furthermore, productive schooling entails more than raising test scores.

I want to be clear that, as a practitioner–academic for over a quarter-century, I share the commitment of colleagues across the nation to improve schooling. While these words may ring defensively, I write them to separate myself from the predictable academic challenge to the premature or selective implementation of any body of research findings. The familiar pattern of a burst of romance followed by frustration and disappointment appears to describe the trajectory of the effective schools enthusiasm (I was about to write the word "movement"). Notwithstanding recent criticism of the research methods, findings, and efforts to create effective schools, there is much to be learned from an analysis of what has and has not been done, and from what is and is not known about local district initiatives in building effective schools. Experience outstrips research in districts implementing improvement policies; this experience may offer clues to other local policymakers and furnish promising leads for researchers to pursue. Several problems with the research on and practices in effective schools have already become evident.[3]

No one knows how to grow effective schools. None of the richly detailed descriptions of high performers can serve as a blueprint for teachers, principals, or superintendents who seek to improve academic achievement. Constructing a positive, enduring school climate remains beyond the planner's pen. Telling principals what to say and do in order to boost teacher expectations of students or to renovate a marginal faculty into one with esprit de corps remains beyond the current expertise of superintendents or professors. Road signs exist, but no maps are yet for sale.

There is no agreement on definitions. Half a dozen methodologically identical studies have produced as many different definitions of effectiveness. The concept of "climate" varies with the researcher and practitioner using it. Moreover, some feel that the term "leadership" is undefinable. "Instructional leadership," for some, resides in the role of principal; for others, in the teaching staff; and for others, it is beyond definition.

The concept of effectiveness is too narrow. Tied narrowly to test scores in lower-order math and reading skills, school effectiveness research and programs ignore many skills, habits, and attitudes beyond the reach of paper-and-pencil tests. Educators and parents prize other outcomes of schooling that transcend current definitions of effectiveness. Some of these outcomes are sharing, learning to make decisions, developing self-esteem, higher-order thinking skills, and a sense of the aesthetic.

Research methodologies leave much to be desired. Most of the studies
   that use multiple variables and regression models of analysis have
   failed to control for school populations and previous history of
   achievement. Similarly, because most studies sample a district
   at one point in time, determining which variables cause which
   outcomes is a thorny, if not impossible, obstacle. Do high faculty
   expectations produce higher student achievement, for example,
   or are the higher staff expectations a result of improved student
   test scores? Furthermore, because many studies are done on
   "outliers," generalizing to the larger population of mainstream
   sites is, at best, risky.
Most research has been limited to elementary schools. With a few
   exceptions, effective schools research has occurred in the
   lower elementary grades. Junior and senior high schools are
   organizationally and culturally quite different from the lower
   grades.
Little attention is directed to the role of district leadership.
   Concentration upon the local school site and the principal's
   leadership dominates the research. This implicitly ignores the
   pivotal role that school boards and superintendents play in
   mobilizing limited resources, giving legitimacy to a reform effort
   and the crucial interplay between central office and school site
   that can spell the difference between implementation success and
   failure. Few researchers stress the fact that schools are nested in
   larger organizations that constrain while permitting choice at the
   local site. Thus, the broader perspective of district administrators
   is often missing from the researchers' analyses of effective
   schools. Yet, with all of these shortcomings in the literature on
   high-performing schools, school boards have mandated and
   superintendents have implemented effective school programs,
   showing little concern for the danger of converting correlations
   into policies.

   Coincident with the rising interest in these research findings has been
a gradual trend toward higher test scores among elementary students who
previously had registered declines. The National Assessment of Educational
Progress reports that reading scores have risen.[4] Big city districts publish
tests scores that register gains in skills. In my judgment, however, these
changes reflect a steep rise in the learning curve of boards of education and
school chiefs, rather than a causal linkage with school improvement programs. Administrators have discovered that forging tighter organizational

linkages between what teachers teach and the content of test items results in higher reading and math test scores.

Let me now divide the discussion into three parts. I will discuss district policies to improve overall productivity (as measured by test scores), implementation strategies, and unanticipated consequences. Let me remind the reader that this is an exploratory analysis, since few effective schools studies have focused on district-level policies or given explicit attention to implementation strategies; the thrust of the research has been on the school site and classroom. Hence, citations will be few.

DISTRICT POLICIES

Districts that have embraced the mission of improving schools along the lines suggested in the literature of effective schools—that is, goal setting, targeting academic aims, establishing and maintaining high expectations, frequent monitoring, and so on—have assembled a roughly hewn set of policies drawn from state mandates, other districts, and previous experience. They are conceptually simple and targeted like a rifle shot on lifting test scores. These policies promote a tighter coupling between organizational goals and the formal structure, while relying on a traditional top-down pattern of implementation. Sometimes, at the behest of a school board, but more often at the instigation of a superintendent, these policy decisions trigger a similar pattern of activities in all participating districts.[5]

This pattern includes the adoption of the following policies:

1. School board and superintendent establish district-wide instructional goals, often stated in terms of student outcomes—that is, improvement in test scores.
2. School board revises student promotion policies in line with stated outcomes for certain grade levels; board strengthens graduation requirements by making course content more substantive, increasing amount of seat-time during classes, and adding extra subjects.
3. Superintendent mandates planning process for each school. Each staff produces school-wide and individual classroom goals targeted upon student outcomes and aligned with the district goals.
4. The district curriculum for kindergarten through 12th grade is reviewed to determine if the objectives for subject matter and skills, the textbooks and other instructional materials, and both

district and national tests are consistent with what is taught in classrooms.

5. Superintendent revises district supervisory practices and evaluation instruments used with teachers and principals to align them with district goals and the literature on effective teachers and principals.
6. Board and superintendent create a district-wide assessment program to collect information on what progress, if any, occurs in reaching system, school, and classroom goals. Information is used to make program changes.
7. Superintendent introduces a staff development program for teachers, principals, central office supervisors, and the school board. The program concentrates on effective schools and teaching, goal-making, assessment procedures, evaluation of staff, and the steps necessary to implement each of these.

Few districts have installed all these policies at once or in a sequence resembling the one above. Often, superintendents begin on a pragmatic, ad hoc basis with, for example, goal-setting and test analysis. They then become aware of the crucial need to achieve a match among curriculum objectives, promotion policies, district goals, and test items. Or, in the overhaul of staff evaluation, a school board member or central office administrator will ask if the new instruments and procedures should be keyed in to district goals for student performance, thus forging another linkage. Though serendipity plays a part, the drift toward organizational tautness is unmistakable.

From images popular in the academic journals of schools as loosely linked amorphous enterprises with plenty of slack, a counterimage now emerges from such districts of organizations tightly coupled in both goals and formal structure, targeted sharply on academic productivity. District officials pursuing policies that fasten individual schools snugly to the central office believe they have found just the right hammer to pound in a nail.

There is a growing acceptance among practitioners that these policies work. Like a popular television show that begets clones in order to achieve a larger share of the audience, school boards and their executives seek out what works elsewhere and use exactly the same procedure in their own districts. Findings from the effective schools research spread through informal superintendent networks, national conferences of school board associations and administrators, journals read frequently by school officials, and other information on what pacesetter districts do. But the fact remains that no studies have yet shown which policies, independently or in combination, produce the desired effects. No research has yet demonstrated which strategies for executing policy decisions yield the desired results. While improved student performance on tests after the introduction of such policies has created some believers, it has not yet been established that the policies themselves have caused the improvement. Even more important, success in lifting scores exacts a price from the organization that few policymakers have yet calculated. In this brief summary of district policies aimed at improving system-wide effectiveness, I have failed to mention the bread-and-butter items, the staples of district policymaking: money and personnel.

Money

Born in the backwash of the 1966 Coleman Report and coming of age during a retrenchment on a scale unequaled since the 1930s, the effective schools research implicitly asserts that money does *not* make a difference. People do. Spending more is less important than strategically redirecting existing funds to promote effective staff performance.[6] Given today's shrinking enrollments and fiscal retrenchment, the prospect of converting ineffective schools into effective ones for pennies is most attractive. This message, however, is accurate only in a severely restricted sense. In my own experience and that of colleagues, a district-wide school improvement program involves large expenditures. While there are substantial indirect costs and modest direct ones in initiating a limited school *effectiveness* effort, far more important is the larger issue of total district resources available to fund an entire *improvement* program of schooling. Teacher salaries, recruitment of new teachers, retention of gifted senior faculty, and the addition of instructional leaders to an administrative cadre are also linked to district improvement.

The primary costs of initiating and implementing system-wide policies to increase productivity arise from retraining staff, hiring consultants, and reassigning central office supervisors and administrators. Since 1979, New York City's School Improvement Program has spent over $1 million a year in state and foundation grants on additional staff, teacher, parent, and evaluator time to introduce site-based programs in almost 20 schools. In most instances, however, far smaller sums have bought consultant and teacher time, materials, and supplies. Most costs are hidden, with no extra dollars added to the budget. In Arlington, Virginia, for example, $20,000 was added to the budget to initiate an effective schools project involving 6 out of 21 elementary schools. The 1980 operating budget for the entire school system of 30 plus schools and over 2,000 employees was in excess of $53 million.

Far more money, however, was spent in staff time to design, monitor, and assess annual school plans in relation to goals and objectives; to analyze test items in all standardized and locally developed instruments; to review current curriculum goals and their match with district tests and goals; and to revise existing evaluation tools for teachers and administrators to bring them into line with district goals. I estimate that for the Arlington school system, with a student enrollment of 20,000 in 1974 and 15,000 in 1981, the equivalent of $75,000 to $100,000 in staff time was spent for each of the first few years in getting policies in place, training staff, monitoring results, and returning information to principals, teachers, and the community. Because I had no specific staff assigned to do this work, I assumed a portion of the workload and directed central office administrators to do tasks beyond their assigned responsibilities until school-board-approved reorganizations could realign individuals with the thrust of new policies on goal-setting, annual school plans, curriculum revision, and the like. In Atlanta, Alonzo Grim, superintendent of schools, similarly reorganized and reassigned existing staff in order to concentrate upon student outcomes. Donald Steele, Seattle's former superintendent, lacking funds yet embracing the effective schools approach, assigned central office administrators not involved in instruction to advise individual elementary schools in addition to their regular duties.[7]

These rough cost estimates are for policies implemented in a top-down manner; estimates would differ for implementation efforts that begin with the school site and proceed from the bottom up or for combinations of the two approaches. A careful analysis has yet to be done of direct and indirect costs associated with adopting and implementing district policies designed to improve school effectiveness. I suspect that when such a study is done, it will reveal substantial costs in redirected staff time, a modest investment of additional money, and foregone costs in neglecting other aspects of the district's program.[8]

Personnel

Hiring, training, and evaluating staff and increasing staff awareness of effective schools are the primary personnel tasks. In Arlington, a lowered budget ceiling made hiring new staff impermissible. The school board approved only new jobs supported by federal and state grants. I presume that few districts since the late 1970s have been able to hire new staff except with the help of private or public funding external to the school system.

In the literature on effective schools, establishing a staff consensus over an instructional agenda is a high priority. In each school the principal and teachers shape that agenda and consensus. A principal needs to judge which teachers will work best within that school's culture. In the best of all possible worlds, the principal is free to choose the staff that he or she will need to make a school effective. The world that principals currently inhabit, however, offers severely restricted choices in assembling staff. Reassignment of teachers as a result of shrinking enrollment, the closing of schools, or similar events usually favor senior over junior teachers. When senior teachers come to a school involuntarily, bumping enthusiastic but junior teachers, the faculty's commitment to certain goals, staff morale, and the continuity that is so important in constructing an effective school may suffer. Thus, teacher assignment policies, often embedded in contracts if not in tradition, may work against district efforts to implement effective schools, particularly when the system is retrenching. Although reduction-in-force policies vary across districts, I have observed that principals and personnel chiefs have developed informal ways of abiding by the letter of the policy, while eluding the policy's intent by securing those teachers who might be better matched for one school over another. One tactic used by some principals who need teachers is to scan the recall list of teachers who have been pink-slipped because of shrinking enrollment. Knowing which teachers are viewed as weak, principals keep in daily touch with the director of personnel to determine exactly when to create a new class of students—the trigger for securing a teacher immediately. Invariably, the astute principal creates the class when a weak teacher has been assigned elsewhere and the next teacher on the recall list is more in keeping with what that principal seeks. These informal maneuvers are limited efforts to strike a practical compromise between conflicting policy aims in a district.

Selection and reassignment of principals involves less policy conflict but can generate opposition anyway. According to the growing literature, the principal is central to fashioning an improved school. Most districts allow the superintendent to choose principals for various schools. Career rotation, early retirement, and similar policies generate some turnover in school positions. But dilemmas persist. What can the superintendent do for a school with a high percentage of low-income children, where test scores are unacceptably low and no improvement has occurred for 5 or more years under the same principal? Transferring the principal shifts the problem to another school staff and parent community. Due process and evaluation procedures usually prevent the transfer of a principal because of low student performance; few districts have included in their selection criteria or evaluation policies the clear expectation that principals will improve student academic performance. To move a principal on the grounds that he or she has failed to improve the school's academic performance might be viewed as capricious, unless such a standard was embedded in existing policies and remedial help was offered.

In Arlington, where administrators are unionized, the school board approved the overhaul of the administrative evaluation policy. The new policy called for joint setting of goals and objectives by the superintendent and principal, a clear linkage between district goals and the principal's school goals, and the development by the administrator of a professional improvement plan. Leadership, instructional improvement, and managerial skills were explicitly stressed in the process. My assistants and I met with principals individually two or three times a year to discuss both their professional and school plans and to help them revise their goals, if necessary. Workshops were held on instructional supervision, managing teacher evaluation, assessing school improvement, and analyzing test scores. When I brought before the school board the instance of a principal whom I had evaluated twice as unsatisfactory in instructional leadership and in managing the school program, most of my evidence rested on repeated efforts to improve the principal's instructional management and the persistent erosion of student academic performance over a 5-year period. The school board approved the transfer of the principal to a nonschool post.

Buried in the language of principals as instructional leaders and effective teachers, then, is a crisp accountability for student performance—a steel fist encased in velvet. Boards and superintendents are driven by the inexorable logic of the research findings on effective schools to wrestle with the issue of marginal and incompetent staff beyond passing them from school to school or, as one superintendent put it, "engaging in the dance of the lemons." Because so little has been written or discussed openly about teacher and principal incompetence in terms of technical inability to improve students' academic performance, a district must often devise its own way of dealing with staff who cannot meet the higher expectations for their roles.[9]

Researchers interested in effective schools have yet to examine the crosscutting policy conflicts that occur in selecting, assigning, and evaluating both teachers and administrators when districts embark upon an improvement program, especially when confidence in the schools is low and the climate is hostile to budget increases.

IMPLEMENTATION STRATEGIES

Current practitioner wisdom harnessed to effective schools research cultivates the image of a trim bureaucratic organization that can get the job done—that is, improve test scores. District policies on goals, school plans, revised curricula, analyses of tests, new evaluative procedures, and frequent monitoring of system-wide progress will, according to the growing consensus among boards and school chiefs, produce outcomes that satisfy both professional and community expectations. But little notice has been given to how this will occur. Announcing a decision with a bang of the gavel is not the end of a process but merely the beginning of a sequence of events, many of them unanticipated, in the complicated process of implementation. [10]

A tighter coupling between the central office and individual schools along particular lines—such as goal-setting, monitoring, evaluating, and specifying outcomes—often gets translated into the familiar pattern of top-down implementation. By that, I mean a strategy founded upon the belief that a chain of command, stretching tautly from the board of education to the superintendent, directs principals to lead teachers who, in turn, will raise student academic performance. Proponents of this strategy claim that the use of formal organizational tools such as technical assistance, rewards, and sanctions increases both compliance and productivity. Central office administrators, viewing themselves as having the largest and most accurate picture of district needs, often see top-down implementation as efficient and swift. Their thrust is to set targets, establish control, and reduce discretion. According to this view, increased uniformity in practices will produce improved results. Two key assumptions guide this line of thinking: first, that there is a body of knowledge and expertise that can be used to produce high test scores in basic skills; second, that superintendent leadership and managerial savvy can weld a consensus in a mission and drive the organization toward its achievement. School districts from Portland, Maine, to Atlanta, Georgia, from Milwaukee, Wisconsin, to Milpitas, California, have used this pattern of implementation. These assumptions reflect the bind that superintendents, principals, and teachers find themselves in when they are compelled to act in the face of acute external pressures, yet lack a complete technology to achieve outcomes.

School boards and superintendents commonly use these top-down approaches to translate policies into practice for a number of reasons. Pressure for results pinches the school board and superintendent far more than it does the teacher or principal. Community dissatisfaction with performance leads to far more turnover among board members and superintendents than among principals or teachers. Moreover, the implicit indictment in the literature on effective schools is that if teachers and principals would only alter their beliefs and practices, student performance would improve. To expect teachers and principals, who are street-level bureaucrats at the bottom of every district organizational chart, to agree that they are both the problem and solution is to ask them to become scapegoats for a district's failure to improve academic performance. Few scapegoats have been noted for volunteering. Finally, more often than not, administrators who make the decisions believe that the top-down strategy works. Because time is often short, cries for results are loud, pressures pinch acutely, and routines are already in place, top-down implementation is administratively convenient.

In contrast, implementation strategies adopting a bottom-up approach would concentrate on each school's determining its own agenda, monitoring and evaluating itself, and using district funds in the manner that staff and parents chose. In short, each school would decide for itself how best to reach district goals. Rooted in the literature on organizational development, the bottom-up strategy concentrates on generating among staff a shared vision of what the school might be, creating a team spirit, cultivating mutual trust, and building emotional bonds through collaborative decisionmaking on school issues. Many practitioners and researchers, convinced of the importance of staff commitment, local ownership of decisions, and joint efforts at the school site, have cited instances in the effective schools research where such implementation strategies have produced desired outcomes in test performance. Organizationally, such strategies sustain the existing loose linkages between central office and school; encourage more, not less, principal discretion; and produce redundancy and, for efficiency engineers at the top of the organization, untidy arrangements. Superintendents who find this arrangement congenial lean heavily on informal communication, use networks within the district, and adroitly handle organizational rituals and traditions. Although infrequent in occurrence, bottom-up approaches do appear in the literature on effective schools.[11]

So far, I have implied that a top-down strategy of implementation means that directions drafted in the central office will be executed in each school across the district. Similarly, a bottom-up approach means that school-generated decisions unique to each setting will vary from school to school in the district. Mixes of top-down and bottom-up strategies, which are not necessarily tied either to district or school-based applications, also occur. Consider Figure 3.1.

For example, a superintendent can direct principals in each school to set goals, plan and establish programs, and assess outcomes. By directing from the top a process to occur at each school without prescribing the content of the decisions, a variation on the familiar bottom-up approach emerges. In short, seeking tighter coupling of district practices to school action does not necessarily mean mandating the same effort district-wide; it can be triggered by superintendent mandate but proceed gradually on a school-by-school basis.

FIGURE 3.1. Implementation Strategies

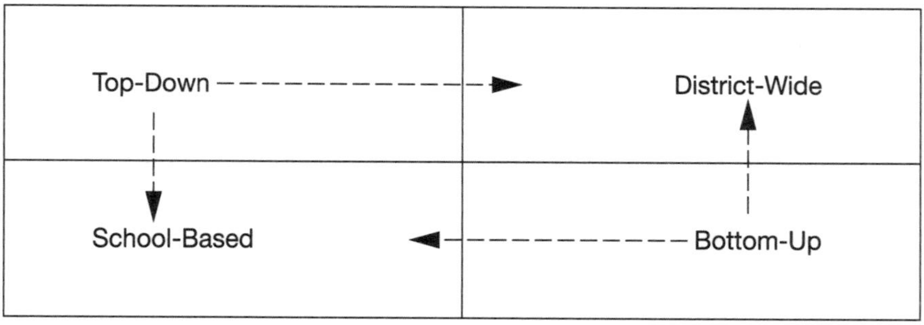

Whichever strategy is proposed, policymakers need to address critical issues concerning voluntarism, in-service training for teachers and principals, incentives, sanctions, and related points. It is still not clear which implementation strategies are most effective because few researchers have investigated the connections between strategies and outcomes. Most researchers have recognized the tangled complexity of such diverse elements as context; roles; individuals; organizational factors such as size, history, and culture; quality of leadership at both district and school levels; timing; and other critical determinants of successful implementation. Beyond recognizing this complexity, few researchers have proceeded further than to construct inventories and taxonomies of essential points in establishing causal relationships between strategies and outcomes. Three issues illustrate the larger complexity involved in implementing policies aimed at making schools effective.[12]

Choice or Mandate

Many practitioners and researchers believe that volunteers bring high energy and a positive outlook to producing an effective school, while draftees only find fault and complain. What, then, do superintendents do with schools mired in low performance for years, whose principals and faculties express great reluctance to join in an improvement program? Mandates, as many school officials know, can produce compliance with the letter of the order without also leading to improvement. Even when the superintendent, in a heavy-handed compromise between choice and coercion, advises a principal to volunteer, some grudging level of compliance is about all that can reasonably be expected.

The strategies adopted by various school districts offer little guidance. In New York City, the chancellor invited Ronald Edmonds, one of the effective schools researchers, to introduce a school improvement program based upon his research, and in which voluntarism played a major role. Schools were invited to participate, and from the pool of volunteers Edmonds and his staff chose a number for the project. In Milwaukee, the superintendent designated 18 schools with the poorest test scores for the effective schools project. In New Haven, Milpitas, and Seattle, all schools participate in the program. In Arlington, elementary schools other than the six initially selected may choose to enter the program and receive the services. Of course, superintendents employ mixes of choice and coercion. Generally, however, tight-coupling strategies favor mandating involvement, whereas bottom-up approaches favor allowing staffs to choose. Although superintendents' beliefs are strong as to which approach works, no body of evidence yet supports one tactic or the other.

Local context and superintendents' beliefs about change, rather than actual evidence, may often determine whether requiring schools to participate or offering them a choice is the tactic to use. In Arlington, the six schools which were at the bottom in academic performance formed a natural grouping. For two of the six, for example, opting out of participation would have left the school board and me vulnerable to legitimate parent complaints that principals and teachers were insensitive to deteriorating student achievement and resistant to improving the situation. The tradeoff in requiring all six staffs to join the program was apparent in the varying levels of enthusiasm for the initial effort and, in some cases, foot-dragging reluctance. In districts where there is a history of voluntary piloting of new approaches, tradition dominates. Thus, the issue of choice or mandate may hinge less on evidence than on local contextual conditions and on policymakers' beliefs about which implementation approach works. The issue of choice needs explicit attention if for no other reason than to assess the anticipated tradeoffs.[13]

In-Service Training

In mobilizing for an improvement program, the primary means of delivering help to schools is technical assistance. The implicit theory of change embedded in in-service programs is that faculties and administrators, as individuals and small groups, need additional knowledge and skills in order to implement research findings: Change individuals and the school will become effective. But consideration of the impact of the school structure upon individual behavior is often missing from any discussion or analysis of in-service training.

Organizational regularities involving teachers and students, principals and teachers, school staff and district office, parents and school—not to mention how the school is organized for instruction and its use of time—are rarely included in the usual technical assistance packages offered as part of school improvement.

Some researchers have suggested directions for altering a few organizational norms that shape teacher behavior. Judith Little, for example, has shown that breaking down teacher isolation and cultivating a norm of collegiality can lead to improvement in teaching practices.[14] New work norms of teachers observing one another, talking frequently about pedagogy, and engaging in joint planning stimulate the sharing of values that nourish school improvement.

What is offered to teachers is all too familiar. Most teachers and principals know the concepts in the research on effective teaching and schools, insofar as classroom instruction and school-wide leadership are concerned, although the language and emphasis may be unfamiliar. For teachers listening to lectures and reading articles there is little that is complex in the research or that calls for major shifts in classroom practice, although evidence that teachers practice these concepts may be lacking.

On the other hand, the literature on instructional leadership calls for extensive in-service education for principals on the components of managing an instructional program, such as establishing and communicating a mission for the school, supervising instruction, and creating a positive climate. This emphasis does not mean that principals are unaware of instructional management or that they do not perform the function. However, principals themselves report that they give such managerial activities less time because the nature of the job forces them to concentrate on noninstructional tasks, such as maintaining school stability and coping with the often competing interests of the central office, school faculty, parents, and others. In addition to principals' self-reports, observational studies confirm that instructional management is secondary to noninstructional tasks in the daily whirl of a principal's life.[15]

Few training sessions for teachers or principals, however, make either aware that the sharpened expectation for the principal to exert leadership will end the silent agreement between administrator and faculty to honor each other's separate domain. A principal who shifts into a mode of visiting classrooms daily, monitoring student achievement monthly, and evaluating teacher performance quarterly may become a threat to some teachers. Similarly, few in-service sessions deal with dilemmas touching teachers and principals who are asked to implement programs about which they have had little say and with which they may disagree, such as using test results as the major standard for judging success.

How is technical assistance delivered? Researchers agree that the one-shot workshop in the district office, with no follow-up, is at best symbolic, and at worst trivial. Numerous studies of in-service training state that encouraging teachers and principals at each school site to leave their fingerprints on the training format and content—even to the point of reinventing the obvious—is linked to improved staff performance. While partisans of organizational development note such findings, others have observed that local-site staff training permits teachers to adapt new knowledge and skills to their unique circumstances. Continuous sessions with ample and direct follow-up activities are commonly recommended in these studies.[16]

Who does the training? In New York City schools these liaisons, as they are called, are veteran teachers or supervisors in the system who are familiar with both the formal and informal structure of the city's public schools. They work with staffs a few days a week in planning, implementing, and evaluating school improvement plans focused sharply on Edmonds's five factors of effectiveness: strong administrative leadership, orderly school climate, high expectations for student achievement, basic skills emphasis, and frequent monitoring of pupil progress. In the process, they line up consultants and, whenever possible, provide expertise themselves. Arlington uses a team of central office teachers and supervisors in reading, math, and writing who spend concentrated periods at a school on particular tasks, such as coordinating the entire reading and writing program across grades, providing materials, and working with the school staff on a consulting basis for the rest of the school year. Other districts train a cadre of teachers from participating schools so that each school has an on-site trainer who is a resident member of the staff. Some school systems hold a series of workshops at a central location throughout the year, with follow-up done by designated supervisors. The common pattern, however, still seems to be a series of uncoordinated workshops for principals and teachers, with pounds of reading material circulated and a pat on the back.[17]

Technical assistance attempts to increase the capacities of the participants to do a productive job. It is the linchpin of any school improvement. Modest sums of money are needed. For programs aimed at delivering the training during the year at the school site, $3,000 to $4,000 a year per school is probably sufficient to purchase the consultant time, materials, and substitute teacher time involved in getting a program solidly started. For programs using liaisons split between two or three schools, the cost would be higher initially, unless those liaisons are reassigned supervisors or other central office personnel who have themselves received some training.

Incentives and Sanctions

In top-down implementation, formal and informal incentives and sanctions are organizational tools available to superintendents to shape what happens and to introduce managerial control into an ambiguous set of arrangements. With test scores as the coin of the realm, public recognition of school improvement—by such means as certificates of achievement awarded by the board of education or school-by-school scores published in newspapers—acts as an inducement for principals, teachers, and students. School board recognition of the academic achievement of both schools and individuals—such as higher test scores or winning of academic olympics—attracts media and citizen notice; far more important, however, is the fact that the top authority takes the time to acknowledge and honor academic excellence. Principals who behave in a manner consistent with descriptions of instructional leadership and produce higher test results become candidates for promotion. Similarly, teachers who develop reputations for consistently turning out classes with high test scores are sometimes viewed as potential principals.

Securing parental support becomes easier when a school's performance is anchored in standardized test data that reveal promising achievement. For individuals who derive pleasure from a heightened sense of professionalism, attending workshops, reading materials unavailable to other staff, and participating in an effective schools program are rewards in themselves. For others, improved student performance at either the school or the district level encourages a sense of belonging and involvement in a larger, worthwhile effort. The last two are among the informal rewards associated with bottom-up implementation. An important incentive is the powerful feeling that can grow in a staff that works together and succeeds in producing higher test scores. The sense of shared purpose and pride in group achievement fuels further effort, increases participants' self-esteem, and enhances their confidence in tackling tough jobs. Wise superintendents, aware of the influence of their positions and sensitive to the power of both formal and informal rewards, also know that their participation in teacher and principal work sessions tells staff and parents what is important in the district.

Sanctions also exist. When test scores plunge without recovering, the implied, if not actual, consequence for teachers and principals may well be criticism that escalates into warnings or even threats of removal. The effective schools research points inexorably to the conclusion that children *can* achieve. When test scores fail to rise or continue to decline, teachers and principals receive the blame. Although such severe penalties as removal seldom occur, the unspoken threat remains.

Union contracts and due-process requirements protect instructional staff from swift termination on the basis of test results, but the pattern of long-term class or school deterioration has been used to institute charges of incompetence.

The issues of choice, in-service training, and incentives and sanctions are a few of the thorny questions that arise when embracing and executing policies presumably anchored in research findings. Another element missing in the literature on effective teaching and effective schools is the role of district leadership.

Leadership

Most studies of effective schools stress the pivotal role of the school principal. The research says that no school can be labeled effective (again, using the criterion of test scores) unless its principal exerts—and here the words vary—a strong administrative presence, an active style, or some other trait demonstrating leadership. But no study that I have seen lays out empirically derived principal behaviors that produce the desired outcomes. Instead, there are recipelike prescriptions stemming from personal experience, case studies of principals, or inferential leaps based upon theories or data drawn from other organizations. Thus, the connective tissue, the set of behaviors that principals engage in to develop a school climate that supports academic achievement–to gain staff commitment, to engender high expectations, to supervise individual teachers and the entire instructional program, while carrying on the varied and complex duties connected with maintaining order in the school–none of these complex, interacting behaviors has been linked in the literature to the production of higher test scores. So far, only a general notion of leadership is a correlate of high student achievement. Practitioner faith and folk wisdom sustain the conviction that school-site leadership makes a difference. Research has yet to catch up with this lore to either inform, shape, or contradict practice. [18]

Faith and folk wisdom also suggest that the superintendent exerts a critical role in establishing the district agenda, communicating the mission of the district to both the staff and community, creating a system-wide climate favoring achievement, targeting essential personnel and funds, and monitoring and assessing the overall program in order to implement school board policies directed toward school improvement. As with the principal, experience-based knowledge about superintendents as instructional leaders exceeds the present state of research-produced knowledge. The accounts by or about superintendents embracing an effective schools approach describe attitudes and activities typical of an earlier generation of superintendents– teacher–scholars who were deeply interested in the instructional process and active in schools and classrooms. A century ago, superintendents had to teach teachers what to do in classrooms; they inspected what was taught, listened to children recite, taught classes, and, in general, were unmistakably visible in the school program. That model of superintendent as instructional leader gave way to a managerial approach that has dominated the superintendency for the last three generations. With the mounting interest in using effective schools research, the older model of a school chief knowledgeable about both curriculum and instruction and visible in the schools beyond the symbolic tour is reasserting itself.[19]

Given that the literature on effective schools suggests that no school can become effective without the visible and active involvement of a principal hip-deep in the elementary school instructional program, then it also seems likely that no school board approving policies aimed at system-wide improvement can hope to achieve that condition without a superintendent who sustains a higher than usual involvement in the district's instructional program. Of course, there will be districts that have some effective schools regardless of the superintendent's familiarity with instruction, just as in a school with a principal who is uninvolved with the instructional program and sees his or her task as keeping the ship afloat, there will nevertheless be first-rate teachers who maintain high standards of instruction. Moreover, the superintendent can delegate many tasks to subordinates; he or she cannot be everywhere at once, any more than a principal can.

The size of a school system is also a factor. Can the Chicago superintendent with a half-million students perform as an instructional leader in the same way as her colleague in Alexandria, Virginia, who deals with fewer than 10,000 children? Yes, but large districts require far more symbolic and shrewd instructional leadership targeted upon principals rather than teachers. The superintendent's personal, active involvement in the district instructional effort seems to be a necessary condition. I state the above as a proposition derived from the logic of existing practice in improving school productivity. No facts yet exist on superintendent behaviors that cause district improvement. Because of the absence of studies investigating the superintendent's role in improving schools, the literature leaves us with discussions of the ineffable quality of leadership.

At a time when budget, program, and staff cuts and school closings are affecting most districts, when a crisis of confidence in schools is attracting media attention, and when administrators are privately and publicly bewailing the lack of money and the restrictions upon their power, policymakers and academicians are calling for inspired leadership. If the research on effective schools has yet to produce reliable prescriptions tested in numerous crucibles, the literature on leadership for both principal and superintendent reveals a similar barrenness. Long on rhetoric and dictates, much of what is written leans heavily on perceptions of what school leaders do. Within the last decade a few scholars have produced behavioral descriptions of principals and superintendents. Yet the tasks that administrators choose to work on, the language they use, the discretion they employ, the symbols they manipulate, the incentives they extend, the style and commitment they project—all dance beyond the grasp of researchers. There are also organizational theorists who argue plausibly that formal leadership is a myth constructed by those who need to attribute influence to incumbents. Hence, what principals and superintendents do daily to create the conditions for instructional improvement and to influence students directly remains in the shadows of research-produced knowledge, though honored by practitioners and sought by parents.[20]

I prefer to acknowledge that leadership is ineffable rather than to embrace popular recipes that worked once in someone else's kitchen. My experience and that of other superintendents, however, presents some untested propositions that researchers and policymakers may find worthy of consideration.

First, no superintendent can secretly improve a school district. The source of formal authority for a superintendent's initiative is the school board, which needs to approve the general direction and to work in tandem with the superintendent. Self-evident as this may seem, the commonplace needs to be stated.

Second, the superintendent sets the agenda and develops the mission, using his or her managerial skills to decide when to open the gate to ideas and when to close it, when to veto and when to support—in short, how to develop policy.

Third, the superintendent establishes a climate which nurtures instructional improvement in the district. Once the superintendent becomes identified with the mission of school improvement, even symbolic visibility in schools and classrooms carries weight. Encouragement and support (without conceding anything on expectations) for principals and teachers, such as protecting the instructional day and nourishing professional development, are also important.

Fourth, the school chief uses a number of managerial tools to implement the mission: targeting limited resources on activities that promise a payoff; placing like-minded, skilled staff in key positions that will advance the district's mission; and actively participating in monitoring and assessing the instructional program.

Such behavior on the part of the superintendent describes a high-profile, active involvement in the instructional side of school operations. Will it produce improved student academic performance? Maybe. Experience-derived knowledge says yes, but no body of independent evidence yet exists to demonstrate that engaging in these tasks will yield dividends. What these assertions about superintendent behavior suggest is that some degree of direction and top-down implementation is necessary in launching an improvement program. Once launched, however, the improvement process can travel many routes, ranging from organizational development techniques employed with small groups to tightly managed, orchestrated tasks resembling a chess game. Personal preference and belief systems seem to determine the course adopted.

This description of superintendent behavior is narrowly targeted on the academic performance of students. The goals of schooling, however, go well beyond test scores. If the mission of a district embraces many goals, some of which may require substantial changes in teaching practice such as developing student initiative, decisionmaking, and cooperativeness, other leadership tasks may also be involved. Since a great deal of existing pedagogy and principal behavior is shaped by the structure within which both teachers and administrators work, improved academic achievement is well within the margin of change set by organizational boundaries. Hence, changes directed toward test scores are incremental and very different from a major overhaul of the entire district's instructional program.

Whether or not such leadership activities as described here have, indeed, produced the higher academic achievement reported in districts across the nation has yet to be demonstrated. But it is clear that there are many unanticipated consequences of tightly coupling the central office to the local school and of concentrating on raising achievement on tests.

UNANTICIPATED CONSEQUENCES

Increased Uniformity

The school effectiveness literature stresses the importance of managing the instructional program and coordinating the curriculum at the school site. Yet districts concentrating upon improving academic achievement experience a strong, irresistible tug toward a standard curriculum and system-wide use of the same textbooks and student workbooks. Tailoring supplementary materials to student differences becomes less frequent, as does grouping of students within classrooms on the basis of achievement. The notion of a single, best curriculum and managerial style echoing the pre-1900 years of public schooling reasserts itself. The press toward uniformity is neither good nor bad; every school district must strike some balance between uniformity and diversity in curriculum and program management. My point is simply that adopting the school effectiveness research will drive the curriculum and school management toward uniformity.

The same trend is visible in teaching. The research on effective teaching practices has singled out and emphasized particular techniques as being effective means of improving test results. The boosterism surrounding direct instructional methods, such as teaching the whole class at one time, teacher-directed activities, and continual monitoring of student work, presses teachers toward these practices. What the literature has done is to certify direct instruction as the single best way of teaching. But uncritical cheerleading for this brand of teaching stamps whole-group instruction, lecturing, recitation, and seatwork as effective, going far beyond what the research findings promise or even suggest. Moreover, repetitive, low-level intellectual skills are now surrounded by a halo of legitimacy. Filling in blanks, getting test-wise to multiple-choice items, and completing exercises elevate tedious tasks to the status of effective instruction. Concern for student interest, motivation, and the life of the mind diminishes with accelerated use of dittos, seatwork, and pre- and post-tests. Learning becomes a series of repetitive tasks that need to be completed, placed in folders, and marked by the teacher. An increase in drill and routine is justified in the name of direct instruction and concentration on low-order but important basic skills. While mastery learning, the use of individual contracts, and small group instruction through teams stand as alternatives to direct instruction in producing academic gains, such approaches remain largely at the margins of the pedagogical radar screen.

The result is that the ineffable elements of teaching as an art—tempo, improvisation, drama, and excitement of performance—receive little acknowledgment as important qualities and even less attention from district policymakers. The pleasures that teachers derive from their relationships with children, the unpredictable, the unexpected, the unplanned, and the joyful, go unnoticed by partisans of effective teaching. There is a danger in smothering the craft and rewards of teaching in the rush to make instruction scientific and efficient. The dream of an efficient one-best-system of instruction of an earlier generation of reformers appears to have resurfaced with the undisguised fervor for direct instruction.

Narrowing of the Educational Agenda

In the pursuit of improved test scores, areas viewed as nonacademic—such as music, art, speaking, and self-esteem—receive less attention. Partisans of effective schools seem to take the position that if a subject or skill cannot be directly linked to student academic performance, then the burden of proof that it is a legitimate part of a school curriculum rests on those who see schooling in broader terms than spelling bees and multiplication tables.

Narrowing the agenda for public schools was a necessary response to the ballooning expectations of the last half-century. But schools *can* do more than raise test scores of all children. Both citizens and educators must be concerned about shrinking the school district's agenda to the least common denominator.

Increased Conflict Between Teachers and Administrators

Heightened interest in instructional leadership causes a shift in administrator behavior. The principal's weekly presence in classrooms, periodic evaluations, and scrutiny of each class's test achievement boosts teacher anxiety over potential loss of classroom autonomy. The principal's insistence on the use of direct instructional methods may be viewed as a slur on the teacher's ability to make pedagogical judgments. The likelihood of overt conflict increases when teachers feel that their professional domain is being penetrated by administrators who know little of the students they face daily and the craft they practice hourly.

Similarly, latent hostility between principals and the central office is produced by the differences between the view of the district from the principal's office and the view from the superintendent's desk. This conflict sharpens noticeably when the superintendent takes a greater interest in school-wide test scores and holds principals accountable for meeting district goals. Revision in evaluation instruments for administrators raises the spectre that principals' jobs are on the line if they don't produce. Few researchers have pursued this potential conflict as a consequence of adopting policies based upon effective schools research.[21]

Lack of Focus on Schools with High Test Scores

Because the focus of recent efforts is on lifting test scores, little attention is paid to the curriculum, instruction, or organization of schools with median percentile ranks above 95 in math and reading. The presumption is that all is well, yet the analysis of subgroups in high-scoring schools often reveals that there are students who need remedial help. The high achievers in these schools may also receive inappropriate instruction if teachers are using only grade-level materials. And teachers may resist moving them ahead to advanced lessons because of the ripple effects upon the next grade's teachers, whose materials are geared to a certain expected level. Also, low expectations of high achievers—"they are so smart, they will get it on their own!"— often pervade such schools, insulating students from improvement, since the schools look terrific in terms of percentile ranks.

Misapplication of Research Findings

While there is an intuitive and craft wisdom to many of the findings, there are sharp limits on their application to the high school. One limit is that the organizational structure of the high school resembles that of the college more than that of the elementary school. In terms of size, mission, the structuring of time, student–teacher contact, previous training of teachers, and their worldview of what is important for young men and women, the high school is profoundly different from the elementary school. Certainly high schools can become more effective, but to claim that formulas that have proved effective in the lower grades will also be effective in the upper ones is a misuse of research. The Charles Kettering Foundation, for example, sponsors a program that lists 14 attributes of effective high schools. It is a melange of traits drawn from findings on effective elementary schools and from theory undergirding organizational development. The U.S. Department of Education has recently recognized as effective high schools across the country which possess these

14 attributes. Principals are told that if they become instructional leaders, supervise instruction, coordinate curriculum, and evaluate classroom teachers, test scores will improve. Grafts of formulas used in elementary schools will fail, in my judgment, until a more sensitive, grounded organizational analysis is made of the high school. The misapplication of research findings is very tempting to policymakers who hear shrill criticism from taxpayer associations, government officials, academicians, and professional reformers. Conclusions from research studies that demonstrate high positive correlations between certain activities and improvement in test scores are often too seductive for district policymakers pressed to increase productivity to ignore. Accordingly, districts tend to perform the slippery twist that converts correlations into action agendas.[22]

These and other unanticipated consequences raise the obvious question: If productivity improves and parents and policymakers are pleased with higher test results, can we conclude that children are receiving a better education? Inner-city children across the nation who have received a schooling built upon false beliefs in their incapacity to learn are clearly the beneficiaries of effective school efforts.

This fundamental first step is a moral as well as an educational one. No excuses are acceptable.

But improved test scores are simply not enough. To conclude that a school is effective once it demonstrates test-score gains is, implicitly, to conclude that students need to develop no other capacity than to answer multiple-choice items correctly. The concern that drives many schools today—that of improving student performance on achievement tests—is a short-term, useful, but constricting one. The framework for a response to this concern regarding elementary schools comes from research on effective teaching and schools. That framework, I am confident, is useful and will prove successful in lifting test scores. But, while it is a necessary first step, it will prove insufficient in reaching for broader, less easily measured, yet fundamental goals of schooling. The dangers of confusing *means* (test-score gains) with *ends* (multiple aims of schooling) are real. Based upon my experience and an awareness of the inevitable tradeoffs in the implementation of effective school programs, I suggest that the expressed concern regarding test scores be reformulated as a question: *In improving test results, how can the general, more complex and nonquantifiable goals of schooling be achieved?* Such a question places test results in a ranking position in relation to such other important outcomes as problem solving, cooperativeness, independence in decisionmaking, positive feeling for learning, caring for others, an appreciation for the aesthetic, and similar aims.

To evaluate the effectiveness of such complex organizations as schools solely on the basis of a percentile rank is little better than to judge a car's quality solely on the basis of its miles per gallon or a hospital's effectiveness solely by the number of its vacant beds. School officials who have adopted effective schools research, concepts, and language need to use many policy tools to improve school productivity, not just standardized test scores. Tightly coupled organizational procedures sharply focused on academic goals, as measured by test results, are clearly among those tools. Too often, however, those who believe their only tool is a hammer begin to treat everything like a nail. For that to occur now would be, in my judgment, a mistake for the children of the nation.

NOTES

This is a revised version of a paper commissioned by the National Institute of Education on district links with school sites in improving schools. A shorter version of this article, "Effective Schools: A Friendly But Cautionary Note," appeared in the June 1983 issue of *Phi Delta Kappan.* I wish to acknowledge the helpful comments of Steve Swerdlick.

1. Articles documenting the popularity of effective schools research include Bill Bennett and Terry Eastland, "Making a School System Work," *Education Week, 12* (Oct. 1981*),* 24; Cynthia Wilson, "Do Seattle Schools Work?" *The Weekly, 26* (Jan.–Feb. 1983), 26–29; Allan Odden and Van Dougherty, *State Programs of School Improvement: A 50-State Survey* (Denver: Education Commission of the States, 1982); Ronald Edmonds, "Programs of School Improvement: An Overview," *Educational Leadership, 40* (1982), 4–11; "Rating Your Child's School," *Consumers' Research Magazine, 45* (Aug. 1980), 10–13; Thomas Toch, "Pittsburgh Votes New Priorities," *Education Week, 5* (Oct. 1981), p. 5.

2. See James S. Coleman, Ernest Q. Campbell, Carol J. Hobson, James McPartland, Alexander M. Mood, Frederic D. Weinfeld, and Robert L. York, *Equality of Education Opportunity* (Washington, D.C.: CPO, 1966). The immediate background for the surge of interest in effective schools has been described by a number of researchers. See, for example, Stewart Purkey and Marshall Smith, "Effective Schools–A Review," *Elementary School Journal, 83* (1983), 427–452.

3. A number of critiques from academicians have appeared in the last year. The most careful and comprehensive are Stewart Purkey and Marshall Smith, "Effective Schools–A Review," *Elementary School Journal, 83* (1983), 427–452; Brian Rowan, David Dwyer, and Steven Bossert, "Research on Effective Schools: A Cautionary Note," *Educational Researcher, 12* (1983), 24–31; and Michael Cohen, "Instructional Management and Social Conditions in Effective Schools," in *School Finance and School Improvement: Linkages in the 1980s,* eds. Allan Odden and L. Dean Webb (Washington, D.C.: American Educational Finance Association, 1983). Michael Katz provides a historical critique on the current enthusiasm for effective schools in "Reflections on Metaphors of Educational Reform," *Harvard Graduate School of Education Bulletin, 25* (Fall 1980), 4–9. His objection to the lack of attention to district leadership is slowly being overcome. Purkey and Smith, "Effective Schools," use the concept of

"nested layers," that is, the classroom is embedded in a school, which is embedded in a district, and each stratum influences the other. Louis Smith and his colleagues have used the same concept in an article describing the complex history of a school innovation. See Louis Smith, David Dwyer, and John Prunty, "A Longitudinal Nested Systems Model of Innovation and Change in Schooling," in *Organizational Behavior in Schools and School Districts,* ed. Samuel Bacharach (New York: Praeger, 1981). Also, see Charles Bidwell and John Kasarda, "Conceptualizing and Measuring the Effects of School and Schooling," *American Journal of Education, 88* (1980), 401–430. Finally, Philip Hallinger cites district leadership as a factor inducing principals to engage in a surprisingly high level of instructional management. See his "Assessing the Instructional Management Behavior of Principals," Dissertation, Stanford University, 1983.

4. Reading Report No. 11–R–01 (Denver: NAEP, 1981).

5. I draw from my experience in Arlington, Virginia (1974–1981), from my observations of school districts in the San Francisco area that have adopted school effectiveness as a program, and from the following accounts: Alonzo Crim, "A Community of Believers," *Daedalus, 110* (Fall 1981), 145–162; Robert Benjamin's chapter on Modesto, California, in his *Making Schools Work* (New York: Continuum, 1981); Bill Bennett and Terry Eastland, "Making a School System Work," *Education Week, 12* (Oct. 1981) on Portland, Maine; and Cynthia Wilson, "Do Seattle Schools Work?" *The Weekly, 26* (Jan.–Feb.). The Summer 1982 issue of *State Education Leader,* published by the Education Commission of the States, lists the steps that schools, districts, and state agencies should pursue (such as setting goals, cultivating principal leadership, developing staff, and coordinating curriculum).

6. "Improving Schools with Limited Resources," *Issuegram,* July 1982, Education Commission of the States, Denver, Colorado; "Old Debate Revived over Money v. School Quality," *Education Week, 30* (March 1983), 19; Daniel U. Levine and Eugene Eubanks argue that "schools with a solid base of funding, from regular taxes or Chapter I or any other source, do not necessarily require much additional funding for program expenditures." See their article, "A First Look at Effective Schools Projects in New York City and Milwaukee," *Phi Delta Kappan, 64* (1983), 702.

7. Alonzo Crim, "A Community of Believers," *Daedalus, 110* (Fall 1981), 145–162; Cynthia Wilson, "Do Seattle Schools Work?" *The Weekly, 26* (Jan.–Feb. 1983), 26–29. For costs of New York City's School Improvement Programs, see Daniel Levine and Eugene Eubanks, "A First Look at Effective School Projects in New York City and Milwaukee," p. 699.

8. See, for example, the description of New York City's School Improvement Project and the funding necessary to sustain central administration of the program, liaisons for the schools, and other costs, in Terry Clark and Dennis McCarthy, "School Improvement in New York City: The Evolution of a Project," *Educational Researcher, 12* (1983), 17–24.

9. My colleague, Edwin Bridges, is completing a long-term study of how school districts manage incompetent staff. His search of the literature produced very little on either teachers or principals.

10. The literature on implementation grows yearly. Case studies and theoretical contributions have slightly increased our understanding of the complex process of converting policy decisions into practice. See Richard Elmore's "Organizational Models of Social Program Implementation," *Public Policy, 26* (1978), 185–228.

Elmore's taxonomy of implementation models is useful for differentiating the techni-cal-rational approach, currently enjoying a vogue among school policymakers, from the bureaucratic, conflict-bargaining, and organizational development models. Fed-eral and state experience with Title I, PL. 94–142, and special projects since 1965 have demonstrated how legislative intent is persistently twisted into shapes congenial to local needs. The tension between securing compliance and releasing local capaci-ties runs like a red thread through the accounts of these efforts. The projects that were judged effective, according to the intensive case studies of federal programs by Paul Berman and Milbrey McLaughlin, were ones that somehow put their unique stamp upon the federal project's goals, activities, and outcomes. See Berman and McLaugh-lin, "Federal Programs Supporting Educational Change," Vol. VIII of *Implementing and Sustaining Innovations* (Santa Monica, California: Rand Corporation, 1978). In a critique of the literature on implementation of programs, Berman concludes that implementation is determined by so many factors and circumstances that it is idio-syncratic; see Paul Berman, "Educational Change: An Implementation Paradigm," in *Improving Schools*, eds. Rolf Lehming and Michael Kane (Beverly Hills, Califor-nia: Sage, 1981). "Mutual adaptation," a phrase extracted from the Rand researchers' work, has become a shorthand expression for implementation strategies that embrace grassroots participation. Whereas some efforts have employed the findings of imple-mentation researchers that staff commitment and a stake in decisionmaking are of pivotal importance to effective schools policies, most programs implementing effec-tive schools research employ top-down strategies.

11. The New York School Improvement Project is one instance of a top-down strategy employing a school-based approach. For an analysis of bottom-up and school-based strategies, see Jane L. David, *School-Based Strategies: Implications for Government Policy* (Palo Alto, California: Bay Area Research Group, 1982).

12. See Michael Fullan, "Implementing Educational Change: Progress at Last." Paper presented at a conference of National Institute of Education, Airlie, Virginia, Feb. 1982; and Michael Fullan and Alan Pomfret, "Research on Curriculum and Instruction Implementation," *Review of Educational Research, 47* (1977), 335–397. See also David Crandall, Joyce E. Bauchner, Susan F. Loucks, and William H. Schmidt, "Models of School Improvement Process: Factors Contributing to Success." Paper presented at American Education Research Association, New York City, March 1982; and Meredith Gall, "Using Staff Development to Improve Schools," *R & D Perspec-tives,* Winter 1983.

13. Ronald Edmonds, "Programs of School Improvement," *Educational Leadership, 40* (1982), 4–11; and my own acquaintance with efforts in Milipitas, California. Dan-iel Levine and Eugene Eubanks, "A First Look at Effective Schools Projects in New York City and Milwaukee," *Phi Delta Kappan, 64* (1983), 702, recommend mandat-ing school participation if sufficient funds are available but do not mention tradeoffs between choice and coercion.

14. Judith Warren Little, *School Success and Staff Development: The Role of Staff Development in Urban Desegregated Schools* (Washington, D.C.: National Institute of Education, 1981).

15. For teacher staff development and new work norms, see Judith Warren Little, *School Success and Staff Development: The Role of Staff Development in Urban Desegregated Schools* (Washington, D.C.: National Institute of Education, 1981). Among the many

investigators of the role of principals, Harry Wolcott, Donald Willower, and Van Cleve Morris use ethnographic and observational techniques (drawn from the work of Henry Mintzberg) to describe the daily activities of several principals, but instructional leadership—however defined—is often missing from these portraits. See Harry Wolcott, *The Man in the Principal's Office* (New York: Holt, Rinehart and Winston, 1973); Donald Willower, "Managerial Behavior of High School Principals," *Educational Administration Quarterly, 17* (1981), 69–80; Van Cleve Morris, Robert L. Crowson, Emanuel Hurwitz, Jr., and Cynthia Porter-Gehrie, *The Urban Principal* (Chicago: University of Illinois at Chicago Circle, 1981), 14.

16. See Mary Bentzen, *Changing Schools: The Magic Feather Principal* (New York: McGraw-Hill, 1974); for several productive discussions, see the essays in Ann Lieberman and Lynne Miller, eds., *Staff Development: New Demands, New Realities, New Perspectives* (New York: Teachers College Press, 1979); and Judith Warren Little, *School Success and Staff Development: The Role of Staff Development in Urban Desegregated Schools* (Washington, D.C.: National Institute of Education, 1981).

17. Dennis McCarthy and Terry A. Clark, *School Improvement Project, 1981–1982* (New York: New York Public Schools, Office of Educational Evaluation, 1982). Cost estimates and descriptions of the Arlington experience come from my files and a number of extended conversations with Betty Ann Armstrong, curriculum specialist in reading, language arts, and English for the Arlington County Public Schools during 1982–1983. See also David Crandall and Susan Loucks, "Preparing Facilitators for Implementation: Mirroring the School Improvement Process." Paper presented at the meeting of American Education Research Association, New York, March 1982; and Jane L. David, *School-Based, School-Wide Reform Strategies: An Assessment of Their Impact and Promise* (Palo Alto, California: Bay Area Research Group, 1980).

18. A number of researchers have begun to investigate this critical area. Steven Bossert, David Dwyer, and Brian Rowan, all at the Far West Regional Lab, San Francisco, California, have undertaken a series of studies based upon their model of instructional management. So far, they have produced an explication of the model and five ethnographic studies of principals in effective elementary schools. Philip Hallinger, in "Assessing the Instructional Management Behavior of Principals" (Dissertation, Stanford University, 1983), discusses varied principal behaviors in 10 elementary schools in a California district and concludes that the literature on effective schools is essential for improved student performance.

19. See Raymond Callahan, *Education and the Cult of Efficiency* (Chicago: University of Chicago Press, 1962); and Larry Cuban, *School Chiefs Under Fire* (Chicago: University of Chicago Press, 1976).

20. A few studies of superintendent behavior deal directly or tangentially with leadership: David Tyack and Elisabeth Hansot, *Managers of Virtue: Public School Leadership in America, 1820–1980* (New York: Basic Books, 1982); Nancy Pitner and Rodney Ogawa, "Organizational Leadership: The Case of the School Superintendent," *Educational Administration Quarterly, 17* (1981), 45–65; Lars Larson, Robert S. Bussom, and William Vicars, *The Nature of a School Superintendent's Work* (Washington, D.C.: National Institute of Education, 1981).

21. Identification of these potential sources of conflict comes from my observations in school districts implementing effective schools research; Philip Hallinger's

observations in "Assessing the Instructional Management Behavior of Principals" (Dissertation, Stanford University, 1983); and my own experience in Arlington.

22. I obtained these materials in May 1983 while serving as a site visitor for the U.S. Department of Education's recognition program of exemplary high schools. The issue of generalizability surfaces whenever I speak to groups of administrators on effective schools research. I do not claim that the findings of the Kettering Foundation or the Department of Education are irrelevant. But in the few high schools identified as effective that I have observed firsthand, I saw organizational procedures and structural changes quite different from those of the typical high school.

CHAPTER 4

1989—The "At-Risk" Label and the Problem of Urban School Reform

Unless policymakers and practitioners begin to consider how problems involving schools are framed, they will continue to lunge for quick solutions without considering the fit between the solution and the problem. In doing so, well-intentioned educators may perpetuate lies that harm children, rather than help them. As Georges Bernanos warned: "There is no worse lie than a problem poorly stated."[1]

Consider how the problem of at-risk students is framed today. Many families live in poverty. Even though parents try hard to make ends meet, the corrosive effects of long-term poverty splinter families. Children in these families often lack care; to survive, they lie, steal, and fight. They lead stunted lives. Without help, these children will continue their destructive behavior as adults. Thus, if some parents cannot rear their children properly, the public schools must intervene to avert substantial future costs to society and to help each child become a productive citizen.

This description of at-risk students and their families should be familiar. After all, it is almost 200 years old, and it remains today as it was when it first appeared, a formula used by reformers to arouse the public to action.

In 1805, before there were public schools in New York, the New York City Free School Society asked the state legislature to establish a school for poor children. This is how that group framed its request:

> [We] have viewed with painful anxiety the multiplied evils which have accrued . . . to this city from the neglected education of the children of the poor. . . . The condition of this class is deplorable indeed; reared up by parents who . . . are . . . either indifferent to the best interests of their offspring, or, through intemperate lives . . . these miserable and almost friendless objects are ushered upon the stage of life, inheriting those vices which idleness and the bad example of their parents naturally produce. The consequences of this neglect of education are ignorance and vice, and all those manifold evils

resulting from every species of immorality by which public hospitals and alms-houses are filled with objects of disease and poverty.[2]

In 1898, after public schools had been established and compulsory attendance laws had been passed, a staff member of the board of education in Chicago reported to a committee of board members the following concern about truant children:

> All good citizens desire to have these children educated, and we certainly should not permit a reckless and indifferent part of our population to rear [its] children in ignorance to become a criminal and lawless class within our community. We should rightfully have the power to arrest all these little beggars, loafers, and vagabonds that infest our city, take them from the streets and place them in schools where they are compelled to receive education and learn moral principles.[3]

In 1961 former Harvard University President James Conant studied affluent suburban schools and city schools in which most of the students were poor and Black. Conant concluded:

> I am convinced we are allowing social dynamite to accumulate in our large cities. I am not nearly so concerned about the plight of suburban parents whose offspring are having difficulty finding places in prestige colleges as I am about the plight of parents in the slums whose children either drop out or graduate from school without prospects of either further education or employment. In some slum neighborhoods I have no doubt that over half of the boys between sixteen and twenty-one are out of school and out of work. Leaving aside human tragedies, I submit that a continuation of this situation is a menace to the social and political health of the large cities.[4]

For almost 2 centuries, poor children—often non-White and from other cultures—have been seen to pose a threat to the larger society because neither parents nor existing community institutions could control their unacceptable behavior. Fear of having to spend more for welfare payments and prisons drove public officials to compel attendance in schools as a solution to the problem of children we would today label "at risk." Since the early 19th century, this way of framing the problem and this view of compulsory schooling as its solution have reflected an abiding political consensus among federal, state, and local policymakers.

During these years, some poor children from various ethnic and racial backgrounds achieved well in school, but many did not. Why did so many fail to meet the school's standards for academic performance and behavior? Why were so many placed in special classes and segregated from the rest of the school? Why did so many drop out?

FRAMING THE PROBLEM

Compulsory schooling, proposed as a solution to the social problems of children in poverty, produced another problem: growing numbers of children performing poorly in classrooms. Over the last century, educators and public officials have most often defined the problem of low achievement by at-risk children in the following two ways:

- Students who perform poorly in school are responsible for their performance; that is, they lack ability, character, or motivation.
- Families from certain cultural backgrounds fail to prepare their children for school and provide little support for them in school; they are poor, lack education, and don't teach their children what is proper and improper in the dominant culture.

Two alternative views of the problem have been proposed, though much less frequently:

- Children often fail because the culture of the school ignores or degrades their family and community backgrounds. Middle-class teachers, reflecting the school's values, single out for criticism differences in children's behavior and values; they crush the self-esteem of students and neglect the strengths that these students bring to school.
- The structure of the school is not flexible enough to accommodate the diverse abilities and interests of a heterogeneous student body. Programs are seldom adapted to children's individual differences. Instead, schools seek uniformity, and departures from the norm in achievement and behavior are defined as problems. Social, racial, and ethnic discrimination are embedded in the routine practices of schools and districts.

Note that the two most popular explanations for low academic achievement of at-risk children locate the problem in the children themselves or in their families. As evidence of the popularity of these explanations, recall the labels applied to such children over the last 20 years: disadvantaged, culturally deprived, marginal, and dropouts. Almost a century ago, such students were labeled as backward, retarded, or laggards. In short, since the beginnings of public education, poor academic performance and deviant behavior have been defined as problems of individual children or of their families.[5]

When the problems have been attributed to deficits in children, the solutions have involved more intense doses of what the children were already getting or should have been getting: academic preschools, compensatory education, longer school days, higher academic standards, and so on. When the problems have been attributed to deficits of families, the solutions have focused on training adults to do a proper job of rearing their children.

In the 1980s the barrenness of such definitions and solutions is apparent in soaring retention rates and in dropout rates approaching one out of two among the ethnic poor. It is time to consider a less popular way of framing the problem: that the inflexible structure of the school itself contributes to the conditions that breed academic failure and unsatisfactory student performance.

One of the most inflexible of the structures of schooling is the graded school. The graded school categorizes, segregates, and, as a last resort, eliminates those whose performance and behavior deviate too sharply from the norm. The graded school—consisting of one teacher and one class of 30 or so students of roughly the same age who spend about 36 weeks together before moving on to another grade or class—assumes that students possess equal mental and physical capacities, have equal amounts of help available from their families, and will be taught by teachers with equal skills and knowledge. The implicit theory underlying the graded school is that educational quality comes through uniformity. If a teacher teaches a group of students for a certain amount of time, according to the theory, almost all of these students will learn the required amount of knowledge at roughly the same rate and will move on to the next teacher. Those who don't keep pace will simply take a little longer to master the standard course of study.

Hence, the graded school requires a curriculum divided into equal segments, tests to determine whether the knowledge and skills have been learned, and promotion only for those who have attained the minimum levels set for each grade. This organizational scaffolding holds the graded school together.

Such an impulse to standardize student achievement and behavior also nourishes negative beliefs about children on the part of teachers, administrators, and parents. For example, deviations in children's performance or behavior are commonly ascribed to genetic deficits in the child. To end these deviations, children must be grouped by ability. Separate classrooms or programs are established to "remediate" those who deviate too far from the norm. Ultimately, if students' unacceptable performance persists, school officials either terminate the careers of these students or allow the students to drop out.

Despite these problems, the graded school has succeeded beyond the dreams of the 19th-century reformers who invented it. By the early 1900s the graded school was the way to organize education, and so it has remained. It is no accident that the education systems in most developed nations are built on the graded school.

My point should be self-evident. Although the graded school may have moved large numbers of students through a system of compulsory schooling for many decades when a growing economy could absorb early leavers, a substantial number of today's young people from low-income ethnic and racial minorities are unequipped to find jobs when they leave school. Such a waste of human potential is damaging to a society committed to equal opportunity. I believe that one of the unquestioned and unexamined reasons for this waste of individual and social potential stems from the imperatives of the graded school.[6]

I am not arguing that graded schools are solely responsible for the academic failure that can result from attaching labels to students and segregating students in special classes that stigmatize them in the minds of adults and other children. Until recently, Blacks, Hispanics, and Native Americans who attended legally segregated public schools were already viewed by the larger society as different from Whites and unworthy to sit in classrooms with them. Migrants and immigrants from other cultures—marked as different by language, culture, religion, and poverty—have always worn badges of difference and have had to cope with categories created by the school. Finally, over the last 150 years, those children who were physically and mentally impaired have faced a similar process of labeling, segregation, and elimination. For members of these groups, the differences were present before they met their first teacher.

Beyond overt racism, the effects of long-term poverty can disfigure families and children. The grim outcomes of poverty—such as malnutrition, physical abuse, parental neglect, and living in neighborhoods where crime and violence are commonplace—also mark children early and deeply. Children carry these marks to school.

I argue that the graded school unintentionally worsens these social disadvantages by branding students for the duration of their careers through the mechanisms of separate classes and programs. The graded school, with its imperative to sort out differences in order to preserve uniformity, hardens low-status labels (derived from poverty and racism) in the minds of well-meaning teachers and administrators and makes it more difficult for the students to succeed. For those labeled "at risk," graded schools are poised to produce failure.

In generalizing about groups, I do not wish to minimize or ignore the many students who have succeeded by dint of personal resilience and the luck of having one or more teachers who could see strengths when the school saw only failure. My point is that the structure of the school is viewed as legitimate by the community. Thus that structure helps shape not only the attitudes and behavior of administrators and teachers, but also those of students.

THE CASE AGAINST THE GRADED SCHOOL

What evidence is there for my claims that labeling, segregation, and elimination are inherent to the graded school? Let me begin my answer with a brief historical excursion.

The labels I have been discussing refer almost exclusively to children and families. We seldom say that a teacher is culturally deprived, that a school is at risk, or that a school district is disadvantaged or backward. The child and the family are labeled. And, in the last half-century, more efficient ways of blaming the young have been found, especially through the use of intelligence testing and achievement testing.

Invented by leading psychologists in the early 1900s and clothed in the aura of modern science, both types of testing made it possible for schools in the 1920s to respond efficiently to the enormous cultural diversity among their students. Test results were converted into new labels and attached to groups of children. Mentally defective, dull, average, superior, and gifted children were assigned to separate classes in an effort to enable all children to reach their potential. As two reformers in a low-income elementary school in New York City in the 1920s explained, "It seemed fairly obvious to us that, if enough groups were created within a grade, each moving at different rates of speed, every type of child could find his own place."[7]

Even in the 1920s the children who were sent to classes for "dull" and "defective" students came from immigrant, Mexican American, and Black families. Their labels became badges—filed away in cumulative folders to follow them every step of the way through public school. That pattern has continued until the present. Although group intelligence testing is now out of favor in many districts, the impulse to classify differences still demands categories.[8]

More recently, Jane Mercer investigated classes for mentally retarded children. In one community she found more than 2,500 children who were attending Catholic schools in which there were no special classes for mentally retarded children, although many of these children scored low enough on intelligence tests to qualify them for special classes in the public schools. However, the Catholic schools in this community labeled no one "mentally retarded." The public schools had created this label, but it simply did not exist in the parochial schools.[9]

Finally, if such labeling leads to separate classes and programs and if students seldom shake these labels, the cumulative effect will be that fewer of them will complete high school. In the early decades of this century, most students who had been tagged dull or backward left school for good by the age of 14 or after completion of 8th grade. They found jobs, and the labels were left in files and forgotten. The expanding economy in the decades before and immediately after World War I absorbed hundreds of thousands of young men and women who had limited education and strong backs. Just before World War II, the dropout rate was 60% for all students.[10] However, the economic and social penalties for dropping out were not as severe as they are today.

With its mechanisms for labeling, segregating, and ultimately driving out certain students, the graded public school contributes unintentionally to the problem of deviant performance and behavior among children identified as at risk. Unknowingly working in partnership with social and economic forces in a larger culture marked by racial discrimination, unemployment, inadequate housing, and a social safety net that is barely adequate, the graded school is ill-equipped to erase these social effects; it is an organization that, through no ill intent on the part of the people who work within it, is designed to fail most of the children who have historically been labeled at risk.

PAST EFFORTS TO REDESIGN SCHOOLS

In the early decades of this century, reformers expanded the role of the school beyond teaching the basic skills. Reformers wanted to broaden the narrow academic curriculum and end the regimentation and tedious drill that marked public schools in the early 1900s. If the curriculum was too uniform and the mission too narrow for schools in an urban, industrialized society, the solution was to fit the school to the child's needs.

In those decades, reformers introduced such innovations as gymnasiums, lunchrooms, vocational education, medical checkups, extracurricular activities, field trips, greater informality in relations between teachers and students, rugs, rocking chairs in primary classrooms, and movable desks in the upper grades. However, fitting the school to the student also fed the passion for testing and ability grouping.

Framing the problem in terms of both the child and the school widened the focus from solutions involving the child alone to solutions in which teachers, administrators, and policymakers assumed responsibility for altering their practices to accommodate differences among children and within a changing society. The actual changes that occurred in these decades, however, often intensified the sorting of children. New tests, more ability grouping, expanded curricula, better counseling, and different promotion policies were designed to fit the school to the child, but seldom were beliefs or practices seriously questioned or redesigned. Seldom was the graded school itself seen as a source of the problem.

Schools have indeed adapted to children over the last half-century. But the core processes, what we might think of as the DNA of the graded school—

labeling, segregating, and eliminating those who do not fit–have largely endured in the persistent practices of testing, ability grouping, differentiated curricula, and periodic promotions.[11] By the late 1970s a coalition of practitioners, researchers, and policymakers was beginning to examine the influence of teacher expectations on learning and the influence of the principal in shaping a school's culture. This new approach, termed the effective schools movement, shifted the focus of efforts to deal with poor academic performance among low-income minorities from the child to the school.

Reformers, embracing the ideology of the effective schools movement, tried to convince school professionals that all children can learn–regardless of background–and that schools can raise individual achievement and group esteem. They argued persuasively that the school–not the classroom or the district–is the basic unit of change. Advocates of effective schools, however, seldom questioned the core structures of the graded schools within which they worked. Their passion was (and is) for making those structures more efficient.[12]

We are now in the midst of those reforms. School-based change, restructuring, and school-site management are hot phrases that few can resist. Yet the results for at-risk children seem minimal. Urban schools have been bypassed by current reforms: Dropout rates continue to climb, low academic achievement persists, and measurement-driven instruction geared to minimal skills continues to gain in popularity.[13]

In saying this, I am not criticizing those hard-working teachers, principals, and superintendents who have created schools that expect the best from children–and get it. Nor am I criticizing school staffs that can point with pride to the improved academic achievement of children who seldom did well in school. These staffs have, in effect, seen the problem as one of making a better school in order to make a better child, and they have made substantial contributions to the lives of their students.

At the heart of the effective schools movement, however, is the unexamined assumption that the graded school best serves all at-risk students. And efforts to shift the responsibility for change from the shoulders of at-risk children to the backs of school professionals have frequently exhausted those professionals, have often been limited to small numbers of schools, and have seldom spread throughout school systems.

THE DIFFICULTY OF REDESIGN

There are several reasons why redesigning schools is so difficult. First, the acute pressure to educate all children requires efficient and inexpensive means of managing students as they move through 12 or more years of public education. The graded school has proved to be a durable mechanism for handling large numbers of children over long periods of time because it has succeeded in standardizing expectations and procedures at a fairly low cost.

Second, many citizens and educators consider the process successful. Some point to the increasing numbers of students who complete high school: three out of four today, as opposed to one out of nine a century ago. Others cite the correlation between expanded schooling in the 20th century and the nation's economic growth, high standard of living, and status as a world power. Whether or not schooling actually causes growth in wealth and power, the connections between the two are deeply embedded in our thinking. Thus there is little apparent desire and even less political will to investigate other ways to provide schooling for American children.

Except, I should add, in national emergencies. Political coalitions do arise to question the status quo when the security or economic health of the nation is threatened. Recall the Soviet gains in science and technology in the 1950s, and consider the current concern over America's loss of economic productivity and our trade deficit. In both cases, national concern about the quality of schools led to legislation, innovation, and increased funding. However, then as now, we simply assumed that the graded school would be the vehicle for improvement; it simply had to work better. Few, if any, questioned the structure or processes that were embedded in this mid-19th-century invention, and fewer still seriously considered alternatives.

Over the last 60 years, only during the civil rights movement of the 1960s have students been seen as poorly served by schools and undeserving of blame. The spillover of that movement from urban slums into affluent suburbs touched many middle-class, nonminority students. Serious questions were raised about who was teaching, about what these teachers believed about students, about what and how they taught, about how they grouped students, and about what effect that grouping had. Finally, questions were asked about the graded school itself. Alternative ways of teaching, organizing the curriculum, and structuring the school were explored and developed. Many of these alternatives persist today in special education, in Head Start, in dropout-prevention programs, in alternative schools, and in a variety of similar inventions. Many other alternatives failed to endure because of their own inadequacies; most have simply disappeared.

Alarms are sounding again about at-risk children being ill-served by schools, about low academic performance, and about high dropout rates. The current passion for restructuring schools comes from unlikely coalitions of corporate executives, foundation officials, governors, and union presidents—all of whom wish to improve schooling for at-risk children by substituting new arrangements (e.g., teacher-run schools, mentor and lead teachers, more parental choice in selecting schools) for the current ways in which schools are governed.

The reformers mean well, but they miss the target: the graded school itself and the ways in which it contributes to the very problem they seek to solve. No significant improvement will occur in the school careers of at-risk students without fundamental changes in the graded school, and current restructuring proposals will not achieve that end.

Alternatives to the graded school have slipped in and out of fashion but have never disappeared. There have always been one-room schoolhouses in isolated rural areas, but nongraded urban elementary schools have been operating since 1934. Milwaukee introduced nongraded schools in 1942. After World War II, interest in nongraded elementary schools increased. The publication of *The Nongraded Elementary School*, by John Goodlad and Robert Anderson, coincided with rapid growth in the number of schools that were trying the innovation. Between 1960 and the early 1970s nongraded elementary schools (along with a smattering of secondary schools) gained visibility as an alternative to the dominant model. Since the mid-1970s, however, nongraded schools have lapsed into obscurity.[14]

Talk of restructuring has rekindled interest in nongraded schools, grouping across age and ability, team teaching, core curricula, and cooperative learning. However, abolishing grades and changing nothing else would be simple-minded folly; grouping, teaching, and curricular practices also need to be reexamined. Such fundamental changes require endorsement, if not visible support, from the gatekeepers of change within a district: the school board and the superintendent. Such changes will also require time, and the planning and implementation must include teachers, principals, and parents.

INCREMENTAL CHANGE

What if teachers, principals, and district administrators are overwhelmed by the mere thought—much less the task—of redesigning the graded school? Or what if educators are not persuaded that the graded school is a substantial source of academic failure among at-risk students? Whether overwhelmed or unpersuaded, suppose that these very same educators are still convinced that some changes must be made within mainstream elementary and secondary schools. What can they do?

To answer these questions, practitioners would need to know whether there is sufficient knowledge available to make smaller changes that fall short of a complete redesign. They would need to know what, if any, common markers characterize those schools, programs, and classrooms that are successfully serving at-risk students.

Is there enough knowledge of this kind available to practitioners? From both the wisdom accumulated by practitioners over decades of experience and from the knowledge produced by research, enough is known to make substantial changes in schools and classrooms. Some of that wisdom is captured in the work of gifted principals and teachers who have figured out what has to be done and have done it. Some of it occasionally appears in syntheses of research aimed at lay and professional audiences, such as *Schools That Work: Educating Disadvantaged Children*, the booklet prepared by the U.S. Department of Education.[15]

However, no formulas exist as yet to explain how to put together the right combination of people, things, and ideas to create a particular setting that succeeds with at-risk students. All that is currently available is general advice: build commitment among those involved in school-based change, help practitioners strengthen their skills in working together, and remember that change should be viewed as a process rather than as a product.

What common markers characterize those successful schools, programs, and classrooms that practitioners have created for at-risk students? By successful I mean schools and classrooms that motivate students to complete school, that increase students' desire to learn, and that build self-esteem and enhance academic performance. Certain features of such schools and classrooms have appeared repeatedly in the research literature, and they coincide with practitioners' wisdom about what works with at-risk students.

1. *Size.* Successful programs serve as few as 50 students and seldom more than a few hundred. All adults and students know one another at some level. In secondary schools these successful programs might be schools-within-a-school or housed apart from the main building. The face-to-face contact cultivates enduring, rather than passing, relationships between old and young. Small programs are also more likely to involve students in program activities, and smaller class size permits more personalized instruction.[16]

2. *Staff.* Teachers volunteer for these programs and classes and make a commitment to educating at-risk students. Teachers develop camaraderie when they share a commitment, personal and cultural knowledge about students, and a willingness to learn from failure.[17]

3. *Program flexibility.* Because these schools and programs are small and are committed to rescuing students from what appears to be inevitable failure, they share a willingness to try different approaches. Ability grouping is uncommon; few, if any, distinctions are made among students; tests are used only to

match students with appropriate materials. Passing and failing are personal benchmarks along a clearly marked road of achievable goals, not public displays in which some move ahead and others stay behind.

Time and scheduling are handled differently in these schools. Secondary teachers frequently spend more time each day with students, and the same teacher may work with a group of students for 2 or even 3 years.

Teaching is flexible, as well. Working with small groups of students and individuals is common; team teaching is widespread. The same high school teacher may teach three subjects and serve as advisor for a handful of students. In-school activity is frequently mixed with paid employment outside the school building. Finally, many of these programs link students with a wide array of social services through teachers, advisors, or special staff members. Hence, teaching is an uncommon mix of many tasks.[18]

4. *Classroom communities.* In these successful schools, the school, program, or classroom becomes a kind of extended family, and achievement and caring for one another are both important. A sense of belonging to a group—in effect, a different culture—is created as a means of increasing self-esteem and achievement. Of course, the community model exists in some special programs in regular schools, in small elementary schools, and in high school athletics, clubs, bands, drill teams, and the like. But this model tends to be rare in large schools and is further limited by the structure of the school schedule, by ability grouping, and by a host of other factors.[19]

These features of schools, programs, and classrooms that have succeeded with at-risk children add up to teachers and administrators working together to make what is, into what ought to be. They must change the size, structure, staffing, and relationships between students and adults. They must alter—dramatically and fundamentally—what occurs routinely between teachers and students.

What about individual teachers in their classrooms? There are at least three directions that teachers could take. First, research on teacher effectiveness links certain teaching practices to gains on test scores. Proponents of the approach called direct instruction or "active teaching," for example, claim that test scores rise when teachers of at-risk students use such an approach to teach reading and math in certain elementary grades. These research findings have frequently been wedded to larger efforts to create effective schools.[20]

Critics of direct instruction have focused on the small amount of subject matter covered; the tedious, routine work; the emphasis on test scores; the inappropriateness of the approach for secondary school subjects; and the low expectations for the teaching of reasoning and critical thinking at the elementary level. Yet, for elementary teachers concerned about the skills of their at-risk students, this research—harnessed to the folk wisdom of veteran teachers—suggests that familiar techniques of managing a class and of introducing and explaining material will pay off in rising test scores—if that is a goal.[21]

Other choices are available, as well. There are instructional approaches that build on the strengths that at-risk children bring to school. Teachers can make connections with the life experiences of students from diverse cultural groups and can exploit what we know about active learning and student involvement to develop students' reasoning skills. Such approaches enhance the home language of children and connect children's experiences with school concepts and abstract ideas.[22]

Finally, teachers can turn to the growing body of evidence that mixed-ability and mixed-age groupings within and across classrooms have positive effects on student motivation and learning. Evidence drawn from the classrooms of at-risk students regarding the benefits of nongraded early primary units, combination classes, and cooperative learning suggests that there is a technology of instruction to fit heterogeneous classrooms.[23] In order to move in this direction, teachers will need to know the cultural backgrounds and experiences of students. If they are part of a larger school effort, they will need to manage several groups of students of varied abilities during the school day.

Are schools and classrooms that embrace these approaches very different from mainstream schools, where silence, reprimands, worksheets, and uniformity dominate the school day? Indeed, they are. Does this mean more work for the principal and teacher? Indeed, it does. Will this produce deep satisfaction from overseeing student growth? Indeed, it will.

Many teachers and principals have made these kinds of changes. The work is both exhilarating and exhausting. It helps, of course, if colleagues share similar aims for improving classrooms. It is far better if the principal endorses such classroom changes and provides material and emotional support. Even better is the situation in which the district office, the superintendent, and the school board not only endorse, but actively nourish, such schools and classrooms. Going it alone is tough but not impossible. Others have done it, but they have paid a high price. The rewards are intensely personal and sharply felt, and they last a lifetime. There is, then, a tiny window of opportunity open to teachers and principals who, unaided by state and district policymakers, nonetheless wish to improve the lives of at-risk children.

How sad it is, though, that so much rhetoric about fundamental change has produced so little energy for redesigning the graded school. The message I must close with has often been conveyed by well-intentioned citizens and educators: In the absence of fundamental reform, teachers and principals who desire genuine reform will have to go the extra mile.

The larger issue and my central point, however, is this: The basic design of the graded school has trapped both staff members and at-risk students in a web of shared failure. We must reexamine the institution of the graded school and determine the degree to which it is the source of high rates of academic failure among at-risk students. The popular understanding of the problem, which locates the source of failure within the children and their families, is bankrupt. There is, after all, no worse lie than a problem poorly stated.

NOTES

1. Georges Bernanos, *Last Essays of Georges Bernanos* (Chicago: Henry Regnery Co., 1955), 153.

2. Emerson Palmer, *The New York Public School: Being a History of Free Education in the City of New York* (New York: Macmillan, 1905), 19.

3. *Forty-Fourth Annual Report of the Board of Education* (Chicago: Public Schools of the City of Chicago, 1898), 170.

4. James B. Conant, *Slums and Suburbs* (New York: McGraw-Hill, 1961), 2.

5. Stanley Zehm, "Educational Misfits: A Study of Poor Performers in the English Class, 1825–1925" (Doctoral dissertation, Stanford University, 1973).

6. For early evidence of the connection between the graded school and dropouts, see William T. Harris, "The Early Withdrawal of Pupils from School: Its Causes and Its Remedies," *Addresses and Journal of Proceedings*, National Educational Association (Peoria, IL: N.C. Nason, 1873), 266; and E. E. White, "Several Problems in Graded School Management," *Addresses and Journal of Proceedings*, National Educational Association (Worcester, MA: Charles Hamilton, 1874), 34.

7. Elisabeth Irwin and Louis Marks, *Fitting the School to the Child* (New York: Macmillan, 1924), 70.

8. Seymour Sarason and John Doris, *Educational Handicap, Public Policy, and Social History* (New York: Free Press, 1979), 296–354.

9. Jane Mercer, *Labeling the Mentally Retarded* (Berkeley: University of California Press, 1973).

10. Russell W. Rumberger, "High School Drop-outs: A Review of Issues and Evidence," *Review of Educational Research* (Summer 1987), 101. For examples of the literature that connects school processes to dropping out, see Michelle Fine, "Why Urban Adolescents Drop Into and Out of Public High School," in Gary Natriello, ed., *School Drop-outs* (New York: Teachers College Press, 1987), 89–105; and Gary Wehlage and

Robert Rutter, "Dropping Out: How Much Do Schools Contribute to the Problem?" in Natriello, pp. 70–88.

11. For a discussion of the persistence of 19th-century policies and practices, see John Goodlad and Robert Anderson, *The Nongraded Elementary School* (New York: Harcourt, Brace and World, 1963), Chs. 1, 2.

12. See, for example, Kenneth Clark, *Dark Ghetto: Dilemmas of Social Power* (New York: Harper & Row, 1964); and Ronald Edmonds, "Effective Schools for the Urban Poor," *Educational Leadership* (October 1979), 15–24.

13. *An Imperiled Generation: Saving Urban Schools* (Princeton, NJ: Carnegie Foundation for the Advancement of Teaching, 1988).

14. See, for example, Charles Silberman, *Crisis in the Classroom* (New York: Random House, 1971); and John Goodlad and Robert Anderson, *The Nongraded Elementary School* (New York: Harcourt, Brace and World, 1963), Chs. 1, 2.

15. U.S. Department of Education, *Schools That Work: Educating Disadvantaged Children* (Washington, D.C.: U.S. Government Printing Office, 1987). See also Ken Macrorie, *20 Teachers* (New York: Oxford University Press, 1984).

16. *An Imperiled Generation: Saving Urban Schools* (Princeton, NJ: Carnegie Foundation for the Advancement of Teaching, 1988), 21–24.

17. See Shirley Brice Heath, *Ways with Words* (New York: Cambridge University Press, 1983); and Mary Anne Raywid, "Drawing Educators to Choice," *Metropolitan Education* (Fall 1987), 7–23.

18. U.S. Department of Education, *Dealing with Dropouts* (Washington, D.C.: Office of Educational Research and Improvement, 1987); and *An Imperiled Generation: Saving Urban Schools* (Princeton, NJ: Carnegie Foundation for the Advancement of Teaching, 1988), 24–33.

19. James Comer, *School Power* (New York: Free Press, 1980); idem, "Home-School Relationships as They Affect the Academic Success of Children," *Education and Urban Society, 16* (1984), 323–337; Peggy Farber, "Central Park East: High School with a Human Face," *Rethinking Schools*, May/June (1988), 6–7; and Lisbeth Schorr, *Within Our Reach* (New York: Anchor Press, 1988), 241–245.

20. Jere Brophy and Thomas Good, "Teacher Behavior and Student Achievement," in Merlin Wittrock, ed., *Handbook of Research on Teaching* (New York: Macmillan, 1986), 328–375.

21. Ibid.

22. James Banks, "Ethnicity, Class, and Cognitive Styles: Research and Teaching Implications," paper presented at the annual meeting of the American Educational Research Association, Washington, D.C., 1987; and Kathryn Au, "Participation Structures in a Reading Lesson with Hawaiian Children: Analysis of a Culturally Appropriate Instructional Event," *Anthropology and Education Quarterly, 11*(1980), 91–115.

23. Robert Slavin, *Cooperative Learning* (New York: Longman, 1983); and Gaea Leinhardt and William Bickel, "Instruction's the Thing Wherein to Catch the Mind That Falls Behind," *Educational Psychologist, 22*(1987), 177–207.

CHAPTER 5

1990—Reforming
Again, Again, and Again

Everything has been said before, but since nobody listens, we have to keep going back and begin again.

—Andre Gide

At first glance, Gide's quote sounds arrogant—much like saying that America is the land of the forgetful. I do not mean it that way. I interpret his words as a simple recognition of how most people either ignore or forget the past and need to be reminded that much, indeed, "has been said before" about why planned changes keep reappearing (Roth, 1988). To skeptics who may question whether reforms do, in fact, recur, I will offer three examples to make that point. Then I will explore how scholars have tried to explain why school reforms return. Finally, because these familiar explanations ignore or omit extensive evidence, I offer alternatives that embrace the counterevidence.

The point is to spotlight an issue—the inevitable return of school reforms—that has become so familiar as to enter the folk wisdom of policymakers and practitioners. Why is highlighting this issue important? Public officials' eagerness to reform schools has continued unabated in this century, especially since World War II. Policymakers have ready explanations for why schools are so hard to change and why previous reforms have failed. These explanations, drawn from experience and biases, may or may not be informed by historical research or alternative ways of viewing the past.

The state-engineered school reforms of the 1980s, for example, have sought a regeneration of the American economy. This vision was anchored in popular views of the recent past (the 1960s and 1970s), when educators supposedly had permitted academic standards to slip from their high position in earlier decades. Yet, a generation ago, school critics and policymakers in the 1950s argued that Deweyan ideologies had so permeated the public schools of the 1930s and 1940s that the curriculum had become virtually useless in providing the nation with scientists and engineers (Honig, 1985; Ravitch, 1983).

Reform visions often depend on a view of the past as a series of failures that killed a golden age of schooling. Critics' claims about what happened in schools in earlier decades and policymakers' assumptions about the past often become rationales for reform. Thus, the stakes for policymaking are high because such questions about why reforms failed in the past and why they return go to the heart of present policy debates over whether federal, state, and district mandates to alter schooling will ever get past the classroom door. I begin with three examples of recurring school reforms.

CLASSROOM: TEACHER-CENTERED INSTRUCTION

Much has been reported about the durability of teacher-centered instruction, sometimes called "chalk-and-talk" or "frontal teaching," even in the face of determined efforts to move classroom practices toward student-centered approaches (Applebee, 1974; Cuban, 1984; Goodlad, 1984; Hoetker & Ahlbrand, 1969; see also Applebee, Langer, & Mullis, 1987; Stake & Easley, 1978; Suydam, 1977; Westbury, 1973).

Currently, educators and parents are expressing intense interest in such instructional reforms as cooperative learning, greater student participation in classroom tasks, and increased teacher and student use of computers. In each instance, deeply held values about how teachers should teach, the role of content in classrooms, and how children should learn clash. Such debate over classroom pedagogy is familiar.

For many centuries, these two traditions of how teachers should and do teach have fired debates and shaped practice. What I called teacher-centered instruction has been variously labeled as subject centered, "tough minded" (James, 1958), "hard pedagogy" (Katz, 1968), and "mimetic" (Jackson, 1986). What I called student-centered instruction has been variously labeled child centered, "Tender minded" (James, 1958), "soft pedagogy" (Katz, 1968), and "transformative" (Jackson, 1986). Both traditions of teaching are anchored in different views of knowledge and the relationship of teacher and learner to that knowledge. In teacher-centered instruction, knowledge is often (but not always) "presented" to a learner, who—and the metaphors from different cultures vary here—is a "blank slate," a "vessel to fill," or "a duck to stuff." In student-centered instruction, knowledge is often (but not always) "discovered" by the learner, who, again using different metaphors, is "rich clay in the hands of an artist" or "a flourishing garden in need of a masterful cultivator."

In America, over a century and a half ago, pedagogical reformers condemned teacher-centered instruction with its emphasis on a textbook from which students recited already-memorized information, and with teachers doing most of the talking to the entire group and asking rapid-fire questions. Criticism of teachers requiring students to memorize chapters of a text or the entire U.S. Constitution began to appear by the 1840s and 1850s. The metaphor of the mind as a garden (rather than a storehouse) reentered the debates on how teachers should teach (Katz, 1968). Motivating children through their interests introduced notions of the whole child well before the Civil War. Object teaching, an instructional innovation that leaned heavily on what students observed in the world, sought to arouse students' curiosity. Schooling, these reformers argued, should be connected to the real world. Innovative educators introduced animals, flowers, and early photographs into classrooms. Recall also that the first kindergartens, with their heavy emphasis on play, cultivation of emotions and expression, and use of real-world objects, were founded just after the Civil War (Dearborn, 1925; Shapiro, 1983).

The next generation of reformers also tried to end teacher-centered practices. Progressives, some of whom were determined to make schools into child-centered places, fought against regimented instruction as early as the 1870s and into the 1900s. Child-centered progressives wanted more student involvement, active learning, informal relations between teachers and students, and connections to the larger world outside the classroom. Innovative methods such as using small groups, activity projects, joint student–teacher planning of classroom work, and bringing into classrooms just-minted technologies of film and radio were reformers' ways of making early 20th century classrooms child centered. Few of these changes entered classrooms and remained as intended (Cremin, 1988; Goodlad, 1984; see also Cremin, 1961; Cuban, 1984).

Within the present moment of reform another generation of reformers is fighting against a technical, subject-centered form of instruction expressed in mastery learning, measurement-driven curricula, and bookkeeper-like accountability. Those researchers and practitioners who herald cooperative learning, active student involvement, and the virtues of desktop computers that interact with students bring new meaning to Yogi Berra's observation: "It's déjà vu all over again."

CURRICULUM: THE ACADEMIC AND THE PRACTICAL

It comes as no surprise, then, that the centuries-old traditions about the forms of teaching that are embedded in different values about knowledge and its relationship to teachers and students would have generated tensions about what content should be taught in schools. We are now in the full flush of state-driven reforms that aim for a common core of academic knowledge. We

hear that 17-year-olds can't figure out math problems, locate Siberia, or tell
the difference between the Bill of Rights and a bill of sale. Higher graduation
requirements now mandate that all students take more academic subjects.
Yet this passion for a core of subject matter shared by all would be familiar to
Horace Mann and other mid-19th-century school reformers who introduced
the common school curriculum in the first eight grades.

So, too, would the current passion for all students studying the same academic content be familiar to Harvard University President Charles Eliot,
who chaired the Committee of Ten in 1893. That committee urged upon all
high schools 4 years of English and 3 years of history, science, mathematics,
and a foreign language. The committee further recommended that:

> Every subject which is taught at all in a secondary school should be taught in
> the same way and to the same extent to every pupil as long as he pursues it, no
> matter what the probable destination of the pupil may be, or at which point
> his education is to cease. (Krug, 1961, p. 87)

Since then there have been repeated efforts to reduce the tension between
having all students study academic subjects for their liberal values and introducing technical or practical subjects that may reflect different futures in the
job market. Progressives challenged the one best academic curriculum. They
saw boredom, mechanical instruction, and huge numbers of students leaving school at ages 12 and 13. They were anxious to fit the curriculum to the
student rather than the student to the curriculum. They redefined an equal
education, from all students being forced to take the same practical academic
curriculum to all students taking different courses to cultivate their varied
interests, capacities, and vocational futures (Cremin, 1961; Tyack, 1974). The
familiar comprehensive junior and senior high school, with its many courses
of study, is a consequence of these turn-of-the-century reformers' success in
altering the curriculum.

Severe criticism of these reforms came in the 1950s with another generation of change masters whose curricular values were captured in the
titles of their books: *Quackery in the Public Schools* (Lynd, 1953), *Educational
Wastelands* (Bestor, 1953), and *Second-Rate Brains* (Lansner, 1958). The National Science Foundation, established in 1950, launched major changes in
science and math curricula led by university specialists. James B. Conant's
studies of secondary schools in the mid-1950s underscored the necessity
for providing rigorous academic content for able, college-bound students
(Silberman, 1971).

By the mid-1960s, however, broad political and social movements aimed
at freeing the individual from bureaucratic constraints and helping ethnic

and racial minorities end their second-class status had swept across schools. If desegregation, compensatory education, and magnet schools became familiar phrases, so did free schools, open classrooms, flexible scheduling, and middle schools. Many (but not all) of the previous decade's curricular reforms evaporated by the early 1970s as efforts redoubled to differentiate courses and schools for low-income and minority children. Alternative schools, broadened vocational programs, and new curricula that blended academic and practical subjects dotted the school landscape in efforts to recapture students who had been either relegated to the margins of a secondary education or pushed out of schools (Powell, Farrar, & Cohen, 1985; Ravitch, 1983).

By the late 1970s and early 1980s, professional and lay activists were hearing a renewed call for traditional academic curricula in high schools. Demands for academic excellence were translated into more required subjects, a longer school year, more homework, and higher test scores. More students took chemistry, geometry, and foreign languages; fewer students registered for vocational courses. In California, a pacesetter among states in mandating core academic subjects for all students, voters responded warmly to State Superintendent Bill Honig's message for traditional schooling. Honig, a graduate of an academically selective San Francisco high school, said that "a traditional education worked for us, why shouldn't we give at least a good a shot at the common culture to today's children" (Honig, 1985, p. 55).

For almost a century, this enduring curricular tension between values embedded in academic and practical subjects has ebbed and flowed among groups of reformers whose versions of an equal education in a democracy have differed (Kliebard, 1986). The invention of the comprehensive high school and the junior high school in the first quarter of this century fashioned a workable compromise between these competing values that both professional educators and the lay public have since endorsed. Yet each time this debate over values has resurfaced, policymakers have refashioned that compromise by creating or deleting courses of study. As we enter the last decade of this century, this refashioning is again under way.

CENTRALIZING AND DECENTRALIZING AUTHORITY

As a final example of the persistence of reform, consider the resiliency of the issue of centralizing and decentralizing authority in governing schools. Over a century ago, there were more than 100,000 (yes, 100,000!) school districts in the nation. In big cities, school boards had 50 or more members. Frequently, board members doled out teaching jobs to constituents. The system was seen as democratic and responsive to voters by its supporters but to critics–the good-government reformers of the Progressive movement–the system was inefficient and corrupt. To bring order to this uncontrolled localism, progressive reformers proposed consolidating many tiny rural districts into larger ones and centralizing power into the hands of smaller, efficient school boards that would hire trained professionals to run the schools (Cremin, 1961; Cronin, 1973; Katznelson & Weir, 1985; Reese, 1986; Tyack, 1974).

By the early 1960s, the wisdom of these solutions to governing schools had come under attack. Civil rights activists questioned the legitimacy of small school boards in big cities where officials were distant from the lives of minority children in poverty. Calls for schools and educators to be more responsive to their communities swelled into proposals for community control and administrative decentralization (Gittell, 1967; Levin, 1970). Values of participation and equity lay at the core of the impulse to decentralize authority to govern schools. Philadelphia, Washington, D.C., Los Angeles, Chicago, and other cities divided their school systems into districts with regional superintendents in charge. The 1-million-student New York City system was divided into 32 community districts in an effort to shift power closer to parents (Ravitch, 1974). However, by the mid-1970s, the surge of interest in decentralization had spent itself.

In the 1980s, again, centralizing authority gained support from state policymakers who pursued school improvement through legislation. Within a few years, however, a slow recognition grew that state-driven reforms were not penetrating individual schools. Talk spread of unresponsive state bureaucracies incapable of improving local schools. New reform proposals to decentralize decisionmaking were heavily influenced, first, by the research literature on the individual school as the unit of change and, second, by corporate executives who pointed to their organizations, where decisionmaking occurred at the site at which products were made or services delivered (Kearns, 1988; Purkey & Smith, 1983). Policymakers introduced "school-site councils," "school-based management," and "restructured schools." In 1989, the Illinois legislature authorized Chicago to place each of its 595 schools under the management of an 11-member school-site council that included both parents and practitioners. New York City continues to seek ways of retaining its 32 community districts, but without the mismanagement and patronage that have seeped into the governance of a few districts (Daniels, 1988). So, again, the tension persists between the values embedded in centralization and decentralization in governing schools.

In offering these three instances of reforms resurfacing repeatedly in the 20th century, I have set the stage for the central question: Why do these reforms keep reappearing?

WHY DO REFORMS APPEAR AGAIN AND AGAIN?

I begin with an explanation anchored in the rational model of organizational behavior, because it is widely shared by those interested in school improvement. Readers of *Educational Researcher* are familiar with the common practice, among some academics, of bashing rational explanations as ill fitted to the realities of organizations and their environments. Bashing is usually a preface for offering a favored explanation that will, the author believes, convince readers. This is no such preface. I offer a brief examination of the rational model of organizational action because it is pervasive among policymakers, administrators, practitioners, and researchers.

The need to rationalize organizational behavior can be seen in sustained attempts at district and state levels to align curricula with texts, tests, and instructional goals; it can be seen in the accelerating passion for more testing at state and national levels; it can be seen in the spread of classroom evaluation practices drawn from teacher effectiveness research and patterns of systematic curriculum construction laid down by academics who see education as a science; it can be seen in the fickle love affair between the federal government's initial support and later shrunken enthusiasm for research and development centers and laboratories; and, finally, it can be seen in the passion for scientifically conducted evaluation studies to prove, once and for all, that a particular teaching method, machine, or curriculum improves student performance. The rational model may be a favored target for abuse in academic journals and studies, but it is alive and well in the world of school reform (Elmore & McLaughlin, 1988; Honig, 1985; Kliebard, 1975, 1979, 1986; Slavin, 1989; Timar & Kirp, 1988).

A RATIONAL EXPLANATION FOR RECURRING REFORMS

The return of school reforms suggests that the reforms have failed to remove the problems they were intended to solve. Analysts ask: Are we attacking the right problem? Have the policies we adopted fit the problem? Have practitioners implemented the policies as intended? Another set of questions concern whether the solutions designed to correct the problems identified by policymakers were mismatched. Right problems, wrong solutions? Or vice versa? Are we dealing with the problem or the politics of the problem?

Other analysts seeking a rational basis for policy examine the thought processes of policymakers. What analogies and metaphors do they use as a basis for forming policy? For example, historically policymakers have used business firms and their perceived efficiency as desirable models for schools to copy. In the early decades of this century, reformers urged corporate models of governance and managerial techniques on public schools (Callahan, 1962). In the 1980s, it has been common for school funding to be reframed from a cost to an investment in "human capital." Also, explicit comparisons between school sites, as places where services are delivered, and corporate profit centers, where both autonomy and accountability reign, have been common. District and state policymakers increasingly use the language of corporate boardrooms (Committee for Economic Development, 1985).

Take the current passion for policies that encourage choice. Broadening parent choice in public schools is a solution. What are the problems that this reform is supposed to solve? To listen carefully to policymakers who promote this reform, choice will, in the words of Minnesota Governor Rudy Perpich, "improve students' academic skills and attitudes and lower the dropout rate" (Perpich, 1989). According to Perpich and other advocates around the country, permitting parents to choose the school they wish their children to attend introduces competition where a monopoly once existed. "By allowing market forces to work in our educational system, families are empowered to make discerning choices about their schools. And they compel schools to be more responsive to the people they serve" (Perpich, 1989). Buried in the thinking of choice advocates is the analogy of the marketplace, where competition for private goods and services leads to both consumers and businesses profiting. Policies of choice are aimed at ending substantial problems within public schools. How these reform policies of choice will end low academic performance and high dropout rates, however, is unclear. The connection is mysterious, although the warm public response to policies of choice and their potent image argue compellingly that there is a mother lode of political gold to be mined there.

Some researchers and analysts have tried to disentangle the values, arguments, and issues that mark the solution of choice to the perceived problem of inadequate public schooling (Elmore, 1987; Kerchner & Boyd, 1987; Raywid, 1985). Few, however, have yet distilled the linkages between choice and its impact on school-site decisionmaking, staff morale, the remaking of curriculum, and the delivery of instruction. Citing exemplars of choice where schooling has improved is useful, but as incomplete as showing Chartres Cathedral to a novice architect and saying: "Here is what can be done."

Those who believe in rational approaches to organizing change would argue that if policymakers only asked tough questions, thought through issues analytically, examined their beliefs, or avoided playing the politics of the problems while carefully using available research findings, school reforms would not keep returning like bad pennies. This rational explanation suggests that policymakers are in control. They have both the knowledge and technical expertise within their grasp to solve problems just like surgeons doing heart bypass operations.

Reforms return because policymakers fail to diagnose problems and promote correct solutions. Reforms return because policymakers use poor historical analogies and pick the wrong lessons from the past (Katz, 1987). Reforms return because policymakers fail, in the words of Charles Silberman 2 decades ago, "to think seriously about educational purposes" or question the "mindlessness" of schooling (Silberman, 1971, pp. 10–11). Reforms return because policymakers cave in to the politics of a problem rather than the problem itself. Reforms return because decisionmakers seldom seek reliable, correctly conducted evaluations of program effectiveness before putting a program into practice (Slavin, 1989). In short, were policymakers to pursue a rational course of analysis and decisionmaking and, where fitting, use research and evaluation results properly, there would be no need for the same solutions to reenter the policy arena. The rational explanation is compelling but flawed; it is useful but limited; it is popular but often criticized. Why?

The rational explanation frequently leans heavily on two images: the pendulum and the cycle. Policymakers who believe that history repeats itself or who say that those who are ignorant of the past are condemned to repeat its errors often use the pendulum image. They tend to be critical of swings in national moods about schooling. Few question the existence of such periodic movement; it is their unpredictability in when they begin and end that upsets those deeply interested in rationalizing organizational behavior. There are, unfortunately, at least two unexamined flaws in the popular metaphor.

First, the pendulum swing seemingly returns exactly to the same spot it left. Although there is motion, there is no change. Things predictably return to what they were at a prior time. The facts, however, about both the pendulum and lack of change undercut the image. Physicists have discovered that even in the supposed orderly swing of a laboratory pendulum there are microscopic erratic movements that suddenly erupt without apparent explanation and that the disorder creates complex patterns unseen before. Even a simple pendulum swing was far more complicated than anticipated (Gleick, 1987). If physicists were surprised about the pendulum, ahistorical policymakers would similarly be surprised about the vast changes that have occurred in schooling over the last century and a half of pendulum swings.

The expansion of schooling to embrace all groups of children, regardless of background, throughout the 19th and 20th centuries is a trend-line of almost revolutionary proportions that has marked the United States as unique in the family of nations. The introduction and spread of the graded elementary and secondary school in the mid-19th century and the virtual elimination of the one-room schoolhouse by the late 20th century were dramatic changes that altered the face of public schooling in this nation. By the middle of the 20th century, schools contained libraries, lunchrooms, space for health clinics, industrial and manual training shops, and playgrounds; they were very different places than schools in 1900. Large, politically appointed school boards gave way to small, professionally oriented ones; untrained teachers and administrators were replaced by state-certified and professionally trained practitioners; the classical academic curriculum expanded into varied curricula supplemented by a stunning array of extracurricular activities; class sizes of 50 and more fell to half that. All of these changes occurred within less than a century (Cremin, 1988; Kaestle, 1983; Tyack, 1974). No, the image of a pendulum swing, a stable glide from one point to another without alteration, fails to account for either the erratic motions of such a swing or the enormous changes in public schooling that have occurred over the last century.

The second flaw in the pendulum metaphor is that the image requires a powerful external force beyond the control of policymakers and practitioners to set the pendulum in motion. After all, a playground swing just doesn't start moving by itself; something has to give it a shove. Is it the Russians launching a space vehicle? The Japanese economy outperforming that of the United States? The need for a potent outside force to get the pendulum moving suggests helplessness on the part of supposedly rational policymakers to either halt the swing or redirect it. The pendulum metaphor seemingly accounts for the same reforms returning but ends up weakening the rationality of policymakers by suggesting how impotent they are in reshaping the environment in which schools are embedded.

If the pendulum metaphor contains flawed thinking about rationalizing school organizations, what about the cycle image? The image of a cycle has a rich history in human affairs. Philosophers, historians, and informed observers have generated complex images that speak of ancient civilizations and golden ages arising and disappearing and of cycles that ebb and flow, accumulating a residue of change over time (Dewey & Dakin, 1947; Eliade, 1954; Gould, 1987). Cycles, of course, do not have to go through preset evolutionary stages like an egg–caterpillar–chrysalis–butterfly. Cycles can be compared to upward or downward spirals or waves that vary in amplitude and frequency, or to the irregular growth of a coral reef. Nonetheless, cycles appeal to the rational mind with their hint of predictability. Because people, organizations, and nations go through phases of a cycle, the next stage can be anticipated.

One of the most highly developed arguments for recurring cycles that can be easily applied to schooling has been set forth by two historians–father and son–named Arthur Schlesinger (senior and junior). Both have gone so far as to predict when things will change from one chord of a national rhythm to another (Schlesinger, 1986). I analyze their argument because the cyclical image is so deeply embedded in the minds of practitioners, researchers, and policymakers who work within the rational tradition that it is worthwhile to take one of the more popular versions and examine it.

Schlesinger argues as follows. In most democracies, economic factors such as level of unemployment and economic growth determine to a great degree who gets elected. Electoral changes produce public officials with ideas that can be labeled in this society as conservative or liberal insofar as what role the government should play in the lives of citizens. For example, liberals, in their eagerness to use government to solve social and economic problems, pile up reforms.

The first 2 decades of this century belonged to liberals in the Progressive movement. But in the wake of World War I, reform energies flagged. Although progressive sentiment still persisted during the 1920s, the decade became overtly conservative under Presidents Harding, Coolidge, and Hoover and the "politics of public purpose gave way to the politics of private interest" (Schlesinger, 1986, p. 32). Becoming rich and pursuing what is best for each person became prized outcomes. The concern for individual interests in the 1920s evaporated with the onset of the Great Depression, when liberals acted through the federal government to minimize the worst effects of the economic disaster. Impulses to help the poor, aged, and helpless were transformed into social programs. Reform energies, however, were redirected by World War II, and they ebbed in the immediate postwar years.

In the Eisenhower years, as in the 1920s, private interests surged forward and public action receded. The search for racial justice in the 1960s triggered the next turn, when liberals under Presidents Kennedy and Johnson sought public ways of solving national ills in the New Frontier and the Great Society. By the early 1970s, Americans had experienced the trauma of Vietnam, race riots, the fall of a president, and campus violence. During the rest of the decade and into the 1980s, according to Schlesinger, a return to cultivating private interests and self-gratification reached its peak in the presidency of Ronald Reagan.

What about the next decade? Because Schlesinger believes that these two-phase cycles of liberal and conservative change in values alternate every generation of 15 or more years, he predicts that liberals will return.

> At some point, shortly before or after the year 1990, there should come a sharp change in the national mood and direction—a change comparable to those bursts of innovation and reform that followed the accessions to office of Theodore Roosevelt in 1901, of Franklin Roosevelt in 1933 and of John Kennedy in 1961. (Schlesinger, 1986, p. 47)

Note that this two-phase cycle is very close to a pendulum swing—conservative to liberal and back again every decade and a half, according to Schlesinger. Whereas most biological or business cycles may have three, four, or more phases, this one has two, making it almost indistinguishable from the swing of a pendulum (Dewey & Dakin, 1947). Nonetheless, applying this cyclical explanation to schooling is common (Carnoy & Levin, 1985; James & Tyack, 1983; Kaestle, 1972; Katz, 1987; Kirst & Meister, 1985; Kliebard, 1988; Presseisen, 1985; Slavin, 1989).

To do so is easy enough if one sees the struggle over reforms as conflicts over values in both the larger society and schools. When value shifts occur in the larger society, schools accommodate. In the years when conservative values stressing private interests ran strong—for example, in the 1920s, 1950s, and 1980s—schools were concerned with producing individuals who could compete. Hence, high academic standards, orderliness, efficiency, and productivity were prized in schools. In years when politically liberal values dominated, such as the early 1900s, 1930s, and 1960s, concerns for minorities, the poor, and other outsiders prompted school reforms that broadened student access to programs, linked schools to work in the community, and reduced academic achievement gaps between groups of students. Each political turn of the cycle left a residue within schools when the rhythm shifted.

What is appealing about this version of a value-driven two-phase cycle that accrues changes as its political rhythm shifts periodically is the power to account for both stability and change and for recurring moods of pessimism and optimism. According to Schlesinger, liberals and conservatives introduce programs that further their values and stimulate optimism; many programs disappear but some leave traces. Yet, schools have changed over the decades. Moreover, reforms do return as the cycle shifts but they wear different clothes. Stability exists amid change.

As seductive as this explanation is, still it fails to account for some of the more complex aspects of schooling. For example, take the centralizing of authority that enshrines the values of control and efficiency. Squeezing everything possible out of every tax dollar spent and making sure that it is spent properly competes with prized values of citizen participation in decisions and professional autonomy that are at the core of decentralizing authority. One could argue that these value-loaded issues are triggered by larger political and economic events and that Schlesinger's cycles even fit here. I think not.

At the turn of the century, political liberals pushed centralizing authority in school boards and professionalizing educators as a cure for inefficient school district rule. But in the 1960s, liberals pushed decentralizing authority as a remedy for distant bureaucrats who were unconcerned about what happened in each school. In the 1980s, both political liberals and conservatives have favored state-driven reforms that have made some state legislatures super school boards mandating tightly worded rules for students and teachers.

Moreover, in the last few years of the same decade, both liberals and conservatives have endorsed school-site councils, school-based management, and plans that permit teachers to have a much larger voice in managing schools. In short, the political cycle of liberal–conservative, of public versus private interests, simply does not fit the evidence (Carnegie Forum on Education and the Economy, 1986; Committee for Economic Development, 1985).

Nor do the swift changes that have swept across the educational landscape since 1945 fit shifts among political liberals and conservatives. Since the end of World War II, unrelenting criticism about inadequate school buildings, flabby curricula, slipping academic standards, and inferior teaching have appeared regularly in national and regional media. Barrage after barrage of public flak produced school reforms even before votes were counted every 2 or 4 years. Consider how both political liberals and conservatives have endorsed the effective schools movement and have pressed for new programs aimed at students labeled at risk for different yet convergent reasons. In short, on many of the issues that seized public attention and commanded policymakers' reactions, political liberals and conservatives often stood as one (Committee for Economic Development, 1985; National Commission on Excellence in Education, 1983; Ravitch, 1983).

How, then, in the face of evidence that does not fit a rational explanation harnessed to political cycles, can I make sense of the periodic return of similar reforms? To broaden the historical analysis of reform over the last century, I offer alternative explanations that are basically hunches. Because there is so much uncritical reliance on the rational explanation, with its artillery of pendulum and cycle images even when counterevidence is available, few policymakers, practitioners, and researchers have explored alternative interpretations and metaphors. I want to enlarge the discussion by offering two other explanations. In the interest of full disclosure, I label both as speculative.

VALUE CONFLICTS: A POLITICAL PERSPECTIVE

Many issues that reappear, such as the struggle over teacher-centered instruction, the academic and practical curriculum, and the centralizing of authority, are value conflicts. When economic, social, and demographic changes create social turmoil, public opinion shifts. Particular values receive renewed attention and get translated into policies and programs by individuals, media, interest groups, and political coalitions. Much pressure is placed on schools to align with public shifts in values. Because tensions between such competing social values as equitable income distribution and allowing individuals to accumulate wealth without restraint, or between democratic participation and efficiency, are already embedded in schools, they rise to the surface when external events trigger individuals and groups to voice policy differences and demand change in schools (Guthrie, 1987).

Such value differences, as they become transformed by media and political coalitions into pressure on schools to change, can seldom be removed by scientifically derived solutions. Although in this culture the value of a solution for every problem, a pill for every disease, is quite strong and highly prized, there are no antibiotics for struggles over values. Value conflicts, then, are not problems to be solved by the miracles of a science of schooling; they are dilemmas that require political negotiation and compromises among policymakers and interest groups—much like that which occurs in the larger society. There is no solution; there are only political tradeoffs.

But why do Americans turn to schools in times of social turmoil? Scholars have offered at least two answers to this question. One is that elite classes or dominant groups in the society that set directions for major social policies charge the public schools with the responsibility for solving national ills. These elite groups do so because the sources of those ills are deeply rooted in the structures of the society, and if the major problems of poverty, racism, drug addictions, and environmental destruction were addressed directly, grave upheavals in economic, social, and political institutions would occur. If schools work on these tasks, slow improvement in the next generation might happen without untoward dislocations (Bowles & Gintis, 1976; Grubb & Lazerson, 1982; Katz, 1987; Perkinson, 1968).

A second answer has been the enduring faith that Americans have placed in schools as an engine of social and individual improvement. Such faith automatically turns policymakers' attention to schools as a tool of reform when social problems emerge. To Andrew Carnegie the faith was complete: "Just see wherever we peer into the first tiny springs of the national life, how this true panacea for all the ills of the body politic bubbles forth—education, education, education." Also to President Lyndon Johnson: "The answer for all our national problems comes down to one single word: education." With this faith in the power of schools to restore national health and permit social mobility, debates about school reform become, indirectly, discourses about the future of society (Cremin, 1988; Meyer, 1986; Perkinson, 1968).

Simply put, when an impulse for reform rises, crests in the larger society, and then spills over the schools, the conflicting values buried deep within schools also receive attention. The political processes already existing in a decentralized system of schooling produce interest groups and individuals perennially pressing schools to alter what they do. The values of these groups and individuals receive renewed attention for a time until public interest fades.

We are in the midst of a series of reform waves now. In the 1980s, spurred by huge deficits and fears of major economic losses to foreign markets, public and corporate officials have reasserted the values of economic efficiency and competitiveness as values to which schools must now heed. Another national crisis has been announced and the schools are rescuers of America's economic vitality. Expectations have risen. Slogans have flourished ("school-based management," "restructuring schools," and "investment in schools"), and programs are under way. Old compromises over school curricula and academic standards are being renegotiated. Change is in the air (David, 1989; Guthrie, 1985; Kearns, 1988; National Commission on Excellence in Education, 1983).

Yet efficiency in schooling has been a golden phrase–a secular Grail–to educators for well over a century. Submerged at times but never far from the surface, the search for increased productivity with fewer resources has fueled dreams of vocational schooling for all and classroom technologies such as film, radio, and instructional television. As a result of the drive for more efficient operations, educators have borrowed repeatedly from their corporate cousins (Callahan, 1962; Cuban, 1986; Lazerson & Grubb, 1974).

The waves of intense public attention to schools reappear because these conflicting values are buried deep within the economy, political processes, and, of course, schools. When economic instability, shifts in population, and social change uncover tensions, individual champions of particular values and coalitions of interest groups surface. Media and other groups translate the unrest into recommended policies for schools to enact. Waves occur on the surface and, in some instances, programs, like the skeletons of long-dead sea animals, get deposited on the coral reef of schooling.

Within each series of waves breaking on the shores of public attention, there are smaller ones. There is the miniwave of rising and falling expectations; there is the miniwave of policy talk where new phrases are coined and become part of reformers' vocabularies only to fall into disuse; there is the miniwave of the change process itself, where talk leads to some policies getting adopted, partially or wholly implemented, and, in the case of a few, incorporated into organizational practices. As miniwaves within the larger wave action, they overlap, often lagging behind or forging ahead of a companion miniwave, producing, over time, one large wave of public attention that comes to a close as another begins (see Figure 5.1) (Cuban, 1986; Downs, 1972; Kaestle, 1972; Meyer, 1986).

The alternating waves of optimism–pessimism used to span 5 to 10 or more years; however, with the spread of instant media the entire pattern, with its minirhythms including the final deposit of a residue in vocabulary, procedures, or an occasional program, may take a few years or even less.

Figure 5.1. Recurring Waves of School Reform

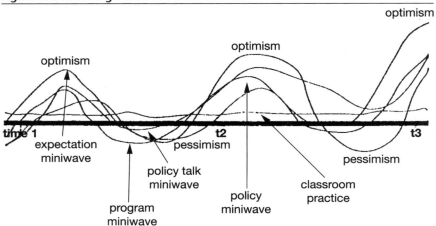

But why do these waves of school reform, with their struggle over value differences, keep reappearing? I have suggested two answers: Dominant social groups getting public schools to work on national ills, rather than risking major dislocations in the society, by addressing directly major social problems; and the shared, enduring beliefs that most Americans have about schools promoting social mobility, creating national harmony, and building solid citizens. Whether as a result of the actions of dominant classes or a durable faith in the power of schooling, the consequences are the same: Policymakers turn religiously to school-based solutions for national problems. If society has an itch, schools get scratched. Or do they?

The nation has no central ministry of education. There is as yet no required national curriculum or test as there is in the rest of the world, where national governments have introduced compulsory public schooling. There is a U.S. Department of Education, but its responsibilities for funding and managing the public schools of the nation are close to nil. It defines the national interest in schooling, collects information, disburses funds to the states, sponsors research, and monitors compliance with laws. Operational responsibility rests with the 50 states. Only one (Hawaii) is a total unit. In the other 49 states, authority for operating schools is delegated to more than 15,000 school districts. With three levels of governance, any single school crisis will be viewed differently by various constituencies. In such a decentralized yet national system of schooling that encourages plural interest groups and much prodding of professionals to alter what they do, it should come as no surprise that many reforms seldom go beyond getting adopted as a policy.

Most get implemented in word rather than deed, especially in classrooms. What often ends up in districts and schools are signs of reform in new rules, different tests, revised organizational charts, and new equipment. Seldom are the deepest structures of schooling that are embedded in the school's use of time and space, teaching practices, and classroom routines fundamentally altered even at those historical moments when reforms seek those alterations as the goal. The itch may be real but the stroking is gentle. Why?

Some scholars believe that recurring reforms rarely transform schools and classrooms because they were never intended to do so. These scholars argue that schools are used to solve social ills because the capitalist system is driven by ideological imperatives that permeate all institutions in the culture. Schools, whether they like it or not, are instruments to express and maintain, not alter, those ideologies. Thus, the overt and covert ways that schools are organized, the curriculum is ordered, and teachers go through their daily teaching routines are what they are supposed to be. Some reforms are for display, not fundamental change. Other reforms that strengthen prevailing beliefs do get implemented (Apple, 1977, 1982; Bernstein, 1977; Carnoy & Levin, 1985; Denscombe, 1982; Popkewitz, 1988; Willis, 1977).

Given these views, school reform rhetoric, policies, and actions are either items to be managed and packaged in such ways as to reinforce things as they are, or that tinker with innovations that will leave untouched the regularities of schooling. What schools do and what teachers do in their classrooms are what they are supposed to do. They perform the social functions assigned by the reigning ideologies and elite classes. Like students, the teachers, administrators, superintendents, and school boards are mere participants in a process willed by larger forces. Schools and classrooms go largely unchanged, although the noise and motion do give an appearance of fundamental reform. Scholars adhering to this view believe that fundamental school reform is, at best, a futile exercise and, at worst, a sham.

Although there is much that I have found both useful and persuasive in these views, there is also evidence that remains unexplained. For example, these scholars argue that a tight coupling exists between the society and its schools—society itches and the schools scratch—implying further that within states, districts, schools, and classrooms similarly strong linkage exists to explain why most people end up doing pretty much the same today as they did yesterday. Yet there is contrary evidence.

There have been many changes of varying dimensions and depth in school organization, facilities, governance, funding, and curriculum over the last century. Such changes include the instances, infrequent though they are, when teachers and administrators have made fundamental changes in their schools and classrooms; the variations in classroom teaching and learning that exist in the same school and within the district—even after allowing for the ubiquitous commonalities; the ways that schools blunt, sidestep, and revarnish reforms imposed by others; and the impact that students and teachers have on the curriculum. All of these examples suggest that schools as institutions and practitioners, collectively and individually, take initiatives and influence their surroundings (Cremin, 1988; Elmore & McLaughlin, 1988; Hansot & Tyack, 1988; Kirst & Meister, 1985; March & Olsen, 1984; Smith, Dwyer, Prunty, & Kleine, 1988; Tyack, 1974). For these reasons, I find it worthwhile to explore another perspective that builds on the political perspective of values conflict discussed above, and attempt to explain why reforms recur even if they seemingly have little impact on what goes on in schools and classrooms.

INSTITUTIONAL PERSPECTIVE

What makes schools different from nonpublic organizations is that they are tax supported and under lay governance. These two deep structural traits mark schools as unique organizations. To retain support from their constituencies who provide children and dollars, state and district systems display multiple and conflicting goals, many of which are stated ambiguously, making them most difficult to measure.

Individuals and groups move in and out of the organization, participating as voters, parents, volunteers, advocates, and critics; the traffic in and out of the organization is constant. Without support from these participants and the constituent groups within its surroundings, a school district would lose its legitimacy and eventually lose its clientele (March & Olsen, 1976; Meyer & Rowan, 1978; Pincus, 1972).

So school organizations try to satisfy what their constituencies believe is proper for schools. The public expects teachers to be certified to teach. The public expects that mathematics offered in the 8th grade will prepare 14-year-olds for algebra in the 9th grade. The public expects transcripts of high school graduates to be considered by colleges. The public expects a principal to be qualified to supervise a staff of 50 teachers and a superintendent to be able to put a budget together for the school board. School system policymakers, in turn, to retain the endorsement of their community, make sure that all of its personnel meet state requirements for their occupations, that schools are accredited, that textbooks come from state-approved lists, and that 3rd graders practice cursive writing like other 3rd graders in nearby districts do. If a significant number of constituencies define a problem in schools as, for example, too many teenagers take drugs, before too long school authorities will have introduced a special drug program or expanded the existing one and appointed a district office coordinator for drug education. In this manner, the school organization signals external groups that it is responsive to their values. If the public loses confidence in the school organization's capacity to act like a system with these rules and classifications, political support and funding shrink swiftly (Meyer, 1980; Meyer & Rowan, 1978).

The unique organizational characteristics of this tax-supported public bureaucracy governed by lay policymakers merge with the imperative to retain the loyalty of the system's constituencies. Both help to explain schools' obvious vulnerability to pressures for change from external groups. When value conflicts arise and external pressure accelerates, both get wedded to an organizational drive for retaining the support of critical supporters; such conditions push school districts to try novel programs, join regional and national efforts to improve curriculum, and adopt innovative technologies so as to be viewed as worthy of continued endorsement. The combined political and institutional perspectives also help explain why districts in different parts of a state, region, and the nation resemble one another in structures, roles, and operations. A district or school that is substantially different from other districts or schools runs the risk of having questions raised about its credibility (DiMaggio & Powell, 1983; Pincus, 1972, Rowan, 1982).

But a school system is also responsible for maintaining order, instructing the young, and producing students who have learned. To ensure that the organization is both efficient and effective, the district has a bureaucracy to coordinate and control what occurs in classrooms and elsewhere in the system. If district policymakers face outward to their publics, administrators face inward. They make sure that there are tight linkages between external requirements and district rules in whether the staff meets state and local criteria for employment, the standards set by regional accreditation associations, and the proper courses necessary for students to attend prestigious colleges. District operations are tightly coupled in meeting legal requirements for bids and purchases, avoiding conflicts of interest, and spending state and federal funds. These linkages are monitored to ensure that they remain intact. Any departures from policy and procedures are scrutinized. Because these categories signal the public that the schools are really schools and are doing what they are supposed to do, careful attention is paid to these items (Elmore & McLaughlin, 1988; Meyer & Rowan, 1978).

The tight coupling vanishes, however, when it comes to the core of schooling—classroom instruction. The transaction among a teacher, students, and content is the basic reason for compelling parents to send their children to school. To determine whether the goals of the district or state systems are being met in the classroom, some level of oversight and control would be expected given the importance attached to the classroom. Although there are ties between classroom and school and between school and district office, there is no tight coupling here as elsewhere in the organization (Bidwell, 1965; Cuban, 1984; Elmore & Mc-Laughlin, 1988; Meyer & Rowan, 1978).

Inspections and tests are the standard bureaucratic tools used to control what teachers do in their classrooms. But teachers work as solo practitioners, isolated from their colleagues. They teach for long periods of time without inspection from their supervisors. Administrators, who depend on teachers to achieve any degree of school effectiveness, basically trust their teachers' craft. They do formally evaluate teacher performance a few times a year, but both parties to the process report that the occasions seem ritualistic even when high stakes are involved. Virtually the same lack of inspection by superintendents, evaluation of performance, and isolation mark the lot of the principal. Similarly, superintendents, who depend on principals to achieve improved school performance, have to trust principals' judgment and skills. The bureaucratic mechanism of inspection exists on paper, but it functions more as a ritual than as a tool for coordination and control (Bidwell, 1965; Dornbusch & Scott, 1975; Dreeben, 1973; Elmore & McLaughlin, 1988; Weick, 1976).

Testing is the other bureaucratic means for controlling what occurs in classrooms. Teachers give their students tests frequently. Most of these are teacher-made or linked to textbook assignments. Seldom, if ever, are the results of these tests used to gauge teacher productivity. Although standardized achievement tests are ubiquitous, it is rare that student scores are used to assess individual teacher performance. Student scores are aggregated at the school and district levels. Because the practice of publishing test scores school by school has become fairly common in cities and many suburbs, there has been growing pressure to hold principals responsible for the school's academic performance, as measured by standardized achievement tests.

Although there have been such pressures, and in particular locations such accountability may be formalized, it has yet to become general practice. So, without either the usual bureaucratic tools of inspection or tests to determine instructional productivity, the daily delivery of instruction is virtually decoupled from administration and policymaking (Duke & Imber, 1985; Meyer & Rowan, 1978; Resnick & Resnick, 1985).

Decoupling classroom teaching from administration and policymaking in the organization occurs because policymakers and administrators need to retain the support of practitioners while maintaining the district's credibility in the eyes of the families that send children to school, citizens who pay taxes, and state and federal bureaucracies that monitor district actions, teachers, students, and others. Without credibility, there is no chance of the schools being viewed as successful. Without teachers' support, few desired outcomes can be achieved. Thus, a bargain is struck over the degree of inspection, how it is carried out, and its consequences (often encased in a contract when unions are present); infrequent and procedurally protected inspection is exchanged for teacher support (Elmore & McLaughlin, 1988; Meyer & Rowan, 1978; Weick, 1976).

Here, then, is an organizational perspective stitched together from the work of a number of researchers that begins to explain why certain school activities and teaching are insulated from externally driven pressures for fundamental changes. The decoupling of instruction from administration and policymaking achieves an autonomy and isolation that teachers find satisfying. They can introduce innovative materials designed by outside consultants, especially if they see the value of their use in class. They can alter the content they teach, even if it is mandated by a state department of education, if they already believe that the topics and content will be in the students' best interest. They also have limited freedom, drawn from their isolation as solo practitioners, to ignore and modify these directives. And they can initiate novel changes. There are limits, of course, on the extent to which principals and teachers can change what occurs in their schools and classrooms, limits set by those very same constituencies whose support of the school is needed. Choice is situationally constrained.

CONCLUDING COMMENTS

Since there is no persuasive explanation for the persistence of reform that goes beyond the rational explanation and 15-year cycles proposed by Arthur Schlesinger, Jr., which neglected counterevidence, I have set forth two other explanations for the reappearance of reforms. These explanations may sound plausible, but they are, after all, only claims, not facts. No body of evidence about past or current reforms yet exists to determine whether these claims have merit.

Reforms do return again, again, and again. Not exactly as before or under the same conditions, but they persist. It is of even greater importance that few reforms aimed at the classroom make it past the door permanently. It is important to policymakers, practitioners, administrators, and researchers to understand why reforms return but seldom substantially alter the regularities of schooling. The risks involved with a lack of understanding include pursuing problems with mismatched solutions, spending energies needlessly, and accumulating despair. The existing tools of understanding are no more than inadequate metaphors that pinch-hit for hard thinking. We can do better by gathering data on particular reforms and tracing their life history in particular classrooms, schools, districts, and regions. More can be done by studying reforms in governance, school structures, curricula, and instruction over time to determine whether any patterns exist. And we can do better by examining carefully the alternative explanations offered here and elsewhere and measuring them against the data. If it occurs to readers that I end with a plea for rationality, that is, serious thinking about rational and nonrational organizational behavior, so be it. If we do not heed the plea, we will continue to mindlessly speculate, and as Gide observed: *"Since nobody listens, we have to keep going back and begin again."*

NOTE

I wish to thank David Tyack, Dan Perlstein, and three anonymous reviewers for their comments on an earlier draft.

REFERENCES

Apple, M. (1977). What do schools teach? *Curriculum Inquiry, 6*(4), 341–358.

Apple, M. (1982). Curricular form and the logic of technical control. In M. Apple (Ed.), *Cultural and economic reproduction in education* (pp. 247–274). London: Routledge & Kegan Paul.

Applebee, A., Langer, J., & Mullis, I. (1987). *The nation's report card: Literature and U.S. history.* Princeton, NJ: Educational Testing Service.

Applebee, A. N. (1974). *Tradition and reform in the teaching of English: A history.* Urbana, IL: National Council of Teachers of English.

Bernstein, B. (1977). Class and pedagogies: Visible and invisible. In J. Karabel & A. H. Halsey (Eds.), *Power and ideology in education* (pp. 511–534). New York: Oxford University Press.

Bestor, A. (1953). *Educational wastelands: The retreat from learning in our public schools.* Urbana, IL: University of Illinois Press.

Bidwell, C. (1965). The school as a formal organization. In J. March (Ed.), *Handbook of organizations.* Chicago: Rand McNally.

Bowles, S., & Gintis, H. (1976). *Schooling in capitalist America.* New York: Basic Books.

Callahan, R. (1962). *Education and the cult of efficiency.* Chicago: University of Chicago Press.

Carnegie Forum on Education and the Economy. (1986). *A nation prepared: Teachers for the 21st century.* New York: Carnegie Foundation.

Carnoy, M., & Levin, H. (1985). *Schooling and work in the democratic state.* Stanford, CA: Stanford University Press.

Committee for Economic Development. (1985). *Investing in our children: Business and the public schools.* New York: Author.

Cremin, L. (1961). *The transformation of the school.* New York: Vintage Press.

Cremin, L. (1988). *American education: The metropolitan experience, 1876-1980.* New York: Harper & Row.

Cronin, J. (1973). *The control of urban schools: Perspective on the power of educational reformers.* New York: Free Press.

Cuban, L. (1984). *How teachers taught: Constancy and change in American classrooms, 1890–1980.* New York: Longman.

Cuban, L. (1986). *Teachers and machines: Classroom use of technology since 1920.* New York: Teachers College Press.

Daniels, L. A. (1988, December 21). Decentralized schools: Inquiries raise concern. *The New York Times,* p. B9.

David, J. (1989). *Restructuring in progress: Lessons from pioneering districts.* Washington, DC: National Governors' Association.

Dearborn, N. (1925). *The Oswego Movement in American education.* New York: Teachers College, Columbia University.

Denscombe, M. (1982). The "hidden pedagogy" and its implications for teacher training. *British Journal of Sociology of Education, 3,* 249–265.

Dewey, E., & Dakin, E. (1947). *Cycles: The science of prediction.* New York: Henry Holt and Company.

DiMaggio, P. J., & Powell, W. W. (1983). The Iron Cage revisited: Institutional isomorphism and collective rationality in organizational fields. *American Sociological Review, 48,* 147–160.

Dornbusch, S. M., & Scott, W. R. (1975). *Evaluation and the exercise of authority.* San Francisco: Jossey-Bass.

Downs, A. (1972). Up and down with ecology—The issue-attention cycle. *Public Interest, 28,* 38–50.

Dreeben, R. (1973). The school as a workplace, In R. M. W. Travers (Ed.), *Second handbook of research on teaching* (pp. 450–473). Chicago: Rand McNally.

Duke, D. L., & Imber, M. (1985). Should principals be required to be effective? *School Organization, 5,* 125–146.

Eliade, M. (1954). *The myth of the eternal return: Cosmos and history.* Princeton, NJ: Princeton University Press.

Elmore, R. (1987). Choice in public education. In W. Boyd & C. Kerchner (Eds.), *The politics of excellence and choice in education.* London: Falmer Press.

Elmore, R. F., & McLaughlin, M. W. (1988). *Steady work: Policy, practice, and the reform of American education* (R-3574-NIE/RC) (pp. 79–98). Santa Monica, CA: Rand Corporation.

Gittell, M. (1967). *Participants and participation: A study of school policy in New York City.* New York: Praeger.

Gleick, J. (1987). *Chaos: Making a new science.* New York: Viking.

Goodlad, J. (1984). *A place called school.* New York: McGraw-Hill.

Gould, S. J. (1987). *Time's arrow, time's cycle.* Cambridge, MA: Harvard University Press.

Grubb, W. N., & Lazerson, M. (1982). Education and the labor market: Recycling the youth problem. In H. Kantor & D. Tyack (Eds.), *Work, youth, and schooling* (pp. 110–141). Stanford, CA: Stanford University Press.

Guthrie, J. W. (1985). The educational policy consequences of economic instability: The emerging political economy of American education. *Educational Evaluation and Policy Analysis, 7,* 319–332.

Guthrie, J. W. (1987). Exploring the political economy of national education reform. In W. Boyd & C. Kerchner (Eds.), *The politics of excellence and choice in education* (pp. 25–47). London: Falmer Press.

Hansot, E., & Tyack, D. (1988). Gender in American public schools: Thinking institutionally. *Signs, 13,* 741–760.

Hoetker, J., & Ahlbrand, W. (1969). The persistence of the recitation. *American Journal of Educational Research, 6,* 145–167.

Honig, B. (1985). *Last chance for our children.* Reading, MA: Addison-Wesley.

Jackson, P. (1986). *The practice of teaching.* New York: Teachers College Press.

James, T., & Tyack, D. (1983). Learning from past efforts to reform the high school. *Phi Delta Kappan, 64,* 400–406.

James, W. (1958). *Talks to teachers.* New York: W.W. Norton & Company.

Kaestle, C. (1972). Social reform and the urban school. *History of Education Quarterly, 12,* 211–229.

Kaestle, C. (1983). *Pillars of the republic.* New York: Farrar, Straus.

Katz, M. (1968). *The irony of early school reform.* Cambridge, MA: Harvard University Press.

Katz, M. (1987). *Reconstructing American education.* Cambridge, MA: Harvard University Press.

Katznelson, I., & Weir, M. (1985). *Schooling for all: Class, race, and the decline of the democratic ideal.* New York: Basic Books.

Kearns, D. (1988). An educational recovery plan for America. *Phi Delta Kappan, 69,* 565–570.

Kerchner, C. T., & Boyd, W. (1987). What doesn't work: An analysis of market and bureaucratic failure in schooling. In W. L. Boyd & C. T. Kerchner (Eds.), *The politics of excellence and choice in education* (pp. 99–115). London: Falmer Press.

Kirst, M., & Meister, G. R. (1985). Turbulence in American secondary schools: What reforms last? *Curriculum Inquiry, 15,* 169–186.

Kliebard, H. M. (1975). Reappraisal: The Tyler rationale. In W. F. Pinar (Ed.), *Curriculum theorizing: The reconceptualists* (pp. 70–83). Berkeley, CA: McCutchan.

Kliebard, H. M. (1979). Systematic curriculum development, 1890–1959. In J. Schaffarzick & G. Sykes (Eds.), *Value conflicts and curriculum issues* (pp. 197–236). Berkeley, CA: McCutchan.

Kliebard, H. M. (1986). *The struggle for the American curriculum, 1893–1958.* Boston: Routledge & Kegan Paul.

Kliebard, H. M. (1988). Fads, fashions, and rituals: The instability of curriculum change. In L. N. Tanner (Ed.), *Critical issues in the curriculum* (pp. 16–34). Chicago: National Society for the Study of Education.

Krug, E. (1961). *Charles W. Eliot and popular education.* New York: Teachers College, Columbia University.

Lansner, K. (1958). *Second-rate brains.* New York: Doubleday.

Lazerson, M., & Grubb, N. (1974). *American education and vocationalism: A documentary history, 1870–1970.* New York: Teachers College Press.

Levin, H. (1970). *Community control of schools.* Washington, DC: Brookings Institution.

Lynd, A. (1953). *Quackery in the public schools.* Boston: Little, Brown.

March, J. G., & Olsen, J. P. (1976). *Ambiguity and choice in organizations.* Bergen, Norway: Universitetsforlaget.

March, J. G., & Olsen, J. P. (1984). The new institutionalism: Organizational factors in political life. *The American Political Science Review, 78*, 734–749.

Meyer, J. (1986). The politics of educational crises in the United States. In W. Cummings, E. R. Beauchamp, W. Ichikawa, Y. N. Kobayashi, & M. Ushiogi (Eds.), *Educational policies in crisis* (pp. 44–57). New York: Praeger Publishers.

Meyer, J., & Rowan, B. (1978). The structure of educational organizations. In M. Meyer (Ed.), *Environments and organizations* (pp. 78–109). San Francisco: Jossey-Bass.

Meyer, M. (1980). Organizational structure as signaling. *Pacific Sociological Review, 22*, 481–500.

National Commission on Excellence in Education. (1983). *A nation at risk: The imperative for educational reform.* Washington, DC: Author.

Perkinson, H. J. (1968). *The imperfect panacea: American faith in education, 1865–1965.* New York: Random House.

Perpich, R. (1989, March 6). Choose your school. *The New York Times.*

Pincus, J. (1972). Incentives for innovation in the public schools. *Review of Educational Research, 44*, 113–144.

Popkewitz, T. S. (1988). Educational reform: Rhetoric, ritual, and social interest. *Educational Theory, 38*, 77–93.

Powell, A., Farrar, E., & Cohen, D. (1985). *The shopping mall high school: Winners and losers in the educational marketplace.* Boston: Houghton Mifflin.

Presseisen, B. Z. (1985). *Unlearned lessons: Current and past reforms for school improvement.* London: Falmer Press.

Purkey, S., & Smith, M. (1983). Effective schools: A review. *Elementary School Journal, 83*, 427–452.

Ravitch, D. (1974). *The great school wars, New York City, 1805–1973: A history of the public schools as a battlefield of social change.* New York: Basic Books.

Ravitch, D. (1983). *The troubled crusade: American education, 1945–1980.* New York: Basic Books.

Raywid, M. A. (1985). Family choice arrangements in public schools: A review of the literature. *Review of Educational Research, 55*, 435–467.

Reese, W. (1986). *Power and the promise of school reform: Grassroots movements during the Progressive Era.* Boston: Routledge & Kegan Paul.

Resnick, D., & Resnick, L. (1985). Standards, curriculum, and performance: A historical and comparative perspective. *Educational Researcher, 14*, 5–20.

Roth, D. (1988). *Calendar quotations.* New York: Workman Publishing Company.

Rowan, B. (1982). Organizational structure and the institutional environment: The case of public schools. *Administrative Science Quarterly, 27*, 259–279.

Schlesinger, A. M. (1986). *The cycles of American history.* Boston: Houghton Mifflin.

Shapiro, M. S. (1983). *Child's garden: The kindergarten movement from Froebel to Dewey.* University Park: The Pennsylvania State University Press.

Silberman, C. (1971). *Crisis in the classroom.* New York: Alfred Knopf.

Slavin, R. (1989). PET and the pendulum: Faddism in education and how to stop it. *Phi Delta Kappan, 90*, 750–758.

Smith, L., Dwyer, D., Prunty, J., & Kleine, P. (1988). *Innovation and change in schooling.* New York: Falmer Press.

Stake, R., & Easley, J. (1978). *Case studies in science education.* Urbana, IL: Center for Instructional Research and Evaluation.

Suydam, M. (1977). *The status of pre-college science, mathematics, and social science education, 1955–1975: Mathematics education.* Columbus: Ohio State University, Center for Science and Mathematics Education.

Timar, T. B., & Kirp, D. L. (1988). *Managing educational excellence.* New York: Falmer Press.

Tyack, D. (1974). *The one best system.* Cambridge, MA: Harvard University Press.

Weick, K. (1976). Educational organizations as loosely coupled systems. *Administrative Science Quarterly, 21,* 1–19.

Westbury, I. (1973). Conventional classrooms, "open" classrooms and the technology of teaching. *Journal of Curriculum Studies, 5,* 99–121.

Willis, P. (1977). *Learning to labor.* Lexington, MA: Heath.

CHAPTER 6

2001—Leadership for Student Learning: Urban School Leadership— Different in Kind and Degree

NATIONALIZING EDUCATION REFORM

In 2001, President George W. Bush appointed a big-city African American superintendent to head the Department of Education, proposed an agenda for spending Title I funds that called for major improvements in urban schools, and asked states to test all children each year between 3rd and 8th grades. Although concentrating on urban schools with high concentrations of poor children, the President urged state and local leaders to raise academic achievement for all students. In doing so, Bush took the current accountability-driven, standards-based school programs he had championed for children in Texas and nationalized the reforms.

From this Republican president the commitment to standards-based reform and urban schools is ironic, but it surprises few observers familiar with the history of American school reform. For the last half-century the unrelenting criticism of public schools has been that they fail to teach basic literacy or develop appropriate moral behavior and character, and they produce graduates with few marketable skills in the workplace. This has largely been a critique of urban schools in which the ethnic and racial mix in these communities may change from one decade to the next, where less experienced and underqualified staff work in deteriorating physical plants that serve chronically poor neighborhoods coping with drug abuse and crime.

This urban-based critique—richly amplified in the media—has been slapped onto all American schools. Popular culture films and television shows from *Blackboard Jungle* (1955), with lethal adolescents overwhelming a genial teacher, to the television show *Boston Public* (2001), in which a teacher disciplines his class with a gun, have helped Americans think that all urban schools—except the one down the block—are like those portrayed in the media. Few pundits point out that these depictions of urban schools capture only a partial and exaggerated picture of what occurs in these schools. Nor do these critics say that what is portrayed too often suggests that all schools are like those depicted in film or television.

Equating inadequate urban schools with all public schools has encouraged sloppy thinking about American education. When it comes to criticism of American schools, for the last half-century, the urban tail has wagged the public school dog.

Pause for a moment and reflect on the flawed logic of those who tar all public schools with the urban brush. For example, if all American schools are lousy, including ones in cities, how can they have produced graduates who have entered and succeeded at colleges and universities which are highly admired by the rest of the world? And, how can the critics also ignore the rise in American economic productivity, global competitiveness, and unrivaled prosperity increases that have surged across the nation in the 1990s and that stem from those very same inadequately prepared high school and college graduates?

Fusing fears over particular urban schools with pervasive criticism of the entire public school system badly biases thinking about reform. When the U.S. Secretary of Education, supporting the President's "No Child Left Behind" plan, writes that "anyone who opposes annual testing of children is an apologist for a broken system of education," he equates reaching the "hard to teach—education shorthand for economically disadvantaged, limited English-proficiency, and special education students," or those concentrated in urban schools—with reaching all suburban and rural children (Paige, 2001).

What's wrong with crossing the city line and aiming for all children? First, the merging of criticism of poor, often racially isolated, schools with all schools ignores the substantial achievements of administrators and teachers in tens of thousands of fine schools, including ones in cities. Second, the diversity among cities—the major differences between, for example, San Diego and Philadelphia—are ignored. Third, the blending of urban with suburban and rural schools encourages presidents, governors, and corporate leaders to design solutions for ailing urban schools that become one-size-fits-all reforms treating all American schools as interchangeable cogs in a large machine.

Our nation's urban schools, particularly those in most need, are poorly matched to current popular reforms and leadership formulas packaged like brand-name products for schools across the country. For those who lead urban schools, different expectations, different obligations, and different city histories require far more moxie, skills, and political finesse than that required of their colleagues in middle- and upper-class, racially isolated suburbs. The all-purpose reform solution now treats all schools as the same while neglecting the vital linkages between cities, their schools, and the country's economic and social well-being.

LEARNING FROM THE PAST

"What shall we do with our great cities? The whole country is affected, if indeed its character is not determined by the conditions of its great cities." (Cronin, 1973)

The year was 1891. Progressive reformers of the day had hit upon a solution to make cities great: Improve schools so that they can build strong American citizens by assimilating immigrants, increasing literacy to reduce poverty, and preparing workers eager to enter industry and business. To have schools achieve these purposes, new leadership and major reforms in school governance were needed. In the years bracketing the turn of the 20th century, progressive reformers yanked schools out of urban political machines, downsized large appointed city school boards that dispensed patronage, and ended the bribing of school officials. They recruited civic-minded business and professional gentlemen (with an occasional woman) to serve on boards of education, and urged that these small boards hire professionally trained administrators to manage the schools. For well over a half-century after these reforms, university-educated superintendents and principals served elected (and some appointed) school boards that were insulated from partisan politics. Civil-service regulations guided school boards' hiring of school staff, virtually ruling out nepotism and patronage, while impartial and public bids reduced considerably the bribing of school officials in buying textbooks, building schools, and transporting children.

Beginning in the post-World War II years, however, another generation of reformers blasted public schools for inadequately dealing with international and domestic threats to the nation. During the 1950s, critics berated public schools for failing to keep pace with the scientific and military progress of the Soviet Union. The United States needed to produce more engineers and scientists to defend the nation in the Cold War. Educators responded by raising academic standards and increasing the number of math and science courses. Academic excellence became the beacon for educational leaders to follow.

The international threat, however, soon gave way to a serious domestic problem that another group of critics believed school leaders should solve. As the civil rights movement spread from the South to the rest of the nation in the wake of the *Brown v. Board of Education* decision (1954), attention shifted from the Soviet threat to the inferior schooling Black students received in the South and across the nation. Desegregation, rural and urban poverty, and dreadful conditions in so many urban schools housing minority students sparked another generation of reformers who sought equality in education. Civil rights marches, school boycotts, and the ouster of urban superintendents ricocheted across the nation's cities. Federal wallets opened and educational leaders designed urban school programs to lift those at the bottom of society into the middle classes.

Yet by the mid-1970s, critics charged that the War on Poverty, like the one in Vietnam, had been lost. Reformers who wanted schools to reduce social injustice and improve the life chances of poor Black and White children had failed, according to fault finders. To worsen matters, these fault finders believed schools—especially those in cities—had abandoned their mission of teaching basic knowledge and skills, respecting authority, and maintaining discipline. Incidents of violence in urban schools, illiterate high school graduates, and shabby teaching became front-page news and subjects of Hollywood films.

At about the same time, rising inflation, increased unemployment, and U.S. firms losing market share to Japan and Germany seized the policy-making agenda. The workplace was being transformed by computerization. From manufacturing to processing insurance claims, a New Economy for an information-based society emerged. As the revolution in the nature of work swept across the private and public sectors, schools seemed stuck in the past. If schools, especially those in cities and low-income suburbs, where over one-third of all children went, could not produce sufficient graduates to enter an entirely new workplace, then the nation's global competitiveness was endangered.

Copying Successful Businesses

Since the *A Nation at Risk* report (1983) judged public schools so mediocre as to jeopardize the economic future of the country, blaming educators has become common fare in the media. In the past 2 decades, a broad coalition of corporate executives, public officials, and business groups has pressed educational leaders to copy successful businesses. School leaders should do what successful corporate leaders have done: trim bureaucracies, focus on measurable goals, manage through incentives and penalties, and hold employees accountable for reaching desired goals. Presidents, mayors, business executives, and parents have said (and say again and again) that public schools must focus on preparing students for jobs.

Responding to scorching and unrelenting criticism, educators in suburbs, rural districts, and big cities, beginning in the early 1990s, have embraced systemic reform. They have established standards-based curricula, aligned the curricula to tests, monitored test scores closely, and rewarded and punished teachers, principals, schools, and students when scores rose and fell.

Confusing Setting Standards with Standardization

The swift spread of this brand of reform has become an early 21st-century formula for reforming American public schools. The theory behind the current reform formula predicts that systemic school reform will produce graduates who can secure high-paying jobs for themselves while ensuring that American businesses can compete in the global economy. The theory also contains two assumptions: All public schools can profit from this approach, and any good leader can put these changes into place, regardless of location. Both assumptions, embraced by President Bush and many other political and business leaders in their school reform packages, are flawed.

All public schools are hardly alike. In 50 states, almost 15,000 public school districts with almost 90,000 schools serve almost 50 million students. The social, academic, and cultural diversity among districts and within districts—think of New York City, Los Angeles, and Chicago with high schools that send 90% percent of their graduates to college and others where no more than 10% continue their education—is stunning. Generally speaking, however, what now exists in the United States is a three-tiered system of schooling. Across the nation, there is a first tier of schools, about one in 10, that already exceeds the high academic standards and test score threshold set by the states. Another four to five of those 10 schools—the second tier—either already meet or come close to their state standards and cutoff scores on tests. The rest, the third tier, don't. Most of these latter schools are located in urban and rural districts with high concentrations of poor and minority families.

Yet the current reform recipe is to hammer this three-tiered system of schooling into one mold. Forcing all schools to fit the same mold, however, ignores those students already meeting and exceeding those standards. Reformers confuse setting standards with standardization.

REFORMING SCHOOLS—THE CURRENT AGENDA

Current reforms, for example, do little for the thousands of elementary schools that perform far above the new standards in such places as La Jolla, California, Arlington, Texas, and Newton, Massachusetts. Nor does systemic reform do much for the hundreds of high schools such as New York City's Bronx High School of Science, New Trier High School in Winnetka, Illinois, or San Francisco's Lowell High School.

These reforms are aimed at the large number of urban schools struggling with students who perform in the lowest quartiles of academic achievement and often drop out. Publicly admitting this is politically risky because the majority of voters who are middle class, White, and live in suburbs might be distressed to see such targeted use of their tax dollars. Nor do these reforms, with their underlying aim to make schools an arm of the economy, touch upon the broad and historic purposes of tax-supported public schools: promoting democratic equality and molding citizens who contribute to their communities beyond being efficient employees.

Also needing inspection is the second assumption buried in the current reform agenda. In looking back over the last century, each generation of reformers sang one refrain again and again: The nation's schools need more and better school leaders.

Expecting More from Superintendents

Amid the rush toward accountability-driven reforms, the refrain has swelled into a loud chorus demanding every superintendent to manage bureaucracies efficiently, lead principals and teachers in instructional matters, and mobilize political coalitions of teachers, parents, and students to move schools from being inadequate and just good enough to ones that are excellent.

These expectations imply that leading city schools is the same as leading suburban, small-town, and rural schools. That is not the case at all. Crucial differences distinguish urban school leaders from those in other districts.

First, while the early history of suburbs has been one of searching for racial and ethnic homogeneity, larger homes, and better schools, cities have been (and are) cauldrons of diversity that have both enriched and enervated schools. Century-old conflicts over assimilating immigrants, using English as the sole language of instruction, desegregating schools, and reducing poverty have been proxies for dealing with issues of color and class, both mainstays of urban schooling. Leading urban districts—from San Diego to Harrisburg, Pennsylvania—have demanded from superintendents a keener sensitivity to inequalities and a well-developed capacity to deal with racial isolation, ethnic conflict, and economic disparities as they affect academic achievement both in the schools and the city itself. Yet no urban superintendent can afford to ignore the current wisdom, forged by corporate executives and public officials, that high academic standards and improved test scores lead directly to well-paying jobs, even when the concentration on tests produces winners and losers in the academic sweepstakes.

As a result of public demands for improved academic achievement among those students who have historically done least well in school, persistent issues of race, ethnicity, language, and class have required urban superintendents in small and large districts like Compton, California, or Baltimore to expand their customary repertoire of political, managerial, and instructional roles to cope with the abiding conflicts that arise time and again. For many urban superintendents, unequipped or unwilling to deal with these issues, the job is overwhelming. Frequent turnover among school chiefs created the false image of an impossible job and a turnstile superintendency. Those urban superintendents who thrive in the post learn to lead by consciously blending the political, managerial, and instructional roles to cope with the conflicts arising from issues of race and class as they affect test scores and the broader purposes of public schooling.

The second distinguishing characteristic for big-city school superintendents is the strong belief that schools can help restore a city's economic, cultural, and social vitality. The once great American cities that were taken for granted in the early decades of the 20th century declined dramatically in post-World War II decades as they lost their appeal (and business) to suburbs—particularly with the increase in the tendency to cast poverty and crime in racial terms during the 1960s. As Cleveland Mayor Michael White said, "Big cities [became] a code name for a lot of things: for minorities, for crumbling neighborhoods, for crime, for everything that America moved away from." The mistaken belief that cities were ungovernable took hold (Siegel, 1997).

Not until the early 1990s with major shifts in work and the economy did some cities begin to see a reverse migration from suburbs and employers relocating because of lower land and labor costs. Boston, Chicago, and San Francisco have begun to regain their cachet of greatness while other cities such as Austin and San Jose have become magnets for technology-based businesses. "Like a mighty engine," former New York City Mayor David Dinkins said, "urban America pulls all of America into the future" (Siegel, 1997).

For many urban politicians, the quality of public schools plays a key part in attracting employers and young families to their neighborhoods and sustaining the vitality of cities. Their reputations as mayors in large and small cities are deeply affected by the quality of their schools. Some superintendents, unlike their peers elsewhere, have become key players in the revival of urban America and urban politics. Thus, President Bush appointing the Houston, Texas, superintendent as his Secretary of Education acknowledges symbolically this current truth.

These differences counter the prevailing assumption buried within standards-based reform that school leadership is the same across districts. Leading urban schools, unlike leading other districts, is intimately tied to a unique and complex mission: Through improved schooling, reduce the dire consequences of racial and ethnic isolation and the impact of poverty on academic achievement, while increasing the life chances of families and their children to succeed economically and to contribute to their communities. An unfortunate byproduct of this distinct mission is the nourishing of the pervasive myth that schools alone can improve the life chances of poor children. They cannot.

Changing Governance Systems

Beginning in the mid-1990s, these differences in leadership requirements slowly and openly became acknowledged. Major changes in urban school governance geared to improving academic achievement have begun to alter urban school districts. In some cities, such as Baltimore, Chicago, Boston, and Cleveland, mayors have appointed school boards and superintendents; in these places schools have become another department of the city's administration. In Philadelphia, Detroit, and New York, mayors exercised substantial influence in picking school board members and exerted increasing control over school matters. In other cities, school boards, losing confidence in the ability of rise-from-the-ranks superintendents to manage big systems, have chosen noneducators to lead their districts: A former governor is Los Angeles' superintendent; a corporate attorney leads the New York City schools; former U.S. generals have led Seattle and District of Columbia schools; and an ex-U.S. Attorney is school chief in San Diego.

These reforms in urban school governance (mostly White, middle- and upper-middle-class suburbs and rural districts have not moved in this direction) are further evidence that cities impose broad and diverse challenges upon those who seek to lead urban districts. The history, demography, governance structures, and cultures in urban districts matter a great deal. Moreover, even among urban contexts, differences matter. Running the Los Angeles schools (with almost 750,000 students), for example, is very different from running the Boston schools 3,000 miles away (with over 60,000 students).

DISPELLING SOME URBAN MYTHS

Establishing that urban district leadership differs both in kind and degree from leadership of other districts is less difficult than eliminating the pervasive fictions that distort discussions about how to lead them. These myths are serviceable, that is, they advance the agendas of those interest groups that wield them as truths, but fictions are unhelpful in designing and implementing policies. Three obvious fictions need elaboration.

1. Big-city school districts are ungovernable.
2. The superintendency is a revolving door that brings in and tosses out school chiefs one after the other.
3. Schools alone can improve the life chances of poor children.

Big-City School Districts Are Ungovernable. During the social tumult of the 1960s and the fiscal retrenchment of the post-Vietnam era, escalating crime, swelling welfare rolls, and reduced city services were amplified in media stories of Whites fleeing to suburbs, uncollected garbage, and random violence on city streets. Cities were melting down. No mayor or city council, critics claimed, could grasp the complexities, solve the problems, or even mobilize the necessary resources to arrest the decline of one city after another. The idea that big cities were ungovernable stuck.

These problems inevitably affected schools. The notion that a superintendent, reporting to an elected school board of five to nine individuals, could govern, say, New York City with over a million students, and almost 80,000 teachers in nearly 1,200 schools, strained belief. Racial and ethnic conflicts over desegregation, community control, school violence, high dropout rates, and abysmal academic performance, again richly documented by journalists, left the strong impression that urban districts were too large to be manageable. New superintendents entering on the heels of a departing school chief only to exit a few years later further sealed the impression.

In the early 1990s, however, a slow turnaround occurred in some of these apparently ungovernable cities. Candidates for mayor in New York, Philadelphia, Chicago, Denver, and Seattle took office after campaigning aggressively on platforms seeking to make their cities livable. Crime decreased. Investors saw opportunities for building offices and homes on cheap land abandoned by businesses decades earlier. Younger families and retired couples began moving back into cities. After serving two or more terms, these mayors trumpeted their victories in making cities attractive to businesses, residents, and tourists. Cities, they said, were governable again.

And so were schools. Efforts throughout the 1970s and 1980s to break up large urban districts into decentralized regions and subdistricts made them more manageable. Throughout the 1980s and early 1990s, while many urban superintendents churned out reform after reform only to depart, there were superintendents who worked closely with business and civic-led coalitions to engineer changes and stayed to see that they were implemented. Pittsburgh, San Francisco, and San Diego had leaders who built teams, delegated authority, and stayed for a decade or longer shepherding reforms into schools and consolidating their successes. Since the mid-1990s, school leaders in Chicago, Philadelphia, Boston, and Seattle have also developed cadres of educators who worked closely with mayors, business leaders, and parents to weld together broad support for their reform agendas. Viewing cities and their schools over a longer time span reveals the fiction that big-city schools are ungovernable and that the superintendency was merely a turnstile.

The Superintendency Is a Revolving Door. Among executives in most private and public institutions, the prevailing wisdom is for leaders and their teams to initiate reforms, and to serve as long as it takes to implement and consolidate the changes amid inevitable conflict. To make the case that reforming big-city schools is an impossible job, however, many policymakers, writers, and researchers cite endlessly reports that big-city chiefs serve between 2 to 3 years before being ousted or resigning. They confuse *turnover* rates among groups of big-city superintendents with how long individual superintendents served in a post (*completed tenure*). When researchers have looked back at a century of "completed tenures" in the nation's 25 largest urban school districts, they found that tenure in these districts had indeed shrunk from an average high of 14 years in 1900 to just under 6 years in 1990. But a median of 6 years served in a big-city district is almost three times more than the 2 plus years that opinionmakers repeat again and again (Yee & Cuban, 1996).

For every city that has superintendents entering and exiting every few years—New York in the 1990s, for example—there are other cities that have superintendents who have served 5 to 10 years: Tom Payzant in San Diego and later in Boston, Gerry House in Memphis, CEO Paul Vallas in Chicago, Walter Amphrey in Baltimore, and David Hornbeck in Philadelphia. (House served 8 years and left the district in 2000, the same year that Hornbeck resigned after serving 6 years. Vallas resigned in 2001 after 5 years.)

The myth of a revolving door urban superintendency is serviceable to professional associations since it drives salaries up and symbolically reinforces the image of hiring a superhero who welcomes an incredibly hard job with a high casualty rate. Nonetheless, the often-repeated claim that most urban superintendents serve a couple of years and depart is, in a word, false. Another equally serviceable fiction is the belief that schools by themselves can overcome the grim effects of poverty, racism, and community neglect.

The Schools Alone Can Improve the Life Chances of Poor Children. Public officials, corporate leaders, and media scolds find it useful to hold schools solely responsible for curing ills that are located in the larger society. The current concentration on accountability-driven school reform assumes that if students, teachers, and principals in big-city schools would work harder than they have in the past, then test scores would improve, more students would earn diplomas, and jobs in an information-based economy will await graduates.

Certainly there is some truth in the assumption. Much has been written about the prevailing low expectations for academic performance urban principals and teachers have held regarding poor and minority students. Studies have shown again and again how children in large schools easily get lost in the impersonal throng of students and hectic schedules of overworked, underpaid staffs. Other studies reveal that schools that seldom meet academic standards suffer few consequences. This research gives credibility to the belief that harder work and higher standards will translate into higher student academic achievement.

What weakens the assumption, however, are other facts that policy-makers, business leaders, and journalists neglect to mention. Anyone who has visited an urban elementary or secondary school for at least one week (not a drive-by visit) to sit in classes, listen to teachers and students, and observe lunchrooms, playgrounds, corridors, and offices would begin to appreciate a simple but inescapable truth: An urban school is deeply influenced by the neighborhoods from which it draws its students. Also of importance is that tax-supported public schools in a democracy are more than training grounds for future employees. Schools are expected to instill in students civic and social attitudes and skills that shape how graduates lead their lives in communities. Schools are expected to build respect for differences in ideas and cultures. These are historic aims of public schools that have been largely neglected in the rush to direct schools to be engines for the larger economy.

Yet the present agenda for urban school reform, narrowly concentrating on raising test scores and getting jobs, largely ignores the pervasive influence upon the school of the community's particular racial, ethnic, and social class strengths and limitations. In middle-class and wealthy neighborhoods, focusing only on what the school can do is reasonable since these families have the money and networks to provide help for their children with academic, health, or emotional problems, and live in communities where civic institutions thrive. That is not the case in poor communities. Families lack personal and institutional resources. They depend upon the school and other public agencies. In short, in cities, schools can't do it alone. This fundamental fact is ignored in the popular accountability-driven reforms.

A reform agenda focusing on pressing students, teachers, and principals to work harder is rational in the sense that these are precisely the ones who work in schools. There is also a political calculus that restricts the reform agenda to schools. To pledge school improvements by including families and neighborhoods would entail major expenditures by cities such as recon-ceptualizing schools as youth-serving agencies rather than places where the single most important job is to produce higher test scores. It would mean reorganizing existing city cultural, civic, and social services. Reformers stammer when faced with the scale of such changes.

Of course, broadening the urban agenda to encompass a community-based strategy to school improvement does not mean that students, teachers, and principals should be held less responsible for working hard to achieve their goals. Nor does this recognition of a school being nested in the larger community suggest that there should be different standards for those who are well off and those who are poor. The obvious fact that schools are entangled in their communities only makes clear the tasks that face urban school leaders. They need to mobilize civic and corporate elites and educate these opinion setters to the plain fact that raising academic achievement in big-city schools involves far more than designing merit-pay plans, threatening teachers and principals, or withholding diplomas for students who failed a graduation test. Few suburban or rural superintendents face such tasks.

AN INITIAL AGENDA FOR ACTION

This essay argues that the key assumptions driving standards-based school reform and accountability testing (all schools are basically alike and a one-size-fits-all leadership can solve America's school problems) are inapplicable to urban schools. The tasks facing urban school leaders differ both in magnitude and kind from guiding other school districts. Moreover, the web of fictions surrounding urban school reform mires ongoing efforts to improve schooling.

This, then, is a brief for spotlighting the importance and singularity of urban leaders in pursuing school reform. It also offers a glimpse of the tough tasks ahead for those who believe in the civic and moral obligations that accompany making both cities and schools far better than they are for those who have been so ill-served in the past.

For those who ask what comes next, following is an initial agenda for civic, business, and educational leaders committed to urban school improvement:

1. *More (and wisely spent) resources need to be plowed into urban schools.*
   There is simply no way around the fact that to achieve the
   mission of tax-supported public schooling in a democracy,
   educating urban children will cost far more than is spent now.
   Critics who cite Washington, D.C., or Newark, New Jersey, as
   examples proving that the problem is not money, per se, but how
   it is spent by clogged bureaucracies, need to stay a few weeks
   in schools and classrooms in Boston and San Diego, and other
   reasonably well-managed urban districts. There, they would see
   clearly that insufficient resources are allocated to teaching and
   learning in urban schools.

2. *Press the public schools to go beyond vocational preparation.* Urban
   schools do more than crank out graduates to fill entry-level
   posts in the old and new economies. They equip students with

the civic, moral, and personal skills and behaviors to live in a multicultural society. Civic, business, and educational leaders need to openly endorse and programmatically strengthen these larger purposes in urban schools.

3. *Provide special programs.* Urban schools struggling with large percentages of low-performing poor and minority students require unique in-school and out-of-school strategies that address the complexities of teaching and learning in cities. What works in middle- and upper-class suburbs cannot be cloned for urban classrooms.

4. *Reframe urban school reform as a civic project.* Incorporate an array of city-, neighborhood-, and community-provided social, medical, library, cultural, and recreational services in and out of school that are rooted in principles of youth development and that seek broader goals for youth beyond raising test scores.

5. *Concentrate on recruiting large numbers of urban teachers and principals.* Train these new leaders within urban schools through year-long paid supervised internships and intensive summer programs in cooperation with local colleges and universities. Pay premium salaries to those teachers and principals who complete the program and stay at least 5 years in the district.

Such an action agenda is only a beginning, of course. It sets a direction rather than offering a blueprint. Very few policymakers, researchers, practitioners, or business and civic leaders can spell out clearly what exactly has to be done to improve urban schools. Combining experimentation and practitioner street smarts will help school leaders chart a course. And it is the direction that matters. Professional educators and lay leaders know in their hearts that for the sake of the next generation, the vitality of cities, and the health of society, urban schools must do far more than raise test scores and prepare workers. They must prepare students to live in a multicultural society where individual character, community involvement, and civic competence are as essential as job skills and academic degrees.

REFERENCES

Cronin, J. (1973). *The control of urban schools.* New York: Free Press.

Elmore, R., & Burney, D. (1998). The challenge of school variability: Improving instruction in New York City's Community District #2. *CPRE Policy Bulletin.* Available at http://www.gse.upenn.edu/cpre/frames/pubs.html

Henig, J. (1998). *The color of school reform. Race, politics, and the challenge of urban education.* Princeton, NJ: Princeton University Press.

Hess, F. (1999). *Spinning wheels. The politics of urban school reform.* Washington, DC: Brookings Institution Press.

National Commission on Excellence in Education. (1983). *A nation at risk: The imperative for educational reform.* Washington, DC: U.S. Government Printing Office.

Paige, R. (2001, May 13). Why we must have testing. *The Washington Post,* p. A18.

Shipps, D. (2000). Echoes of corporate influence: Managing away urban school troubles. In L. Cuban & D. Shipps (Eds.), *Reconstructing the common good in education: Coping with intractable American dilemmas.* Stanford, CA: Stanford University Press.

Siegel, F. (1997). *The future once happened here.* San Francisco, CA: Encounter Books.

Stone, C. (1998). *Changing urban education.* Lawrence: University Press of Kansas.

Tyack, D., & Hansot, E. (1982). *Managers of virtue.* New York: Basic Books.

Yee, G., & Cuban, L. (1996). When is tenure long enough? A historical analysis of superintendent turnover and tenure in urban school districts. *Educational Administration Quarterly, 32,* supplemental.

PART III

MERGED PERSPECTIVES IN REFORMING CLASSROOM PRACTICE

CHAPTER 7

1993—Introduction to
How Teachers Taught

Over a 25-year period I worked as a high school social studies teacher and administrator in four school systems. Since 1981, I have been a university teacher and researcher. Over these years, basic questions on schooling rose that seemed unanswerable or had no convincing answer either in my experience or in the research literature. Here are a few of the questions that have puzzled me.

In the last 2 decades I have been in many classrooms. During the times I watched teachers in secondary schools, a wave of recognition swept over me. What I saw was almost exactly what I remembered from junior and senior high school classrooms that I had sat in as a student in the 1940s and as a beginning teacher in the mid-1950s. This acute sense of something familiar about how teachers were teaching occurred in many different schools. How, I asked myself, could teaching *seem* unchanged over a 40-year period?

During the decade I served as an administrator in two school districts, I had to deal with another question that troubled me: In institutions as apparently vulnerable to change as schools, why do so few instructional reforms get past the classroom door? Policymakers, foundation officials, and academics propose different ways of operating schools and teaching students; schools respond by embracing new reading programs, novel ways of organizing a school, and curricular innovations. School boards and administrators triumphantly display the new programs they have adopted and the innovations that keep them abreast of brand-new ideas in education. Yet many of those very same policymakers, officials, and academics scold teachers for their stubbornness in maintaining conventional styles of teaching inconsistent with the newly adopted policies, programs, and materials. The questions I ask, then, seem linked. The apparent uniformity in instruction irrespective of time and place appears connected to the apparent invulnerability of classrooms to change.

In an article I published in 1979, I sought answers to these questions through a study of curricular change and stability since the 1870s. In examining how various forces had shaped the curriculum and classroom instruction over the previous century, I used the metaphor of a hurricane to distinguish among curriculum theory, courses of study, materials, and classroom teaching. Hurricane winds sweep across the sea, tossing up 20-foot waves; a fathom below the surface turbulent waters swirl, while on an ocean floor there is unruffled calm.[1]

As tricky as metaphors can be, I compared that hurricane to any newly trumpeted curriculum theory and the policy talk that such theories generated. Professional journals, for example, echo arguments for and against a new theory. Letters to editors and sharp rebuttals add to the flurry. Books are written and reputations are made. Conferences host both skeptics and promoters. Professors of education teach the new wisdom to their students. Some school boards adopt policies and start an occasional program consistent with the novel concept. Yet most publishers continue producing texts barely touched by the new theory and most teachers use methods unmarked by either controversy or slogans. I used the metaphor to illustrate distinctions among theory, policy rhetoric, the content of programs, and, most importantly, the impact of all these factors upon teaching behavior.

In that article I wrote that curriculum theories did influence professional ideologies and policymakers' vocabularies, as well as courses of study and, to some extent, textbook content. But I did not find much evidence of significant change in teaching practices. However, I had not systematically or comprehensively examined primary sources in general or in particular school districts. I used, for the most part, secondary sources, and consulted a few primary documents that were available. Based upon this initial review, I found some evidence of a seemingly stubborn continuity in the character of instruction despite intense reform efforts to move classroom practices toward instruction that was more student-centered.

Deepening the paradox, the limited evidence suggested that teaching practices seemed uncommonly stable at all levels of schooling touching students of varied abilities in diverse settings over many decades, despite improvements in teacher education, state credentialing, and scholarly knowledge of teaching practices. In dealing with this paradox researchers have tied more knots than they have loosened. Some writers assert that student-centered instruction has been embraced by teachers, while others argue that such classroom changes have seldom been institutionalized. Common to all research is a dearth of evidence about what teachers have done in classrooms.[2]

The lack of evidence about whether or not instruction had evolved over time drove me to ask a basic question: How did teachers teach? If the answer I sought was to have weight and clarity, the fragmentary data about what teachers did in their classrooms needed to be brought together with reform efforts to alter practices. This study begins that task.

A framework for understanding different kinds of school and classroom reforms is a useful tool for trying to answer the question of how teachers taught and what classroom changes occurred over a century.

REFORMING SCHOOLS AND CLASSROOMS

To understand the deeper meanings of past and present efforts to improve teaching, and to connect broad policies of school improvement with class-room teachers' behaviors, I divide the reforms of the past century into *incremental* and *fundamental* changes.[3]

Incremental Reforms

Incremental reforms are those that aim to improve the efficiency and effectiveness of existing structures of schooling, including classroom teaching. The premise behind incremental reforms is that the basic structures are sound but need improving. The car is old but if it gets fixed it will run well; it needs tires, brakes, a new battery, and a water pump—incremental changes. Illustrations of incremental changes within schools would include adding another curricular track to the three or four that already exist in a high school; introducing merit pay; decreasing class size from 30 to 28; adding two more counselors to a secondary school or an assistant principal to an elementary school; improving attendance procedures for the school; and changing parent conference times to accommodate single, working parents.

In the classroom, incremental changes would include new units for teaching civics or handwriting; in-service workshops to teach teachers to use a classroom computer to keep attendance and record grades; or introducing teachers to various techniques of maintaining classroom discipline.

Fundamental Reforms

Fundamental reforms are those that aim to transform, i.e., alter permanently, those very same structures. The premise behind fundamental reforms is that basic structures are flawed at their core and need a complete overhaul, not renovations. The old jalopy is beyond repair. We need to get a new car or consider different forms of transportation—fundamental changes. If new courses, more staff, summer schools, higher standards for teachers, and increased salaries are examples of incremental enhancements to the structures of public schooling, then the late-19th-century innovations of the progressives in the kindergarten and junior high school are instances of fundamental changes in the conduct of schooling. Other examples would be the broadening of the school's social role in the late 19th and early 20th centuries to intervene in the lives of children and their families (for example, in the areas of medical and social services) and giving parents the option of enrolling their children in private or public schools.

Applied to the classroom, fundamental changes would aim at transforming the teacher's role from that of a central source of power and knowledge to the role of a coach who guides students to their own decisions, who helps them find meaning in their experiences and in what they learn from one another and from books. Teaching becomes structuring activities that enable students to learn from subject matter, one another, and the community. Teaching becomes less telling and more listening. Student learning becomes active and includes groupwork, play, independent work, and artistic expression. There is less seatwork and listening to the teacher explain. Such changes would represent fundamental alterations in the ways teachers think about the nature of knowledge, teaching, and learning, and about their actions in the classroom.

Some of these examples of incremental and fundamental innovations in teaching practices have stuck—that is, they have been institutionalized. Many, however, have not. The overall mortality rate for classroom reforms is high. Some reforms survive birth only to linger on for a few years and then pass away. Other reforms get incorporated into routine classroom activities. What accounts for the survival of some and not others?

Transforming Fundamental Changes Into Incremental Ones

The kindergarten, junior high school, open-space architecture, and the use of computers are instances of actual and attempted fundamental changes in the school and classroom since the turn of this century that were adopted in many schools and yet, over time, either were marginalized into incremental changes or slipped away, leaving few traces of their presence. How did this occur? Familiar examples of this unplanned process are the curricular reforms of the 1950s and 1960s, which were guided in large part by academic specialists and funded by the federal government. These reforms were aimed at revolutionizing teaching and learning in math, science, and social studies, and millions of dollars were spent on producing textbooks and classroom materials and on training teachers. Using the best instructional materials that scholars could produce, teachers would coach students to understand how scientists thought, to experience the pleasures of discovery in solving math problems, conducting laboratory experiments, and using primary sources to understand the past. Materials were published and placed in the hands of teachers who, for the most part, had had little time to understand what was demanded by the novel materials or, for that matter, to practice their use.

By the end of the 1970s, when researchers reported on what was now occurring in classrooms, they found the familiar teacher-centered instruction aimed at imparting knowledge from a text and little evidence of student involvement in critical thinking, problem solving, or experiencing how scientists worked. These federally funded *efforts* did, however, leave a distinct curricular residue in textbooks published in the 1970s. An attempt to revolutionize teaching and learning became, in time, new textbook content.[4]

A more complicated way in which fundamental reforms become incremental changes is what George and Louise Spindler call "substitute change." They studied a small school in a southern German village called Schonhausen for over a decade. Initially a rural area, the village was undergoing changes in land ownership and wine production, that is, the creation of larger plots and introduction of machines to till and harvest grapes. Moreover, shifts in population were urbanizing the area.

For decades, the school curriculum had emphasized the land, the village community, and family values. The federal and provincial ministries of education, however, mandated a new curriculum and textbooks based upon life in cities, the importance of modernization, and high technology. The Spindlers studied the village and its school in 1968 and returned in 1977 after almost a decade of reform.

What surprised the Spindlers was that in spite of the clear attempt by ministry officials to make a village school more modern and more responsive to urban life, children, teachers, and parents continued to make tradition-based and village-oriented choices. In the school, trips that had once taken classes on day-long strolls in the countryside gave way to role-playing a petition to the village council. Much of the earlier content about the beauty of the land was lost but the cultural goals and values nourishing the traditions of the village were maintained. How?

The Spindlers found that the way teachers taught and how they maintained classroom order sustained village traditions in the face of curricular reforms. For a play about the village political process, a reading recommended in the new curriculum, the teachers substituted a romantic folktale from the previous curriculum. Thus, the focus of the classroom activity remained on the importance of life in the village. An *effort* to alter fundamentally the values of villages in that part of Germany so as to make them more responsive to urban life was transformed into an affirmation of village values.[5]

Another way of transforming fundamental reforms is to shunt them to the periphery of the regular school. For example, innovative programs that reduce class size, reconceptualize the student-teacher relationship, integrate subject matter from diverse disciplines, and structure activities that involve students in their learning often begin as experiments in regular classrooms but, over the years, migrate to out-of-the-way programs in the main building or faraway sites. The schools have, indeed, adopted and implemented programs fundamentally different from what mainstream students receive, yet it is the outsiders–students labeled as potential dropouts, vocational students, pregnant teenagers, those identified as gifted, at-risk students, and handicapped pupils—who participate in the innovative programs. Thus, some basic changes get encapsulated, like a grain of sand in an oyster; they exist within the system but are often separated from mainstream programs.[6]

These organizational processes that maintain continuity are seldom conspiratorial or even due to conscious acts on the part of school officials. Such transformations occur as a consequence of bureaucratic, political, and cultural processes deeply embedded in the different levels of schooling as they interact with the larger society. They occur as a result of deep-seated impulses within the organization to appear modern, to convince those who support the schools that what happens in schools is up-to-date and responsive to the wishes of their patrons. Thus, pervasive and potent processes within the institution of schooling preserve its independence to act even in the face of powerful outside forces intent upon altering what happens in schools and classrooms.[7]

How much of this framework for distinguishing between incremental and fundamental reforms and what happens to them over time applies directly to how teachers teach? It is easy to sketch out an argument that captures the broad outlines of how macropolicies get adapted after they are adopted. It is far more difficult to account for teachers' behaviors in varied classroom settings over an entire century.

To apply this framework to describing how teachers taught, I investigated teaching practices before, during, and after reform impulses in the 20th century aimed at fundamentally changing what teachers routinely do. In doing so I hope to give a clearer sense of what has persisted and what kinds of changes have occurred in classrooms.

But what are we to look for in classrooms marked by a bewildering variety of student and teacher behaviors? While no single study can do justice to the intricate complexity of classroom teaching, there is a useful tool for revealing a portion of that complicated terrain. The device of describing instruction as a continuum stretching from teacher-centered to student-centered instruction contains a limited but useful set of indicators describing important dimensions of what teachers do in their classrooms. While this continuum cannot capture the richness of the classroom environment or the intersection of curriculum and instruction, it nonetheless offers a glimpse behind the closed doors of classrooms that existed decades ago and allows us to map, in a preliminary fashion, their pedagogical topography.

Before proceeding further, I need to state plainly what I mean by teacher- and student-centered instruction. Teacher-centered instruction means that a teacher controls what is taught, when, and under what conditions within a classroom. Observable measures of teacher-centered instruction are:

- Teacher talk exceeds student talk during instruction.
- Instruction occurs frequently with the whole class; small-group or individual instruction occurs less often.
- Use of class time is largely determined by the teacher.
- The teachers rely heavily upon the textbook to guide curricular and instructional decisionmaking.
- The classroom furniture is usually arranged into rows of desks or chairs facing a chalkboard with a teacher's desk nearby.

Student-centered instruction means that students exercise a substantial degree of responsibility for what is taught, how it is learned, and movement within the classroom. Observable measures of student-centered instruction are:

- Student talk about learning tasks is at least equal to, if not greater than, teacher talk.
- Most instruction occurs individually, in small groups (2 to 6 students), or in moderate-sized groups (7 to 10), rather than being directed at the entire class.
- Students help choose and organize the content to be learned. Teachers permit students to determine, partially or wholly, rules of behavior, classroom rewards and penalties, and how they are to be enforced.
- Varied instructional materials (e.g., activity centers, learning stations, interest centers) are available in the classroom so that students can use them independently or in small groups.

Use of these materials is scheduled, either by the teacher or in consultation with students, for at least half of the academic time available. The classroom is usually arranged in a manner that permits students to work together or separately, in small groups or in individual work spaces; no dominant pattern in arranging classroom furniture exists, and desks, tables, and chairs are realigned frequently.

I view these differences in teacher- and student-centered instruction as tools to help map what happened in classrooms. These instructional patterns have long histories.

For centuries, at least two traditions of how teachers should and do teach have fired debates and shaped practice. What I call teacher-centered instruction has been described as subject-centered, "tough-minded," "hard pedagogy," and "mimetic." What I call student-centered instruction has been labeled at different times as child-centered or "progressive," "tender-minded" or "soft" pedagogy, and as "transformative." While they are far from identical with these earlier notions, my definitions overlap with them sufficiently to be located in views of teaching that are millennia old.[8]

The two traditions of teaching are anchored in different views of knowledge and the relationship of both teacher and learner to that knowledge. In teacher-centered instruction, knowledge is often (but not always) "presented" to the learner, who—and the metaphors from different eras and places vary—is a "blank slate," a "vessel to fill;' or "a duck to stuff." In student-centered instruction, knowledge is often (but not always) "discovered" by the learner, who is "rich clay in the hands of an artist" or "a garden in need of a masterful gardener."

Using these two historical traditions of teaching as tools for understanding constancy and change is limited because they lack precision. Much detail is missing about what happens when a teacher teaches within a tradition. Nevertheless, even with these shortcomings, these traditions can help sort out, however simply, various teaching patterns, especially if the patterns are arrayed on a continuum. Of even greater importance is to weigh these shortcomings against the fact that so few studies have captured what teachers have done in classrooms over time.

In using these constructs, I do not assume that actual changes in practice moved solely from teacher- to student-centered instruction; traffic flowed both ways, regardless of reformers' intentions. Individual teachers stopped at various places along the way. Nor do I assume that changes in teaching behavior were an all-or-nothing embrace of an entire approach. Quite often, as this study will show, teachers incorporated into their repertoires particular practices they found useful. Hybrids of familiar and new practices turn up repeatedly in classrooms over the last century. In 1929, for example, an elementary school teacher whose only classroom innovation in years was to divide her class into two groups for reading, teaching some students in front of the room while the rest worked at their desks on an assignment, nevertheless added a new teaching tool to her repertoire. Likewise, a high school history teacher who in 1933 began using examples from contemporary political life to enliven his students' study of the French Revolution was modifying his routine practices.

While pedagogical progressives of those decades might have winced at my wording and labeled such changes as trivial, these teachers had selectively adopted child-centered practices. A continuum needs to have space for the hybrids of progressive teacher-centered instruction, just as it must have space for the various types of student-centered instruction more familiar to promoters of that approach.

The various adaptations of student-centered pedagogy that teachers over the last century have selectively incorporated into their practices are just as puzzling, if not as interesting, to policymakers and scholars, as those reforms teachers have ignored. Scholars also must unravel the mystery of what kinds of changes these hybrids are. Does an expanded arsenal of teaching approaches that meld student-centered techniques with a dominant teacher-centered approach mean that these are simply incremental changes, enhancements to the prevailing style of teaching? Or does it mean that these are incremental steps toward a fundamental shift in the emphasis of the individual teacher's approach? Although I take up these questions later, I raise them now to alert readers to the fact that many puzzles remain for scholars and policymakers to explore.

Despite these puzzles, observers can still categorize instructional patterns of individual teachers by careful attention to visible areas of classroom decisionmaking over which teachers have direct influence. These classroom indicators are evidence of the dominant form of instruction, especially when they combine to create patterns. Such indicators include:

1. Arrangement of classroom furniture;
2. The ratio of teacher talk to student talk;
3. Whether most instruction occurs individually, in small groups, or with the entire class;
4. The presence or absence of learning or interest centers that are used by students as part of the normal school day;
5. The degree of physical movement students are allowed without asking the teacher; and
6. The degree of reliance upon texts and use of varied instructional materials.

In describing classroom practices I had to narrow my scope. This study excludes descriptions of the emotional climate in classrooms and informal relationships between teachers and students. No judgments are made about the effectiveness of teacher- or student-centered instruction, nor are comparisons made among teaching practices. I assume that instances of effective teaching, however defined by scholars or practitioners, occur within both traditions. The central research issue for me is to determine how stable certain teaching behaviors were over the last century in the face of mighty efforts to move teaching toward student-centered instruction, not to determine the relative value of either approach in achieving desirable outcomes. But in trying to be objective about the two traditions of teaching, I cannot check my values and experiences at the door like a coat and hat. As a historian, I face dilemmas. A few words about these dilemmas may help the reader assess the worth of this study.

In seeking to be objective about the two traditions of instruction and their hybrids, I describe carefully my evidence and its sources and assess their strengths and limitations. I have met at least one condition of objectivity by telling readers at every step of the way how I carried out this study. In striving for impartiality, I have also tried to avoid describing teacher-centered instruction with such loaded phrases as "traditional teaching," "frontal teaching," or "conventional instruction," or student-centered instruction in terms such as "permissive" or "lacking academic standards."

While I work toward the ideal of objectivity in the methods I use and believe in the worth of that ideal, it is difficult to attain because I value certain kinds of teaching over others. I state my preferences for teaching approaches here so that readers can understand the value conflicts I face, as a historian seeking to be fair in describing and analyzing reforms aimed at altering teacher-centered instruction, and as a teacher and reformer eager to improve what happens in classrooms.

I began teaching in 1955. If an observer had entered my high school social studies class in Cleveland's Glenville High School a year later that person would have easily categorized my instruction as wholly teacher-centered. My students sat in rows of movable chairs with tablet arms; we carried on, more often than not, teacher-led discussions interspersed by my minilectures and occasional student reports, or a class debate, or a game to break the routine. Over 90% of instructional time was spent teaching the whole group.

By the early 1960s, I had begun to incorporate into my repertoire such techniques as student-led discussions, dividing the class into groups for varied tasks, creating instructional materials first to supplement and later to replace the textbook, and other approaches that could be loosely called "the new social studies."

In the early 1970s, one class of the five that I taught daily would spend the entire 50-minute period going from one teaching station to another. I used these stations at least once a week, sometimes more, depending on how much material I had developed. Most of the week, however, was spent on teacher-led discussions, supervised study periods, group meetings for particular projects, student reports, minilectures, and other nontraditional approaches. I had become much more informal in interactions with my students. They sat in a horseshoe arrangement of desks and chairs with the open end of the horseshoe facing my desk and chalkboard. Movement in the class and easy exchanges between me and students during small-group work and whole-group discussions spoke of a relaxed social organization in the classroom. I still decided, for the most part, what was to be studied, what methods were to be used, and how time and classroom space was to be allocated. At the same time, however, I was giving students a small but growing role in choosing topics within the larger framework I determined, in deciding how to use their time within the classroom when they had tasks to perform, and in making other instructional decisions.

Where along the continuum between teacher- and student-centered instruction did I fit? My dominant pattern remained teacher-centered but I had begun a journey in the mid-1950s and moved substantially toward the student-centered end of the continuum by the early 1970s. When I began teaching as a professor in 1981, the mixing of approaches began to be deliberate and explicit. When I returned to the high school classroom in 1988 for a semester to teach U.S. history to low-achieving students, the mixing of teaching approaches was even more evident. Over the years, then, I have come to see that I had developed a teaching hybrid that included features of student-centered instruction yet retained a dominant teacher-centered pattern.

Since the early 1960s I have also been deeply involved in improving the practice of social studies teaching, preparing new teachers for teaching in schools enrolling mostly poor, minority students, and making organizational reforms in one school district. Furthermore, I have written extensively about what policymakers, administrators, and teachers should do to improve schooling and teaching. So in my roles as high school teacher, administrator, and professor since 1955, I have mixed activism with reflection, practice with theory. That mixing has created many tensions within me; for example, even as I teach as a professor, I have come to value student-centered practices more and more over the years.

As my ideas of how knowledge is formed, learned, and used by both children and adults have changed over the years, so has my teaching. If students construct new knowledge out of their experiences, as I believe they do, then I, as a teacher, must grasp some portion of their experience and connect it to the knowledge I convey to them. How to connect what students already know to what they should know is the challenge facing every teacher. To secure that student understanding requires active student involvement in what is to be learned, different forms of representing that knowledge, and giving students many chances to practice and display what has been learned. This agenda, of course, tilts toward using student-centered practices in classrooms. Has this mixture of teaching practices that I have created over decades made me more effective in helping students learn? In other words, is it "good" teaching? The answer depends on one's definition of good teaching. Since I seek to make students think for themselves and put their fingerprints on any content that is learned in order to apply that content to their lives, I believe that my teaching is "good" teaching and that its effectiveness can be measured. Readers should note, however, that this study focuses on teaching, not on student learning. Any adequate definition of good teaching would require ample evidence of what students have learned as a consequence of the teaching approaches being evaluated.

This overview of my career as a teacher brings into focus a few of the dilemmas I face as a researcher committed to the ideal of objectivity in scholarship while practicing the art of teaching and also trying to introduce school and classroom reforms. I have tried to control for my biases in this study by using different forms of evidence, investigating different sites, and sampling from different periods. These devices are ways of reducing the effects of my preferences. The compromises that I have constructed to deal with the tensions of the competing, even conflicting values of a scholar, a practitioner, and a reformer may not please each reader, but I feel that readers should be aware of how I dealt with these inevitable quandaries.

Given the limits of this study, an obvious question arises: If this inquiry avoids defining what is "good" teaching or how some teachers succeed better than others at creating a classroom atmosphere where students want to learn, then what will be the practical uses of this research? This is a fair question because it raises the issues of the intersection between research and practice and the uses of historical investigation.

Because researchers, policymakers, practitioners, and reform-minded citizens know so little about which instructional practices have remained stable and which ones have changed over the last century, investigating certain classroom practices can illuminate both the potential for and the limits to altering how teachers teach. Exploring the terrain of the classroom since the 1890s should reveal what is durable and what is transient, what can be changed and what is invulnerable to reform. By learning more about the instructional quark that is the classroom, policymakers, practitioners, and scholars can come to have reasonable expectations about what teachers can and cannot do, what schools can be held accountable for, and what is beyond their reach. Thus the outcomes of this study, however modest, should offer practical direction for the periodic surges of reform that sweep over public schools.

I also see an indirect, subtler use for this study of classroom practices. Powerful metaphors for schooling dominate the thinking of practitioners, scholars, and policymakers. J. M. Stephens writes that a common metaphor for schools is the factory. This image exalts rational decisionmaking, suggesting that schools are mechanical; each part of the machine is connected to the others by an assembly line and can be fixed or improved. Switch to the metaphor of farming, Stephens says, and schooling looks different. Through an ancient, stable process, farmers predict what the sun, the climate, seeds, plants, and insects are likely to do each year. By understanding the durability of the process and working within its limits, he argues, farmers can improve production. But, he continues, farmers cannot ignore these "older organic forces [they] have little control over." They have to work with and through them. The agricultural metaphor is a fundamentally different image of teaching and schooling that has direct consequences for what reform-minded policymakers believe can and cannot be done with and for classroom teachers.[9]

Many policymakers, scholars, and practitioners carry these or similar images in their heads. Such pictures shape their decisions. Historical maps of teaching practices over the last century have at least the potential for determining the accuracy of these metaphors and, in turn, suggesting directions for the periodic reforms undertaken by citizens and professionals alike.

Two specific questions guide this study:

- Did teacher-centered instruction persist in public schools during and after reform movements that had as one of their targets the installation of student-centered instruction?
- If the answer is yes, to what extent did it persist and why? If the answer is no, to what extent did instruction change and why?

In order to answer these questions I have drawn historical maps of teaching practices in three cities and many rural districts during the 1920s and 1930s; in two cities and one state for the decade between 1965 and 1975; and in one medium-sized school district in a metropolitan area between 1975 and 1981. The two periods of major reform efforts to shift classroom practices fundamentally from teacher- to student-centeredness were (a) the decades in the first quarter of the 20th century, when progressive education became the dominant ideology, and (b) the decade between the mid-1960s and the mid-1970s, when informal education, or "open classrooms," dominated the talk of policymakers, practitioners, and scholars.

To determine how teachers taught, I used a variety of sources:

Photographs of teachers and students in class; textbooks and texts used by teachers;
Student recollections of their classroom experiences; teacher reports on how they taught;
Reports from journalists, administrators, parents, and others who visited classrooms;
Student writings in school newspapers and yearbooks; research studies of teaching practices; and
Descriptions of classroom architecture, room size, desk design, building plans, and so forth.

Historians have to cope with the dilemmas of selectivity of evidence (i.e., what survives and is available may be atypical of the era being studied) and the inherent biases of sources (e.g., a photographer in 1900 posed students to illustrate the "New Education"). To minimize the effects of selectivity and bias I have sought multiple and divergent sources representing two periods of time and a number of different settings, from elementary to high school, from urban to rural.

From these sources I have gathered descriptions of over 1,200 classrooms for the years 1890 to 1990. These descriptions are embedded within a larger set of data from each district and across the nation that indirectly reveal teaching practices in almost 7,000 other classrooms.

The patterns in teaching practice described in this study represent only a fraction of what teachers did in their classrooms. Anyone familiar with a classroom knows the kaleidoscopic whirl that it is—although its pace, intensity, and complexity are often obscured by student compliance with teacher-established routines. (To the casual observer, the classroom may, after 30 minutes of observation, seem humdrum, even tedious.) How, then, can I capture only one slice of this whirl after it has disappeared?

The historian of classroom teaching is in the same bind as the paleontologist who carefully and softly brushes away the dust from a jaw fragment of an apparent human ancestor. The bone is an infinitesimally tiny fragment of the skeleton, the skeleton an even tinier fraction of the population that the scientist wants to describe. The "bones" I have had to work with are classroom photographs, and written accounts by various participants.

Historian David Fischer suggests another image. Studying history is like trying to complete an unconventional puzzle. Take a Jackson Pollock painting and cut it into a puzzle with a thousand parts. Throw out the corner pieces, most of the edges, and half of the rest. The task of putting it all together comes close to describing what historians do.

Trying to put the puzzle together also means trying to make sense of the Jackson Pollock painting. A study of constancy and change in American classrooms over the last century must ask: Why did various teaching practices persist in spite of determined efforts to alter them and why did teachers invent new approaches and integrate them into their daily routines?

EXPLANATIONS FOR CONSTANCY AND CHANGE

There are a number of explanations for stability in teaching practices and instances of teacher-adopted changes. I mention these possible explanations briefly now to alert readers to both the range and character of the arguments. (I will use the words "argument" and "explanation" interchangeably in this context.) The arguments are as follows:

1. Cultural beliefs about the nature of knowledge, how teaching should occur, and how children should learn are so widespread and deeply rooted that they steer the thinking of policymakers, practitioners, parents, and citizens toward certain forms of instruction. Centuries ago, in European and American cultures, formal schooling was instituted in religious institutions with the aim of teaching students to spread the word of the particular gospel and to study its meaning. Books were rare and teaching and learning in church-related schools and colleges depended on those who were informed telling the uninformed what was important to know. Knowledge was a body of beliefs, facts, procedures, and opinions that largely went unquestioned.

For millennia, then, deeply embedded Western beliefs about the nature of knowledge (a body of human wisdom accumulated and tempered over time that must be passed on from one generation to another), teaching (the communicating of that wisdom), and learning (the absorption of that wisdom) have marked efforts to school the young. These beliefs unfolded within the family when it acted as the first school for infants and toddlers. Strengthened by formal religions as they emerged over the centuries, these cultural beliefs shaped the character and direction of religious instruction before the introduction of tax-supported public schools. With the invention of public schools in Europe and later in the United States, teacher-centered instruction, stressing the teacher as the authority who passes on the required knowledge to students, who in turn are expected to take in and digest the knowledge, continued as the dominant form of instruction.

Occasional European and American philosophers and educators over the last 500 years objected to these ingrained cultural beliefs and maintained that education should focus on the child, rather than on a body of knowledge accumulated over centuries. Such reformers viewed the teacher's primary role as that of guiding the unfolding of the child's talents to their fullest and were eager to develop student-centered ways of educating the young. Twentieth-century reformers, for example, introduced the kindergarten, small-group learning approaches, the movable desk, and other child-centered practices into public schooling. These changes have come slowly and have often been diluted by the dominant cultural norms deeply ingrained in these schools.

Thus, it comes as no surprise that most descriptions of classrooms portray the persistence of teacher-centered classrooms consistent with the historical traditions that took shape when men and women lived guided by a deep reverence for the accumulated wisdom of their elders.

2. The organization and practice of formal schooling function to socialize and sort students into varied socioeconomic niches. In the life of a growing child, the school is the only public institution that stands between the family and the workplace. Schools inculcate in children the dominant social norms, values, and behaviors that will prepare them for entry into the larger culture. Schools are organized into bureaucratic, age-graded settings where students are grouped, first by ability, in elementary schools and then by tracks in secondary schools. Schools and the adults who staff these institutions, then, unwittingly distribute dominant cultural knowledge (American history, grammar, math, and so on), inculcate mainstream values (punctuality, the work ethic, competitiveness, and so forth), and channel students into appropriate socioeconomic niches (the upper and middle classes into corporate, professional, and business careers, the lower classes into service and low-grade technical jobs).

Classrooms come to be dominated by particular teaching practices that concentrate on definite content and skills that have to be learned and by student attitudes toward conformity, productivity, and other traits required for minimal participation in social, bureaucratic, and industrial organizations. Mainstream beliefs and values have to be taught; children from other cultures who bring to classrooms languages, habits, and attitudes different from what is taught in school have to be transformed into American citizens. A standard English has to be mastered; classroom habits of turn-taking and remaining quiet for long periods of time, for example, must be learned.

Students who have already learned the necessary etiquette at home meet teachers' expectations. Many are placed in advanced reading groups and, in the higher grades, on college preparatory tracks. For students who come from cultures or socioeconomic backgrounds where these school demands are unfamiliar, adjustment is difficult. Many, but not all, of these students are labeled by teachers and administrators as "slow" learners or misfits and are assigned to particular groups within a classroom or to separate programs.

Certain teaching practices are practical for both groups, but especially for children who come from different socioeconomic backgrounds: arranging desks into rows to secure uniform behavior; relying on textbooks to yield reams of homework for which credit is given or withheld; giving tests and quizzes to permit the teacher to sort students by their achievement or lack of it; and having students follow teacher-directed procedures for seatwork, recitation, and reports. These dominant teacher-centered practices endure because they produce student behaviors consistent with the requirements of the larger society.

3. If educational policymakers had effectively implemented reforms aimed at changing what teachers routinely do, changes in instructional practices would have occurred. When attentive policymakers systematically and thoroughly put into practice policies aimed at fundamentally altering teaching behaviors, classroom practices changed. But where policy efforts were ill-conceived and partially or haphazardly implemented, teachers remained largely insulated from reformers' designs for basic classroom changes.

Flawed implementation of student-centered instructional reforms accounts for a durable core of teacher-centered instructional approaches. Had deliberate and comprehensive efforts been undertaken to implement instructional changes, many more of the reforms begun in the early 1900s and in the 1960s would be apparent in the 1990s. Where implementation was carefully planned and executed, teaching practices changed substantially.

Student-centered approaches, then, infrequently penetrated classrooms because of the inattentiveness, unwillingness, or inability of school officials to convert a policy decision or formal approval of an instructional change into a systematic process that would gain teacher support for classroom adoption.

4. The organizational structure of the district, school, and classroom shaped teachers' dominant instructional practices. The organizational structures of a district and school steered teachers into adopting certain instructional strategies that varied little over time. "Structures" refers to how school space is arranged; how content and students are organized into grade levels; how time is allotted to tasks; and how organizational rules govern the behavior and performance of both adults and students. These structures result from the basic imperative of public schooling: to manage large numbers of students who are forced to attend school and absorb certain knowledge in an orderly fashion. The age-graded school, self-contained classrooms, a curriculum divided into levels, 50-minute periods, and large classes are structures that have developed over time to meet this basic imperative.

The classroom organization nested within the larger school structure assigns to the teacher the task of managing 25 to 40 or more students of approximately the same age who involuntarily spend—depending upon their age—anywhere from 1 to 5 hours daily in one room. The teacher is expected to maintain control, teach certain subject matter, motivate students to learn, vary levels of instruction according to student differences, and display evidence that students have performed satisfactorily.

Within these overlapping school and classroom structures, teachers have rationed their energy and time. They have coped with multiple and conflicting demands by inventing certain teaching practices that have emerged as resilient, imaginative, and efficient strategies for dealing with a large number of students in a small space for extended periods of time.

Rows of movable desks and seating charts, for example, permit the teacher easy surveillance to maintain order. The teacher's desk, usually located in a visually prominent part of the room near a chalkboard, underscores quietly who determines the direction for what the class will do each day. Class routines that require students to raise their hands to answer questions, to speak only when recognized by the teacher, and to speak when no one else is talking establish a framework for whole-group instruction. Requiring students to ask for permission to leave the room bolsters a teacher's control over students and maintains classroom order.

Within these structures, teaching the entire class together is an efficient and convenient use of the teacher's time—a valuable and scarce resource—to cover the mandated content and to maintain control. Lecturing, recitation, seatwork, homework drawn from texts, and weekly tests are efficient, uncomplicated ways of transmitting knowledge to groups and determining whether students have learned the material.

Student-centered approaches where students work together, move freely around the room, and determine certain classroom tasks for themselves make a shambles of classroom routines geared to handling batches of students. These approaches are incompatible with existing school and classroom structures and would require a complete overhaul of basic modes of classroom operation. Few teachers are willing to upset their controlled, familiar world for the uncertain benefits of a student-centered classroom.

This argument stresses that the structures of the age-graded school produce regularities in instruction. Past teachers coped with the dilemmas imposed by these structures, over which they had little control, by inventing creative compromises in the shape of teacher-centered instructional practices.

5. The cultures of teaching that have developed within the occupation tilt toward stability in classroom practices. The occupational ethos of teaching breeds conservatism, that is, a preference for stability and a cautious attitude toward change. This conservatism is anchored in the very practice of teaching, in the people who enter the profession, in how they are informally socialized, and in the school culture of which teaching itself is a primary ingredient.

The aim of teaching is to change children into youth viewed as desirable by parents and society. Yet teachers are wholly dependent on their students for producing successful results. Moreover, as yet there is no societal consensus about what are the desired outcomes of teaching. Understandably, teachers are often reluctant to take risks by modifying practices, particularly by embracing student-centered instructional reforms, which place even more reliance upon students for results.

Who enters teaching is another factor encouraging conservatism within the occupation. Often newcomers seek contact with children, appreciate the flexible work schedule, and, while acknowledging the limited financial rewards, still embrace the service mission built into the occupation. Of the young who enter teaching, women outnumber men. Men often move out of the classroom in search of greater social recognition, more organizational influence, and higher salaries. Attracted by work schedules that permit flexible arrangements with regard to family obligations and vacations, women and men who do remain teachers have few incentives to alter occupational conditions or seek major improvements.

Furthermore, recruits to the occupation lean toward continuity because of their prior school experiences. As public school students for 12 years, future teachers unwittingly served an apprenticeship as they watched their teachers teach.

Thus, classroom practices tend to be stable over time. After all, homework assignments, discussion, seatwork, tests, and an occasional film to interrupt the routine were all methods familiar to teachers in their own schooling and, more often than not, seemed to keep the class moving along. Instead of fundamental changes—such as teaching small groups, integrating varied content into units, planning lessons with students, and letting class members choose what to do—the basic conservatism of the occupation would favor tinkering with methods, polishing up techniques, and introducing variations of existing ones.

6. Teachers' knowledge of subject matter and their professional and personal beliefs about the role of the school in society, about classroom authority, and about children's ethnic and socioeconomic status shape classroom practices. What teachers know about a subject gets converted into teachable language and activities for children. A social studies teacher, for example, not only has content knowledge of, say, United States history, but also knows how to convey, to 15-year-olds uninterested in academic subjects or in going to college, what the Bill of Rights means to teenagers today, through concrete examples drawn from actual court cases. The images a biology teacher uses to illustrate the concept of evolution to sophomores in a college preparatory class are not drawn from a textbook but from the experience the teacher has had with previous students' struggles to understand the concept.

If content knowledge counts, so do the teacher's professional and personal beliefs about how children learn. An elementary school teacher who believes that children working together in small groups can learn from editing one another's writing will organize classroom furniture differently than a teacher who views learning as having pupils memorize editing rules. The teacher who looks for connections between textbook content and daily events because he or she believes that students absorb knowledge more easily when it is related to their lives will depart from the text far more often than others to explore these connections.

Finally, those teachers whose social attitudes lead them to seek contacts with higher- rather than lower-status children, with children more similar to their own ethnic, racial, or religious background, will approach choosing content, managing the classroom, and structuring activities differently in teaching low-income Black or Hispanic pupils than in teaching affluent White or Asian American students.

The knowledge, beliefs, and attitudes that teachers have, then, shape what they choose to do in their classrooms and explain both the constancy and the change that have shaped the core of instructional practices that have endured over time.

Note how the six explanations for how teachers teach include the environment (cultural inheritance and social functions of schools), the organizational (implementation of policies and the structures of schooling), occupational socialization (the nature of teaching, who enters the occupation, and future teachers' long apprenticeship of observing their elders), and, finally, the individual whose knowledge and beliefs shape classroom behavior. Four of the arguments try to explain why teacher-centered instruction endured; two (occasional implementation of classroom reform policies and teachers' knowledge and beliefs) suggest reasons why classroom changes may have occurred.

Earlier I compared my task to that of fossil seekers. Let me shift disciplines to use the image of a 13th-century cartographer trying to map a new world on the basis of what knowledge seafarers brought back, what had been written in books, and informed guesses. The maps he produced contained numerous mistakes and lies, and yet sea captains who used them explored the world and returned with new information that reshaped subsequent maps. This study is in the tradition of 13th-century mapmaking.

NOTES

1. Cuban, 1979.

2. I take up the questions of how historians have viewed stability and change in schools and classrooms in Chapter 1, L. Cuban, 1984, *How teachers taught: Constancy and change in American classrooms, 1890–1980.* New York: Longman.

3. I drew these ideas from Watzlawick, Weakland, & Fisch, 1974. In their book, they use the term "first-order" for changes that I call "incremental" and "second-order" for changes that I call "fundamental."

4. Atkin & House, 1981; Stake & Easley, 1978; Suydam & Osborne, 1977. For other instances of incrementalizing fundamental reforms, see Wolcott, 1977.

5. Spindler & Spindler, 1988.

6. Powell, Farrar, & Cohen, 1985.

7. Meyer, 1986; Meyer & Rowan, 1978; see also Cuban, 1992.

8. James, 1958; Katz, 1968; Jackson, 1986.

9. Stephens, 1967, p. 11. David Tyack pointed out to me that progressive reformers Ellwood Cubberley and Franklin Bobbitt used both metaphors. For other images of schools and classrooms.

REFERENCES

Atkin, J. M., & House, E. (1981). The federal role in curriculum development. *Educational Evaluation and Policy Analysis, 3*(5), 5–36.

Cuban, L. (1979). Determinants of curriculum change and stability, 1870–1970. In J. Schafferzick & G. Sykes (Eds.), *Value conflict and curriculum issues* (pp. 139–196). Berkeley, CA: McCutchan.

Cuban, L. (1992). Stability and change in curriculum. In P. Jackson (Ed.), *The handbook of research on curriculum* (pp. 216–247). New York: Macmillan.

Jackson, P. (1986). *The practice of teaching.* New York: Teachers College Press.

James, W. (1958). *Talks to teachers.* New York: Norton.

Katz, M. (1968). *The irony of early school reform.* Cambridge, MA: Harvard University Press.

Marshall, H. H. (1988). Work or learning: Implications of classroom metaphors. *Educational Researcher, 17*(9), 9–16.

Meyer, J. (1986). The politics of educational crises in the United States. In W. Cummings, E. R. Beauchamp, W. Ichikawa, Y. N. Kobayashi, & M. Ushigi (Eds.), *Educational policies in crisis* (pp. 44–58). New York: Praeger.

Meyer, J., & Rowan, B. (1978). The structure of educational organizations. In M. Meyer (Ed.), *Environments and organizations* (pp. 78–109). San Francisco: Jossey-Bass.

Powell, A., Farrar, E., & Cohen, D. (1985). The shopping mall high school: Winners and losers in the educational marketplace. Boston: Houghton Mifflin.

Spindler, G., & Spindler, L. (1982). Roger Harker and Schönhausen. In G. Spindler (Ed.), *Doing the ethnography of schooling* (pp. 20–46). New York: Holt, Rinehart and Winston.

Stake, R., & Easley, J. (1978). *Case studies of science education* (Vol. 1). Urbana, IL: Center for Instructional Research and Curriculum Evaluation.

Stephens, J. M. (1967). *The process of schooling.* New York: Holt, Rinehart and Winston.

Suydam, M., & Osborne, A. (1977). *The status of pre-college science, mathematics, and social science education, 1955–1975: Mathematics education* (Vol. 2). Columbus: Center for Science and Mathematics Education, Ohio State University.

Watzlawick, P., Weakland, J., & Fisch, R. (1974). *Change: Principals of problem formation and problem resolution.* New York: Norton.

Wolcott, H. (1977). *Teachers and technocrats.* Eugene: Center for Educational Policy and Management, University of Oregon.

CHAPTER 8

2006—Reflections on Two Decades of Computers in Classrooms

INTRODUCTION

Over the past 3 years, I have met with teachers, administrators, state policy-makers, and district board members across the nation, all of whom were eager to talk about their experiences in using computers for instruction. Many had read *Oversold and Underused*; others had heard about the book and the research that I had reported. Many wanted me to answer their questions, tell me where I had erred, and raise issues that I had neglected to cover in the book. In preparing for this talk, I thought of those many exchanges. This talk gives me the chance to offer a few observations on what I have learned from these intense discussions.

I have found that conversations about computers in schools have become less testy, less polarizing, and more engaging in their policy implications than exchanges I had had a decade ago.

Name calling, at least public scorn for anyone who would question the prevailing belief in the magical efficacy of computers in schools, is unfashionable. I found educators and noneducators who deeply believed in classroom computers as engines of learning, willing to listen to critics when concerns were raised about the many goals of schooling in a democracy, the small part technology plays in classroom instruction, and insufficient technical support.

In the past, promoters of new technologies, be they vendors, practitioners, or policymakers, would curtly dismiss these concerns by calling skeptics "Luddites." No more. At least in public. As investments in new technologies continue to mount, as the all-important concept of total cost of operations has sunk into the skulls of policymakers, and as fiscal retrenchment has reduced school budgets, there is far more willingness on the part of ardent promoters to pause and consider answers to tough questions: Do teachers integrate the new technologies into their daily instruction? If not, why not? How much of the technology budget is devoted to on-site professional development and technical support of teachers? What kind of research designs have to be pursued to show that teacher use of classroom technologies has caused gains in academic achievement? That these questions could be asked and thoughtfully considered is encouraging.

I also found in my travels that the idea of the computer as a learning tool is firmly planted in the language used to describe new technologies. Time and again, the refrain that the computer (and its software) is about learning, not technology, came from school board members, teachers, superintendents, and parents. And, from the testimony of those who have written of their experiences, the clever and imaginative ways in which the new technologies can be used routinely both in teaching and learning are more than evident. I count the growing understanding of fitting computers to student learning a small victory for common sense about schooling in America.

Except when it comes to 1:1 computing and the spread of laptops in this nation. I hear again, as I have heard before in the past 2 decades, the claims of technological champions that somehow, in some way, each student having a laptop would revolutionize classroom learning. As satisfying as these discussions over the past few years have been, I worry that the gush of unrestrained enthusiasm for 1:1 computing will shove aside the hard-earned lessons of the past 2 decades about new technologies in classrooms. So let me begin my reflections with 1:1 computing.

1:1 COMPUTING

From 125 students per computer in 1984 to just under five students for each computer in 2003 and now to many districts moving toward a 1:1 ratio, computers in schools are becoming ubiquitous. Sure, a "digital divide" existed between high-wealth and poor schools but it has been closing rapidly in the past decade. In higher education, no such divide exists: 1:1 pervades colleges and universities.

The argument for each student having a laptop goes like this: Each student has a textbook, each has a pen and notebook, each student, therefore, should have a computer. In what business, in what hospital, in what police precinct, in what university, advocates of 1:1 ask, do four or five employees, doctors, officers, or professors have to compete for one computer? None. For God's sake, they say, even when you turn in your rental car, the person has a hand-held computer. If you want productive future employees, give each student a laptop or hand-held device to use in class.[1]

So 2 decades after the introduction of the personal computer to public schools, policymakers, parents, business and civic leaders seek complete access for students—rural and urban, wealthy and poor—to a powerful learning tool.[2]

The uncritical embrace of 1:1 laptops by elites, parents, and many educators is similar to earlier responses to new technologies that promised increased teacher and student productivity, transformed teaching and learning, and improved academic achievement. Before there were computers, school policymakers had introduced film and radio in the 1920s and instructional television in the 1950s as technological marvels to make teaching and learning faster and better. In studying these machines after they entered classrooms, researchers found common patterns:

1. Policymakers, not teachers, made the decision to buy and deploy film projectors, radios, and television.
2. In each case there was initial excitement over how the innovation would revolutionize teaching and learning. Equipment was purchased and put into schools. Then researchers went into schools to see how often and in which ways teachers were using these new technologies in lessons. They found very limited and unimaginative classroom use by teachers. Finally, disillusionment among policymakers spread and teachers were bashed for being resistant to technology.[3]

But information and communications technology (or ICT) is different from film, radio, and television as tools for teaching and learning. First, earlier machine technologies were sparingly distributed among schools, and teachers had to compete for limited film inventories or rigidly scheduled times for initially radio and, later, television programs. Second, these technologies came from the entertainment industry and students listened and watched passively; films and TV had the gloss of something that was fun, not educational.

Computers, however, were initially invented for the military and spread rapidly through manufacturing and businesses as tools to automate work, cut labor costs, and increase employee efficiency. Computers as productivity tools expanded from the workplace into police cars, hospitals, churches, libraries, and virtually every other institution. For schools, the computer has been a boon to administrative work and with its interactivity, a powerful teaching and learning tool for creating knowledge and practicing skills.

Because of these significant differences between film, radio, instructional television, and the computer, comparing these earlier technological innovations with ICT is like comparing horse-drawn trolleys with bullet trains: they are both means of transportation but vastly different in effects upon passengers. So it comes as little surprise as these potent machines become available to each and every student, their champions paint utopian pictures of transformed teaching and learning unlike anything that existed before. In these scenarios, students work alone or in small groups using laptops or small hand-held wireless devices. In school and at home, instruction is individualized. Students consult occasionally with a teacher, but are mostly independent learners.

Based on the history of schools adopting and using earlier technological innovations, however, I question these rose-tinted educational utopias where learning is 24/7. I question these scenarios because well-meaning reformers persistently ignore the multiple roles schools perform in this society, its resilient structures and processes and, most important, what has happened in schools over the past century when such dreams have been launched again and again as well-intended progressive changes.[4]

For many years, I and other researchers, rather than rely upon surveys and self-reports of teachers and principals, have gone into schools to see what has happened when technological innovations enter classrooms. Now that students and teachers have greater access to ICT than any previous technological innovation, obvious questions arise: How do they use them daily for teaching and learning? What have been the outcomes for teachers and students of use? From my studies and those of other researchers who have gone into classrooms for the past 15 years, I offer three statements to answer these questions.[5]

1. Teacher and student use of ICT at home and in school is widespread in doing assignments, writing, preparing lessons, Internet searches, and e-mail, but lags far behind in routine use for classroom instruction. Except for online instruction in many high schools and reports of 1:1 laptop programs, once-a-week use of ICT in classrooms is restricted to a loyal but small minority of teachers.

In my research, I found less than 10% of teachers integrated ICT seamlessly into their lessons on at least a weekly basis. Occasional teacher use of ICT—once a month—had slightly increased in the past decade to nearly 50%, meaning that the percentage of teachers who hardly ever use ICT for classroom instruction remains around 40%. Even with these modest changes, classroom use of ICT remains, at best, limited.[6]

A recent study I did of classroom instruction in three districts (Arlington, Virginia, Oakland, California, and Denver, Colorado) offers system-wide snapshots of technology use. In this study, I collected 1,044 direct observations—not survey responses—of what elementary and secondary schoolteachers in these districts did in their classrooms between 1993–2005. These reported observations included summaries of supervisor visits, student descriptions, journalist visits, actual photos, my direct observations, and other sources. In effect, these were snapshots of lessons in progress. When I sorted through the data I pulled out all of those instances of teachers using technologies as part of their lessons. I counted use of overhead projectors, videos, LCD projectors, calculators, and, of course, computers in classrooms, media centers, and labs. Table 8.1 shows what I found.

At first glance, these data show fairly high percentages of teachers using technology. It helps, however, to sort out which technologies teachers were using in their lessons. And I have done that in Table 8.2.

The results in Table 8.2 show teachers using mixes of old and new technologies with their students. In looking solely at computers used for instruction, percentages of teachers across the three districts range between 8% and 12%. These results, however, tell us nothing about frequency of use or how students use computers in classrooms.

What about those schools with 1:1 access? Has frequency of student use increased? According to teacher, student, and administrator surveys and interviews about laptop programs, the answer is an unqualified yes. Survey evidence is slowly accumulating that teachers and students use computers more often than when they had access to fewer computers in the classrooms, mobile carts, labs, and media centers.

But how much more use and what kinds of use? Journalist accounts and many teacher, student, and parent surveys of 1:1 programs in the state of Maine, Henrico County, Virginia, and individual districts scattered across the nation report extraordinary enthusiasm. Teachers report daily use of laptops and elevated student interest in schoolwork, higher motivation from previously lackluster students, and more engagement in lessons. Students and parents report similar high levels of use and interest in learning. All of these enthusiastic responses to 1:1 programs do have a déjà vu feel to those of us who have heard similar gusto for technological innovations prior to the initial novelty wearing off.[7]

The déjà vu feeling is not only from knowing the history of classroom machines; it is also because the evidence is largely drawn from self-reports. Researchers know the dangers of unreliable estimates that plague such survey and interview responses. When investigators did examine classrooms of teachers and students who reported high frequency of usage, these researchers

TABLE 8.1. Technology Use in Three Districts' Schools, 1993–2005

	Arlington	**Denver**	**Oakland**
Elementary	N = 379	N = 68	N = 49
Reports of technology used	N = 75 (20%)	N = 15 (21%)	N = 8 (15%)
Secondary	N = 220	N = 166	N = 162
Reports of technology used	N = 105 (48%)	N = 50 (30%)	N = 42 (26%)
TOTAL REPORTS	N = 599	N = 234	N = 211
TOTAL OF TECHNOLOGY USED	N = 180 (30%)	N = 65 (28%)	N = 50 (24%)

TABLE 8.2. Specific Technology Use in Three Districts' Schools, 1993–2005

	Arlington	Denver	Oakland
Elementary reports	N = 379	N = 68	N = 49
Overhead projector	N = 23 (6%)	N = 3 (4%)	N = 3 (6%)
Computers in labs or classrooms	N = 31 (8%)	N = 8 (12%)	N = 3 (6%)
Video/LCD	N = 12 (3%)	N = 3 (4%)	N = 1 (1%)
Calculators	N = 6 (2%)	N = 1 (1%)	N = 1 (2%)
Video camera	N = 1 (< 1%)		
Audiotapes	N = 2 (< 1%)		
Secondary reports	N = 220	N = 166	N = 162
Overhead projectors	N = 49 (22%)	N = 14 (8%)	N = 13 (8%)
Computers in labs or classrooms	N = 2 (10%)	N = 20 (12%)	N = 10 (6%)
Video/LCD	N = 22 (10%)	N = 9 (5%)	N = 13 (8%)
Calculators	N = 6 (3%)	N = 6 (4%)	N = 6 (4%)
Slide projector	N = 1 (< 1%)		
Audiotapes	N = 5 (2%)	N = 1 (1%)	
TOTALS	N = 599	N = 234	N = 211
Overhead projectors	N = 72 (12%)	N = 17 (7%)	N = 16 (8%)
Computers in labs or classrooms	N = 53 (9%)	N = 28 (12%)	N = 13 (6%)
Video/LCD	N = 34 (6%)	N = 12 (5%)	N = 14 (7%)
Calculators	N = 12 (2%)	N = 7 (3%)	N = 7 (3%)
Other	N = 9 (1%)	N = 1 (< 1%)	

subsequently found large discrepancies between what was reported and what was observed. So a healthy dose of skepticism about teacher claims of daily use and students' long-term engagement is in order because few researchers have directly observed classroom lessons for sustained periods of time where students use laptops. Until more researchers go into classrooms, it will be hard to say with confidence that teacher daily use of computers has changed considerably with 1:1 laptop programs.[8]

To sum up, in this decade student and teacher access to ICT has expanded dramatically and is approaching 1:1 in many districts. The digital gap has shrunk considerably in public schools. But gaining access—and this is a crucial point—does not necessarily translate into teachers and students routinely using ICT during lessons. Most schoolteachers who use home computers daily have yet to use ICT in their teaching as often as they use overhead projectors or textbooks. I now turn to my second statement.

2. Few marked changes in pedagogy have occurred as a result of abun-dant ICT access. Prior to the spread of 1:1 laptop programs, champions of student-centered or constructivist pedagogy latched onto ICT as a means of reducing the dominant and traditional teacher-centered forms of instruction. Previous data revealed clearly that the introduction of ICT even with coaching and technical support had not altered mainstream pedagogies of more than 5%–10% of teachers. When changes in teaching did occur alongside increased use of ICT–such as with project-based learning–more often than not, they occurred because teacher beliefs and predispositions already had tilted toward student-centered pedagogy.[9]

In listening to current enthusiasts for 1:1 computing, the same hopes for a transformation in classroom practice are front and center. Rather than give you extended quotes, I offer a typical one from a recent review of 1:1 programs in various districts: "Collaborative learning, rigorous authentic learning, inquiry-based learning, and active, engaged learning are consistently associated with 1 to 1 learning initiatives." Repeating learning five times in the same sentence is a bit much but the reviewers concluded, without reservation, that 1:1 laptops would transform pedagogy.[10]

Other researchers, however, have studied how massive infusions of technology do not necessarily translate into teachers altering their daily practices even when 1:1 exists. Consider the work of Judith Sandholtz and her colleagues on the Apple Classroom of Tomorrow, or ACOT, program between 1985 and 1998, an uncommonly intensive, long-term study of computers in classrooms.[11]

The original ACOT project distributed two desktop computers (one for home and one for school) to every student and teacher in five elementary and secondary classrooms across the country, eventually expanding to hundreds of classrooms and schools. ACOT researchers reported student engagement, collaboration, and independent work much as 1:1 researchers do today. But they also found that for teachers to use computers as learning tools, the 1:1 ratio was not necessary. In elementary and secondary classrooms, clusters of computers could achieve the same level of weekly use and maintain the other tasks that teachers and students had to accomplish.[12]

With some teachers, but not the majority, teacher-centered practices shifted slowly to student-centered ones over years as long as teachers worked closely together and had sufficient technical on-site support. On-site professional development where teachers learned from one another made a significant difference in shifting practices, again, over many years. What ACOT researchers found was that teachers created hybrids of student- and teacher-centered practices using computers for certain activities and not others.[13]

ACOT demonstrated clearly that dumping lots of equipment into class-rooms would not magically change teaching; many other things need to come together for teachers to alter their pedagogy. So there is little question that teachers—male and female, old and young—use ICT as personal learning tools at home and at school in researching and preparing lessons, e-mail, and administrative tasks. Nor is there any question that teachers see computers as helpful to their students' motivation and daily work in schools.

Yet major expectations of teachers remain beyond using computers in classrooms. Policymakers and parents expect teachers to make children liter-ate while promoting moral behavior, civic engagement, and job preparation. They also expect teachers to maintain control of students in their classroom, make certain that their students are respectful and dutifully complete their work, and ensure that students achieve curriculum standards as measured by tests. In light of these expectations, abundant access to new technologies can create mixes of teaching practices but will hardly transform pedagogy. Now, I turn to my final statement.

3. Abundant ICT access and small gains in teacher use have yet to reveal any causal link to improved academic achievement. For the past 80 years of research on technology's impact on learning, not much reliable evidence has emerged to give impartial observers confidence that students' use of com-puters or any other electronic device leads directly to improved academic achievement. Of course, saying this contradicts vendor ads, software devel-oper claims, and policymakers' pronouncements—not to mention the high expectations of advocates of 1:1 computing. Attributing test score gains to increased use of ICT and earlier technological innovations has been around for nearly a century and is, at best, misleading and, at worst, false.

Some recent examples of misattribution might help. For example, a small district in Alaska and another in New Jersey enrolling largely poor minor-ity students have continually been championed as sterling models of places where extensive purchase and use of computers have led to substantial gains in test scores. What is often omitted from these accounts, however, is that each district received lots of money to launch system-wide reforms in cur-riculum, teaching, and accountability 3–5 years before schools were wired and computers bought. Yet gains in academic achievement were attributed to computers, not the funding or deep structural and curricular reforms in-troduced years earlier.[14]

What causes enthusiasts to attribute gains in achievement to ICT use? Researchers mistake the medium of instruction—instructional television or laptops—with the instructional method embedded in the video or software and the teacher's approaches to the lesson.

Richard Clark and others have said for decades that personal computers, laptops, and hand-held devices are vehicles for transporting instructional methods. They are not the teaching methods. By teaching methods, I mean practices such as asking questions, giving examples, lecture, recitation, guided discussion, drill, cooperative learning, individualized instruction, simulations, tutoring, project-based learning, and innumerable variations and combinations of these methods.[15]

Confusing ICT with instructional methods in designing a research study produces misleading results. Or as Clark has said: Media like television, film, and computers "deliver instruction but do not influence student achievement any more than the truck that delivers our groceries causes changes in our nutrition." Alan Kay, who invented the prototype for a laptop in 1968, made a similar point when he recently said schools confuse music with the instrument. "You can put a piano in every classroom but that won't give you a developed music culture because the music culture is embodied in people." If, on the other hand, you have a musician who is a teacher, then you don't "need musical instruments because the kids can sing and dance." "The important thing . . . is that the music is not in the piano and knowledge and edification is not in the computer."[16]

Misleading results, however, do not derive only from a research design that confuses the medium with teaching practices. Misleading results also come from confusing correlations with causation. Consider test scores. The typical study of 1:1 laptops, for example, compares test scores of students in classrooms with laptops with students in other classrooms lacking laptops. For those few studies that do control for students' socioeconomic and academic differences, test scores, attitudes toward schools, motivation, attendance, and other outcomes turn out to be more positive for students who have laptops.[17]

Yet these studies seldom hold constant the teacher—that is, the same teacher for laptop and non-laptop classes—or ever isolate and examine how teachers teach during the time of the study. The focus is on the machines. And this is why it is impossible to conclude that test scores rose because students used ICT. It is what critics have said for decades: Confusing the truck delivering the food and eating a nutritious diet; confusing the piano with a music teacher. Researchers designing studies confound ICT—the medium—with the teacher's instructional methods. And when initial gains in test scores occur, they are then attributed to ICT or laptops, not what and how the teacher teaches.

As for outcomes of abundant access and use of ICT, no widespread changes in teaching or test score gains have occurred. For those studies that do make such claims, I argue that a fundamental confusion between medium and method of instruction leads to making misattributions about the effects of technology on academic achievement.

A FINAL WORD

I do not know how many of you will agree with one or more of these statements. Let's say, for purposes of discussion, that I am correct in what I say. So what can practitioners and researchers do about confusing access with actual classroom use and about claiming that 1:1 computing will transform pedagogy and produce increased academic achievement? Since all worthwhile practitioner problem solving and research begins with a question, I offer a few questions for both practitioners and researchers to consider that get away from surveys and interviews and require extended observation in classrooms.

1. How often and in what ways do elementary and secondary teachers use particular software and ICT in teaching reading, math, language, writing, and academic subjects?
2. Do teachers who have used ICT in their classrooms for at least 3 years teach the same or different than they had prior to using ICT? In what ways do they teach the same and in what ways different?

And let me end with the big question that confounds so many champions of technology: If I want to find out whether ICT causes changes in pedagogy and academic achievement, what needs to be done to avoid the historic confounding of machine and teaching method and correlations with causation?

NOTES

1. Rhea Borja, "Researches Weigh Benefits of One Computer Per Lap," *Education Week*, May 10, 2006, p. 10; Nicolas Negroponte of MIT has developed a prototype for a $100 computer for each poor child in developing nations. See http://www.boston.com/news/education/higher/articles/2005/09/28/for_each_poor_child_in_world_a_laptop/

2. David Silvernail and Dawn Lane, "The Impact of Maine's One-to-One Laptop Program on Middle School Teachers and Students," Research Report 1 (University of Southern Maine, Maine Educational Policy Research Institute, 2004); David Ress, "Veteran Laptop Users Nonchalant," *Richmond Times-Dispatch*, May 27, 2004, p. 1.

3. Larry Cuban, *Teachers and machines: The classroom use of technology since 1920* (New York: Teachers College Press, 1986).

4. One typical example of futuristic scenarios of school use of computers is Sharon Cromwell, "The School of the Future," *Education World*, January 12, 1998, available at http://www.education-world.com/a_curr/curr046.shtml

5. The fear of a "digital divide" that swept across the media and stirred policymakers and business leaders in the early 1990s dissolved within a few years as access to

computers climbed among low-income families and access to computers in schools became widespread. That fear joined a concern for the poor with an unvarnished faith in the power of computers to "solve" the problem of poverty, another excursion into using schools to cope with larger economic problems. See Andrew Trotter, "Study Shows a Thinner 'Digital Divide,'" *Education Week*, March 26, 2003, p. 9; Robert Samuelson, "Debunking the Digital Divide," *The Washington Post*, March 20, 2002. http://www.washingtonpost.com/ac2/wpdyn/A53118-2002Mar19?language = printer

6. Larry Cuban, *Oversold and Underused: Computers in Classrooms* (Cambridge, MA: Harvard University Press, 2001).

7. Education Development Center and SRI International, "New Study of Large-Scale District Laptop Initiative Shows Benefits of 'One-to-One Computing,'" June 2004, http://main.edc.org/newsroom/Features/edc_sri.asp; Saul Rockman, "Learning from Laptops," *Threshold*, Fall 2003, www.ciconline.org; David Silvernail and Dawn Lane, "The Impact of Maine's One-to-One Laptop Program on Middle School Teachers and Students," Research Report #1, February 2004 (Maine Education Policy Research Institute, University of Southern Maine).

8. Rhea Borja, "Researchers Weigh Benefits of One Computer Per Lap," *Education Week*, May 10, 2006, p. 10.

9. Judith Sandholtz, Cathy Ringstaff, and David Dwyer, *Teaching with technology: Creating student centered classrooms* (New York: Teachers College Press, 1997).

10. Apple Computers, "1 to 1 Learning: A Review and Analysis by the Metiri Group," February 2006. See: http://www.apple.com/education/k12/onetoone

11. Judith Sandholtz, Cathy Ringstaff, and David Dwyer, *Teaching with technology: Creating student centered classrooms* (New York: Teachers College Press, 1997).

12. Ibid., p. 6.

13. Ibid.

14. Diane Curtis, "A Remarkable Transformation," *Edutopia*, Spring 2003; Rhonda Barton, "In the Chugach District, The Sky Is the Limit" *Northwest Education Magazine*, Winter 2003, 9(2) http://www.nwrel.org/nwedu/09-02/chugach.asp; Jill Anderson, "Filling in the Achievement Gap with Hard Work, Strict Laws, and More Funding," *HGSE News*, March 23, 2006.

15. Richard Clark, "Reconsidering Research on Media in Learning," *Review of Educational Research*, 1983, *53*(4), 445–460; Richard Clark, "When Researchers Swim Upstream: Reflections on an Unpopular Argument about Learning from Media," *Educational Technology*, February 1991, 34–40; Wilbur Schramm, *Big Media, Little Media* (Beverly Hills, CA: Sage Publications, 1977).

16. Alan Kay, "Still Waiting for the Revolution," *Scholastic Administrator*, April/May 2003, 23–25.

17. A particularly rigorous statistical design studying laptop use of cohorts of students over time in a California district that fails to separate instructional methods from the presence of laptops can be seen in James Gulek and Hakan Demirtas, "Learning with Technology: The Impact of Laptop Use on Student Achievement," *The Journal of Technology, Learning, and Assessment, 3*(2), 2005, 3–38.

CHAPTER 9

2007—Hugging the Middle: Teaching in an Era of Testing and Accountability

For nearly a half-century, critics have scolded dithering boards of education for low-performing public schools, condemned school bureaucracies and unions for blocking reform, but stuttered when it came to teachers. In carping at teachers, critics have been caught in a bind. They see too many teachers thwarting necessary changes. Yet critics know that these very same teachers—nearly 4 million strong—are gatekeepers to learning in schools and crucial to the growth of nearly 50 million young children and youth. No technology has yet convinced fault finders, parents, or policymakers that machines can replace teachers. As important as improving boards of education, streamlining bureaucracies, and getting unions to be reform-minded are in making good schools, student learning still depends on what teachers do in classrooms. Inevitably, then, if critics see teachers as the problem these decisionmakers also know that teachers are also the solution.

The paradox of distrusting teachers and then turning around and expecting them to solve the problems of low-performing students has often frustrated critics and reformers. The paradox, however, says little about what teachers do in classrooms once they close their doors. How teachers actually have taught has largely remained a mystery even though nearly all Americans have sat across from teachers' desks. Yes, stories, jokes, paintings, memoirs, interviews, and even television sitcoms have tried to capture both inspiring and ridiculous teachers and in doing so have given tantalizing but atypical glimpses of what occurs during lessons.

Finding out what typically happens in classrooms is important since in today's policy arena, local school boards, state legislators, and U.S. presidents say again and again that without good teaching, students will not learn vital content and skills. Furthermore, policymakers believe that improved reading, math, and science content and skills are the keys not only to reducing the student achievement gap between White and low-income minority students, one that has existed for decades, but also to future economic success.

Thus, parents and policymakers want teachers who have the subject matter and instructional expertise to boost the academic achievement of low-performing students and make the difference between students' dropping out of high school and getting trapped in low-wage jobs, on the one hand, and entering college and eventually snaring a high-paying job, on the other hand. For those committed to improving schools, then, how teachers teach–their classroom pedagogy–is a powerful tool in getting students to learn and succeed.

HOW HAVE TEACHERS TAUGHT?

To answer the question, I present the big picture of pedagogy. From the very beginning of tax-supported public schools in the United States, two traditions of teaching have shaped classroom instruction: teacher-centered and student-centered (Jackson, 1986; Katz, 1968).[1] The teacher-centered tradition of instruction refers to teachers controlling what is taught, when, and under what conditions. Teachers transmit knowledge, skills, and values to students. Were readers to sit for a few minutes in such a classroom, they would note that the furniture is usually arranged in rows of desks or chairs facing the front chalkboard. In such a classroom, teachers talk far more than students, the entire class is most often taught as one group with occasional small groups and independent work, and students regularly use texts to guide their daily work. Scholars have traced back the origins of this pedagogical tradition to the ancient Greeks and religious schools centuries ago and have called it by various names: "subject-centered," "mimetic," "teaching as transmission," and "direct instruction" (Chall, 2000; Jackson, 1986; Katz, 1968).

The student-centered tradition of instruction refers to classrooms where students exercise a substantial degree of responsibility for what is taught and how it is learned. Teachers see children and youth as more than brains; they bring to school an array of physical, psychological, emotional, and intellectual needs plus experiences that require both nurturing and prodding. Were readers to sit for a while in such a classroom they would see that the furniture is arranged and rearranged frequently to permit students to work together in large and small groups or independently. Student talk is at least equal to, if not greater than, teacher talk. Varied materials (e.g., science and art centers, math manipulatives) are spread around the room for small groups and individual students to use. Guided by teachers, students learn content and skills through different tasks such as going to activity centers in the room, joining a team to produce a project, and conducting independent work. Scholars have tracked this tradition to its historical roots in ancient Greece and labeled it over the centuries as "child-centered," "progressive," "teaching as facilitating," "transformative," and "constructivist" (Chall, 2000; Jackson, 1986; Katz, 1968).

Skirmishes Between Advocates of
Teacher-Centered and Student-Centered Approaches

In each case, champions of each tradition believe that all students regardless of background grasp subject matter, acquire skills, cultivate attitudes, and develop behaviors best through its practices. Yet the accumulated evidence of actual classroom practices producing particular student outcomes to support advocates of each tradition has been mixed or unconvincing. Therefore, no preponderance of evidence is yet available to demonstrate the inherent superiority of either pedagogy in teaching the young.[2]

Lacking substantial evidence, ideology and faith drive proponents of each tradition. Fierce rhetorical struggles erupt over which ways of teaching and learning are best for all or some students—often mirroring larger conservative vs. liberal (or orthodox vs. progressive) ideological battles over religion in schools, interracial marriage, child-rearing practices, and television programming. These so-called "culture wars" boiled over in newspapers, books, educational conferences, and scholarly journals before and after World War I and during the civil rights movement in the 1960s (e.g., Zimmerman, 2002). Since the 1970s, occasional outbreaks of these media-amplified fistfights have spilled over from state legislatures and the Oval Office into newspapers, journals, and books with arguments on how best to teach reading, math, science, and history. Again, these battles reflect the ideological divide between political conservatives and progressives over diverse issues such as abortion, school prayer, the right to die, and teaching about evolution (Dionne, 2005; Fiorina, 2004; Hunter, 1991; Lakoff, 1996).

To cite a recent example, in 2003, New York City chancellor of schools Joel Klein mandated "Balanced Literacy"—a progressive whole language approach—as the preferred way of teaching children to read in nearly 750 elementary schools rather than a largely phonics-based approach. Advocates of teaching children to learn the rules of decoding words on paper, waving research studies that proved their way worked better than "balanced literacy," engaged the enemy in the latest skirmish over which pedagogy is best (Kolker, 2006). And in the latest battle in the "math wars" between progressives and conservatives, the National Council of Teachers of Mathematics (NCTM) issued a report in 2006 urging that math teaching in elementary and middle school concentrate on knowing multiplication tables, how to do division and manage decimals. Their earlier report in 1989 called for engaging students in learning concepts thoroughly and applying them to real-world situations rather than memorizing multiplication tables and rules for long division and other familiar ways of grasping mathematics (Garelick, 2005; Hartocollis, 2000). As one former federal education official said:

This is definitely a back-to-basics victory. Emphasizing the building blocks children have always learned . . . and moving away from the constructivist approach some educators prefer, in which children learn what they want to learn when they're ready to learn it. (quoted in Lewin, 2006, p. A18)

These historic traditions of teaching practices, then, are alive and well. Yet in each instance the sharp divide between progressive and traditional ways of teaching blurs in practice because curriculum and pedagogy are entwined in an enduring marriage. For instance, in the past quarter-century, state curriculum standards in math include both traditional and progressive language to describe teaching. Current textbooks in math (e.g., University of Chicago School Mathematics Project, 2003) tilt toward constructivism but do blend traditional practices (e.g., whole class drill on math facts) with progressive ones (e.g., students working in small groups, writing in journals).

Historical Evidence

The polarizing ideologies remain alive and well and occasionally spark debates among parents and educators but the closer one comes to classroom practices, the distinctions become much less clear. The obvious question arises again: How have teachers taught over the past century? In *How Teachers Taught*, a study of these two teaching traditions in urban and rural schools between 1890 and 1980, I collected data from over 8,000 classrooms on common observable features within teaching in urban and rural districts that could distinguish between the two pedagogical traditions. I examined how teachers organized space in classrooms, grouped students, and the activities they structured for their students. I found several classroom patterns (Cuban, 1993).

Between the 1890s and the 1980s, the social organization of the classroom became increasingly informal. In the early 20th century, dress-clad women and tie-wearing men facing rows of 50 or more bolted-down desks controlled every move of students. They gave or withheld permission for students to leave their seat. They required students, even little ones, to stand when reciting from the textbook or answering a question. Teachers often scowled, reprimanded, and paddled students for misbehaving.

Over the decades, however, classroom organization and teacher behavior slowly changed. By the 1980s, few classrooms contained rows of immovable desks. Classrooms were now filled with tables and movable desks, particularly in the early grades, so students faced one another and walls festooned with colorful posters and student work. Jean-wearing teachers drinking coffee smiled often at their classes and students went to a pencil sharpener or elsewhere in the room without asking for the teacher's permission. The dread and repression of the early 20th-century classroom marked often by the swish of a paddle and a teacher's sneer slowly gave way, decade by decade, to classrooms where teachers were kinder, more informal in language and dress, and had a light touch in controlling unacceptable behavior.

By the early 1980s, most elementary and a lesser number of secondary teachers had blended certain student-centered and teacher-centered classroom practices into hybrids of teacher-centered progressivism. With the social organization of the classroom becoming increasingly informal, particularly in the primary grades reflecting new knowledge of child development, most teaching practices evolved into a blending of the two traditions.

Consider grouping. For decades, teachers taught 40 to 70 or more students as one group. Over time as class size fell, the student-centered practice of dividing the whole group into smaller ones slowly took hold among most elementary schoolteachers so that the teacher could work with a few students at a time on reading while the rest worked by themselves in groups or independently. However, small-group work had a harder time taking hold among secondary schoolteachers, though variations in grouping occurred among academic subjects (Grossman & Stodolosky, 1995; Stodolosky & Grossman, 1995).

A similar pattern occurred with assigning groups different tasks. "Activity (or learning) centers" where pairs of students or individual children would spend a half-hour or more reading a book, playing math games, drawing or painting, listening to records or, later, tapes slowly took hold in kindergarten and the primary grades, spreading later to the upper elementary grades. Learning centers, however, seldom appeared in secondary schools.

The use of student projects as activities lasting a few weeks that tie together reading, math, science, and art—think of a 4th-grade class divided into groups or working individually on Native American life—became a standard part of elementary school curriculum and teachers' repertoires. In secondary schools, projects appeared in vocational subjects and periodically in science, English, and social studies classes.

Between the 1920s and 1980s, then, teachers combined two pedagogical traditions in their classrooms in imaginative ways to create hybrids of teacher-centered progressivism. In elementary schools, particularly in primary classrooms, richer and diverse melds of the two traditions appeared with far fewer instances surfacing in middle and upper grades. In high schools—allowing for some variation among academic subjects—teacher-centered pedagogy attained its purest forms.[5]

While the social organization of classroom moved from formal to infor-mal and hybrids of teacher-centered progressivism multiplied, teacher-centered pedagogy still dominated classroom life. As Philip Jackson (1968) noted in his study of suburban teachers in the early 1960s, teacher smiles and friendly looks have, indeed, replaced "the scowls and frowns of teachers past" and "today's teachers may exercise their authority more casually than their pre-decessors," yet "the desire for informality was never sufficiently strong to interfere with institutional definitions of responsibility, authority, and tradi-tion" (p. 29). In short, amid the evolving classroom informality, the growth of hybrids, and teachers' light touch in managing student behavior, deep continuities in teachers' exerting their authority persisted.

In light of my findings for classroom instruction between 1890 and 1980, the two teaching traditions seldom appeared in classrooms as unvarnished types. In schools across the nation where great diversity in children, parental wishes, academic subjects, and teachers were common—even amid "wars" fought in newspapers and conferences over the best way to teach—hybrids of subject matter and practice flourished albeit more so among elementary than secondary schoolteachers. Thus, at the risk of overstating the point, the title of a 1973 song captures the place in which a typical teacher found herself "Stuck in the Middle." But since teachers can choose what they do in their classrooms, I prefer the phrase "Hugging the Middle."[6]

Seeing teachers as carriers of these two traditions mirrors the evidence I collected of many teachers who combined elements of each teaching tradi-tion over the past century. Teacher behavior has been in the middle of a continuum rather than clustered at its polar extremes, as it were, hugging the middle.

HOW ARE TEACHERS TEACHING?

Standards-Based Reform, Testing, and Accountability, 1980s–2005

Since the early 1980s, state- and federally driven reforms aimed at improv-ing student academic achievement have sprinted through U.S. schools. Prompted by low scores of U.S. students on international tests, powerful coalitions of business and civic elites, fearful of losing economic traction in global commerce with too many entry-level employees mismatched to the demands of an ever-changing knowledge-based labor market, pressed state and federal officials to draft schools into preparing the next generation of engineers, scientists, and workers. State after state stiffened graduation requirements and set curricular standards with accompanying tests (Cuban, 2005).

By the late 1990s, however, a swelling movement mobilized by business-minded coalitions seeking a nimble college-educated workforce for early 21st-century labor markets lobbied states vigorously to require demanding curricula, more testing, and accountability. U.S. presidents and state legislators endorsed these educational policies. With the election of former Texas governor George W. Bush as President in 2000, both Democrats and Republicans fashioned the No Child Left Behind law (NCLB), wrapping these state efforts into national policy (Cuban, 2005).

According to surveys of teachers and reports from researchers, policymakers, and journalists, the standards-based, testing, and accountability movement has strongly influenced classroom content and practices in the 1990s and especially since NCLB became law in 2002. Teachers reported spending more classroom time preparing students for state tests and less time on those subjects not on tests. Journalists uncovered that middle and high school students who scored poorly on tests have to double up on reading and math periods and can no longer take other academic subjects. Prodded by federal officials, districts' use of phonics spread in primary grade classrooms. According to observers, teacher lecturing and explaining, and assigning more homework from textbooks had become pervasive (Dillon, 2006; Pedulla, 2003).

These portrayals of classroom teaching track the onrushing freight train of standards-based testing and accountability erasing student-centered approaches. Do these reports of teaching mirror what has occurred in classrooms?

A FOLLOW-UP STUDY OF *HOW TEACHERS TAUGHT*

Beginning in 2004, I have extended the data base I had accumulated for classroom practices between the 1890s and the 1980s to the present day in three districts: Denver, Colorado, Arlington, Virginia, and Oakland, California.[7] The key question was whether earlier patterns in classroom practice extended into the early 21st century, a time when stories and surveys repeated again and again the claim that state and federal policies were shaping both content and classroom practice. *Have teachers in these districts organized their classrooms, grouped students, and taught lessons in response to the policy demands of standards-based reform, increased testing, and accountability measures?* In answering the question, the research has used the design, the framework of two pedagogical traditions-cum-hybrids, and the methods from *How Teachers Taught* (Cuban, 1993).

Methods

This article uses comparative case studies to examine pedagogical patterns in these three districts between 1993 and 2005. Getting data about classrooms in the past quarter-century requires care with several issues. Recapturing lessons that were once taught last year or a decade ago means that historians must cope with fragmentary data since records of classroom lessons or observations are rarely available to researchers. Moreover, interviewing or surveying teachers about how they taught last week or 10 years ago often yields unreliable results. For example, surveys of teachers, the most common and least expensive way of ascertaining classroom practices, remain imprecise and tend to reflect what teachers believe they did, not what occurred when independent observers sat in their rooms (Hook & Rosenshine, 1979; Mayer, 1999; Tibballs, 1996; Viadero, 2005).

Multiple-Source Data Collection

Using the strategy pursued in *How Teachers Taught,* I collected multiple sources within a district drawn directly from teachers, students, principals, administrators, journalists, parents, and others, including researchers, who were either in or entered classrooms and recorded what they saw. In addition, I briefly observed classrooms in each district. Finally, I used teacher and journalist photos of classrooms and ones taken by students for annual yearbooks. In short, I gathered opportunistic samples of classrooms in districts. From these reports, "snapshots" of three districts' classrooms chronicle particular observable features of classrooms: how teachers physically organized space in the classroom, how they grouped students for instructional tasks, and the activities in which students and teachers were engaged. These three features there are ubiquitous, closely connected, and point to either teacher-centered or student-centered traditions or hybrids of both.

Observable Features of Classrooms

Organization of classroom space. Typically, elementary school classrooms are 900 square feet (700–800 square feet for an average secondary school room). Except in uncommon cases where district regulations require teachers to organize classrooms in uniform ways (e.g., for certain reading programs, team teaching arrangements), teachers arrange classroom furniture within the allotted space to express their beliefs in how best to teach, maintain order, and get students to learn. As one teacher put it: "A teacher's room tells us something about who he is, and a great deal about what he is doing" (Kohl, cited in Cutler, 1989, p. 36; see also Hutchinson, 2004; Weinstein 1991).

The most common arrangement of furniture in secondary school class-rooms and upper-grade elementary ones is traditional rows of desks facing the chalkboard and teacher's desk. I call it "traditional" because for the entire 19th century and nearly half of the 20th century, bolted-down desks in rows–later replaced by movable tables and desks–dominated classroom organization. Such a traditional floor plan locates one side of the rectangular classroom at the "front" (usually where the teacher's desk and a chalkboard are located), signaling students that the teacher gives directions, makes assignments, leads discussions, and determines the degree of student move-ment. In this familiar floor plan, the silent message is that teacher-to-student interaction is more important than student-to-student interaction.

In most elementary and some middle school classrooms teachers have departed from traditional space arrangements. Since the 1960s teachers have grouped desks in clusters of four or five, hollow square arrangements, or mixes of rows and clustered desks. There is no obvious "front" to the classroom. Such a floor plan expresses the teacher's willingness to promote student-to-student interaction and student movement within the room. Pro-viding space for a rug and soft chairs where students can sprawl and sit with partitions for learning centers (reading, computers, math, science) signal stu-dents that learning not only occurs in the whole group listening to the teacher but happens in small groups and individually. These arrangements are most often seen in K–3 classrooms but appear in increasing frequency in upper elementary grades as well.

In effect, how teachers configure classroom space teaches students unobtrusively what kinds of interactions are both important and acceptable. Notably, the physical design of the classroom flows into teacher decisions about grouping.

Grouping of students. If the classroom floor plan has clustered desks where students face one another, a rug-covered area, and designated spots for certain tasks (or various mixes of these), then teachers have designed their space to encourage both small group work and independent activity while encouraging student movement (Barth, 1972; Doyle, 1986; Perrone, 1972; Slavin, 1995). In such classrooms, mostly in elementary school grades, mul-tiple forms of grouping occur for different activities. Over the course of a 6-hour day, teachers organize whole group instruction for particular tasks (e.g., morning opening activities with the teacher reading a story), small groups working on different activities (e.g., reading group with teacher while a math group is with an aide or in learning centers), and individual students at their desks (e.g., working on a project or completing a worksheet).

In those classrooms where rows of student desks face the front of the room dominated by a teacher's desk and chalkboards–mostly in high schools–teachers often use the whole group for lecture, demonstration, and discussion. Students also work individually at their desks working on assignments from their textbook, writing essays, and completing worksheets. Occasionally in previous decades but more often in the past 10 years, middle and high school teachers will ask students to move their chairs into small groups for particular tasks. So a mix of grouping patterns exists in secondary schools across academic subjects while whole group instruction remains dominant. Of course, the kind of grouping that the teacher chooses depends upon the teacher-designed activity–tasks that over time accumulate into patterns that track the dominant teaching traditions.

Classroom activities. The basic unit of a teacher's work in a classroom is the activity designed for students. One important consideration is that the teacher is a whirlwind of decisions and tasks over the school day. Researchers have documented 500 to 800 discrete elementary schoolteacher acts a day (some teachers accumulating well over 1,000). Teachers are constant decisionmakers. To make sense of these acts, Table 9.1 describes four types of tasks that teachers specifically design for students: teacher-directed, student-directed, interactive, and miscellaneous (Gallego & Cole, 2001; Gump, 1982; Shuell, 1996).

In thinking about the classification of teacher acts, researchers should acknowledge that most activities are teacher-directed simply because the classroom is a crowd that has to be managed by the teacher who, in Philip Jackson's apt summary, serves as a "combination traffic cop, judge, supply sergeant, and time keeper" because "some kinds of control are necessary if the school's goals are to be reached and social chaos averted" (Jackson, 1968, p. 13). Furthermore, except for parents and lawyers, the teacher is one of the few people in the work world who asks questions to which she knows the answers. Because of the imperative to maintain group order and the teacher's power to control talk in a classroom, most classroom activities are teacher-directed and of relatively short duration, usually between 10 and 20 minutes (Cazden, 1988; Doyle, 1986).

Second, certain activities are more evident in elementary school classrooms than secondary ones (e.g., sharing time, seatwork, learning centers) while other activities are more common in secondary school classrooms (e.g., bench work in science labs, discussions, lectures). Third, activities similar in structure (e.g., small group work, seatwork) will vary by subject matter. Math teachers, for example, use seatwork and small groups differently than social studies teachers (Stodolsky, 1988). Finally, a few teacher-directed activities consume a substantial majority of classroom time, even accounting for differences in level of schooling, students, and varied subject matter. For example, researchers estimate that more than 30 separate

TABLE 9.1. Typology of Teaching Tasks

Teacher-directed activities (mostly teacher talk with some student interaction)	Lecture; demonstration; going over daily schedule of activities including homework; opening activities (song, salute to flag, doing calendar for day and month; taking attendance, making announcements); teacher reading aloud to class; students reading aloud; students reading silently; review for test; checking student work; teacher calling students to board to solve problems; giving test; showing film; seatwork (individualized tasks, diverse tasks, common task).
Student-directed activities (mostly student talk with some teacher interaction)	Small group work; pairs/trios of students; learning centers in elementary school including playtime; reports to rest of class; working on projects (individually chosen or teacher-assigned small groups); bench work doing problems in science labs; student-chosen tasks in computer labs or with computers in classroom; working in library on assignments individually or in small groups.
Interactive between teacher and students (substantial student and teacher talk)	One-to-one question and answer between teacher and student; teacher-directed small group work (math/reading) with teacher interacting one group at a time; competitive games; simulations and role-playing; whole class discussion; recitation; sharing time in primary grades.
Activities not falling into above categories	Transitions from one activity to another; teacher giving permission to move around or leave room; handling disruptive students; recess; going to bathrooms; scheduled field trips; whole school assemblies, etc.

activities occur in elementary classrooms with the majority of classroom time spent in seatwork and the rest in whole-class presentation, recitations, and transitions. Historically, students' tasks have a narrower range in secondary school classrooms than in elementary school classrooms (Doyle, 1986; Fisher et al., 1978; Shuell, 1996).

Using these three interconnected observable markers—with special emphasis on teacher-designed activities—I collected 1,045 classroom reports from 71 schools in three districts between 1993 and 2005 and placed them along the continuum of historical teaching practices. Many reports showed teachers who tilted toward student-centered instruction in how they organized their classroom space, used different groupings, and carried out classroom activities; in other reports, teachers arranged classroom furniture, grouped students, and designed lessons that leaned decidedly toward teacher-centered instruction. But, as in the past, most teachers hugged the middle of the continuum, blending activities, grouping patterns, and using furniture to create hybrids of the two traditions.

Caveats

While the comparative case study research design permits me to answer questions about certain observable classroom practices that emerged across districts and within districts, both design and methodology exclude much about classroom life. In looking at a classroom through a straw one can see some things but not others.

The design, for example, neither investigates teachers' beliefs about the subjects they teach nor students' depth of understanding of subject matter. Nor does the design document the informal bonds between teachers and students or the emotional and intellectual climate of classrooms. The design does not allow me to assess the taught curriculum over time, teacher effectiveness, or what students actually learn.

Moreover, some sources are vulnerable to criticism, especially surveys of teachers and students. Such teacher self-reports contain well-documented shortcomings of respondents' selective memory, inflation of what is considered "good" teaching, and deflation of what is viewed as "poor" teaching. To offset these drawbacks, I collected journalist reports, classroom photos, supervisors' observations, researcher studies, lesson plans, and self-reports. This mélange of sources offers a brief glimpse–a "snapshot"–of teaching practice in particular schools and a district.

Some readers, however, could rightly ask what conclusions one can draw about teaching from the observable features of classrooms: Will documenting furniture arrangements, grouping practices, and teaching activities capture the depth, texture, and character of a teacher's routine instruction for a researcher sufficiently to place that teacher confidently on the continuum of teaching traditions? It is a fair question that needs answering before any broad statements can be made about what happens in classrooms during a period of strong policy intervention by state and federal authorities.

Target Districts

The choice of districts was made to maximize comparisons, regional dispersion, and unique circumstances involving the history of reform in each district. Arlington, Virginia, and Denver were in my original study (Cuban, 1993), and as such I had comparative data prior to the 1990s. I chose Oakland, California, because *How Teachers Taught* did not include a West Coast district, and I had access to historical archives to capture lessons from the 1920s through the 1980s. Contacts in the district made it possible for me to visit many classrooms in 2004 and 2005. Between the mid-1960s and the present, Arlington, Denver, and Oakland experienced national surges of school reform and tailored those reforms to fit their particular settings. The decade of the mid-1960s to mid-1970s, for example, saw squabbles over desegregation disturb each of the three districts. Furthermore, district policymakers designed reforms to loosen the grip of traditional school and classroom practices by building open-space schools, launching informal or open classrooms, and urging teachers to adopt student-centered classroom practices of small group work, learning centers, and project-based learning.

By the late 1970s across the nation, however, passion for desegregation, open-space schools, and open classrooms had ebbed considerably. Parental and policymaker concerns in the three districts over students not learning basic skills, having little homework, and being unready for college produced a climate spotlighting literacy, subject-matter proficiency, and no-nonsense discipline. Spurring this return to traditional practices were business and civic leaders who worried about the United States' global competitiveness because high school graduates were unprepared for college and entry-level jobs in an economy swiftly turning to information and communication technologies.

Within a decade, Virginia, Colorado, and California had mandated higher graduation requirements and new tests. With a growing national and bipartisan fervor for curriculum standards and accountability culminating in the No Child Left Behind Act, again each district accommodated to state and federal mandates (see Table 9.2).

Arlington. Arlington is a midsized urban district across the Potomac River from Washington, D.C., blessed with a long-standing solid funding base for its schools and a string of long-tenured superintendents (only six between 1960 and 2007). Arlington had also avoided court intervention by desegregating its few all-Black schools by the early 1970s, permitting the district to respond wholeheartedly to state-mandated standards and tests. By the early 1990s, however, Virginia business and civic elites—like their counterparts elsewhere—feared that the state was falling behind in producing sufficiently educated graduates to enter college and a swiftly changing

TABLE 9.2. Demography of Three Districts, 1970–2004

Trait	Arlington, Virginia		Denver, Colorado		Oakland, California	
	1970	*2004*	*1970*	*2004*	*1970*	*2004*
Schools	36	31	119	136	90	131
Minority %	28	53	34	79	72	94
Lunch program %	N/A	41	N/A	63	28	63

Sources: Arlington School District (http://www.arlington.k12.va.us); Cuban (1993); *Keyes v. School District* (1973); McCorry (1978); Oakland Unified School District (2001; http://webportal. ousd.k12.ca.us/index.aspx); Yee (1995); and documents in author's possession.

job market. In 1995, the Virginia Board of Education approved new Standards of Learning (SOLs) in English, history/social science, math, and science. In 1998, districts administered new tests to students matched to each of the SOLs.

State and district administrators used test scores to determine whether schools would be accredited, and whether individual students would be promoted or held back in the lower grades and whether they would graduate high school. For the Standard Diploma, high school seniors in the class of 2004 for the first time had to pass six SOLs (or state-approved substitutes) and for the Advanced Studies Diploma, nine SOLs. Because Arlington and other districts began identifying academically struggling high school students in the 9th grade and provided individual help, less than 1% of Arlington's 1,100-plus seniors were barred from graduating in 2004. As the Virginia Board of Education President said, "I see this as our first look at what tomorrow's education may be like in Virginia and not just for seniors." Colorado political leaders also sought tomorrow's education now (Helderman, 2004).

Denver. Responding to state leadership in standards, testing, and accountability was not easy for Denver since the district had experienced 40 years of turbulence that had taken its toll on staff and community. Beginning in the mid-1960s, racial turmoil over desegregation fastened the district's attention upon low-performing, largely Black and Hispanic schools. A marker of Denver's difficulties over these 4 decades is that between 1967 and 2006, 11 superintendents served the school board. In *Keyes v. School District No. 1, Denver* (1973), the U.S. Supreme Court ruled that Denver had segregated its schools and ordered the district to desegregate Black and Hispanic schools. The board of education plan included busing, establishing magnet schools, and other means of reducing race and ethnicity as a factor in students attending school. Not until 1996 was the desegregation order lifted at which time the entire district enrolled mostly Hispanic and Black students (Taylor, 1990).

By the mid-1990s, Colorado leaders, like those elsewhere who were concerned about the links between education and the economy, had taken aggressive action to improve schooling. The governor and legislature had put into place new curriculum standards, tests, and accountability regulations. The Colorado Student Assessment Program (CSAP) tests Denver students every spring in reading and writing grades 3 through 10 while students take math tests in grades 5 through 10. Eighth graders take science tests. The state reports results in percentage of students who perform in four categories: unsatisfactory, partially proficient, proficient, or advanced. In Denver, familiar patterns emerged of largely poor minority schools doing badly on these tests—with occasional exceptions—and a yawning achievement gap between

White and minority students. To Governor Owens, however, "Schools all across Colorado are improving because of the standards and accountability measures like the School Accountability Reports that tell parents about how well their school is educating their children" (Owens, 2005, p. 3). That boiler-plate reasoning in the face of continuing low academic performance in largely poor minority schools also propelled the rhetoric of California policymakers.

Oakland. Once a national leader among states for its educational system, California had fallen upon fiscally hard times after the passage of Proposition 13 in 1978. Since then local school funds drawn from property taxes had shrunk. School services once taken for granted such as reading, art, music, and librarians in elementary schools and counselors in high school disappeared. Fees for athletics, busing, and field trips became common. Class size ballooned. Affluent districts established private foundations to help fund smaller classes and replace lost staff and services. The state steadily assumed a far higher proportion of funding local districts than previously but failed to reach pre-1978 levels. With increased funding came increased state authority for determining curriculum standards, class size, testing students, and accountability for results.

Few state-driven and business-inspired school reforms in the 1980s and 1990s unfolded in a straight line. In California, where state authority over schools is split among the governor, legislature, elected state superintendent, and an appointed state board of education, reforms showered districts in these years. For example, an aggressive State Superintendent of Instruction pressed forward with new curriculum frameworks throughout the 1980s only to run up against a governor reluctant to support these initiatives. The legislature mandated new curriculum standards and tests in the early to mid-1990s only for the governor to repeal one set of tests that had been given for a few years. Then in 1999, another governor pushed through the legislature a new state-wide accountability system called the Academic Performance Index (API) with test scores determining where each school ended up on the Index. Doing well on the Index meant rewards—cash for improving schools—and penalties—state intervention for low-performing schools (Carlos & Kirst, 1997; EdSource, 2001; Wilson, 2003).

All of these state actions directly affected Oakland Unified School District. After nearly 4 decades of turmoil over desegregation, community involvement, the assassination of one superintendent, and continuing low academic performance of a largely minority school population, Oakland school leaders drew constant criticism from civic officials, parents, media, and state policymakers. In 2000, the district took the unusual step of mandating a literacy program called Open Court to be phased into all elementary schools within 3 years. In the same year, Oakland's mayor attempted to shift school governance from an elected school board to City Hall. The battle with the school board ended in a compromise with the mayor appointing three of the seven-member board. Shortly afterwards, without warning, a serious fiscal breakdown occurred (Oakland Unified School District, 2001; Yee, 2004).

In 2003, the startling discovery of a $100 million deficit led to the resignation of a popular superintendent, the legislature lending that amount to the district, and the State Superintendent of Instruction appointing an outside administrator to run the district with the elected school board becoming a mere advisory body. In 2006, the state-appointed administrator left to be replaced by another appointee. That superintendent was the 15th to lead Oakland since 1962 (Yee, 2004).

Expectations from Increased Accountability

Given this background in each of the three districts, one should be able to answer the central research question: Have teachers in these districts organized their classrooms, grouped students, and taught lessons in response to the policy demands of standards-based reform, increased testing, and accountability measures? To many teachers and researchers the answer would be an unequivocal yes. Classroom stories and teacher surveys report again and again that more lesson time is spent preparing students for high-stakes tests, and the narrowing of the curriculum to what is on those tests. As one first-year teacher put it:

> The test is the total goal. We spend time every day doing rote exercises. Forget ever doing hands-on science or math games, or creative writing. We do one hour of sit and drill in each of the subjects of math, reading, and writing. We use a basal reader, math workbook pages, and rote writing prompts. Every day for one hour the whole school does the exact same direct instruction lesson. The children sit and get drilled over and over (Jones, Jones, & Hargrove, 2003, p. 37).

A national survey of curriculum changes revealed that in thousands of schools under threat of being closed for poor performance, administrators restrict students to taking only math and reading classes until their scores improve and then they can take elective subjects. Over 70% of nearly 15,000 districts in the nation have cut back time spent in social studies, science, art, music, and other subjects to create more time for reading and math (Dillon, 2006).

Such stories and scattered teacher reports describe classroom instruction, particularly in largely poor and minority schools, as more focused on meeting prescribed state standards and raising test scores. Journalists report that districts reduced recess time in elementary schools. Teachers say they use fewer student-centered activities (e.g., small group work, discussions, learning centers, and portfolios) because such work takes away precious classroom time from standards-based curriculum and test preparation (Hasiotis, 2006; Herman, 2002; Pedulla, 2003; Pressler, 2006; Viadero, 2006).

From these stories, one might expect that the reports collected in the three districts on classroom instruction would indicate mostly teacher-centered practices of rows of desks facing the teacher and much direct instruction to the entire class at once. Further, in light of these state policy changes, one would expect student-centered features in classrooms such as clustering tables and desks, small group work, and activities calling for much interaction among students and between teacher and students to be less frequent.

It is important to keep in mind that all of the above expectations linked to consequences of federal and state policies on standards, testing, and accountability might (or might not) have altered classroom furniture arrangements, grouping practices, and teaching activities, yet still failed to capture such changes in practice as increased time spent on test preparation and less time on subjects not covered by the tests that have been reported in a multitude of journalist stories, researcher studies, and surveys. That gap between changes in particular classroom features and what teachers report about their lessons is an important point taken up later.

Findings

Organization of Classroom Space

Regarding the organization of classroom space, the data include reports from nearly 500 elementary and secondary classrooms in the three districts (see Table 9.3). Teachers used traditional teacher-directed ways (rows of movable tables or desks facing the front of the classroom) or nontraditional ways (clusters of tables where students faced one another, horseshoe arrangement, etc.).

TABLE 9.3. Traditional Arrangement of Classroom Space in Districts, 1993–2005

School level	Arlington	Denver	Oakland
Elementary			
N (all reports)	78	56	43
In rows	19	14	4
% in rows	24%	25%	9%
Secondary			
N (all reports)	51	128	118
In rows	16	69	78
% in rows	31%	54%	66%
All classrooms			
N (all reports)	129	184	161
In rows	35	83	82
% in rows	29%	45%	51%

While variation in space organization exists among the three districts, the overall historic pattern of elementary classrooms being arranged far more nontraditionally than secondary classrooms is evident in these three districts. The change is also important to note. In Arlington between 1975 and 1981, from 333 reports of elementary and secondary classrooms on arrangement of desks, 47% of those classrooms were arranged in nontraditional patterns. In Denver between 1965 and 1993, from 95 reports of elementary and secondary classrooms, 42% were arrayed in nontraditional ways. For Oakland, from 170 secondary school classroom reports between 1965 and 1992 (mostly taken from photos in high school yearbooks), nearly 20% of the classrooms show desks and tables arranged nontraditionally. When comparing these classroom reports to those from earlier periods in each district, a decided trend toward increased student-centered space arrangements is apparent.

Grouping of Students

How teachers organize the space in their classrooms is linked to how they group for instruction (see Tables 9.4 and 9.5). For that feature of instruction, I have slightly over 1,000 classroom reports for both elementary and secondary classrooms in the three districts. Similar patterns across the three districts (except for one instance) turn up in classroom grouping. I divided the results by elementary and secondary classrooms.

TABLE 9.4. Elementary Classroom Reports on Grouping for Instruction, 1993–2005

	Arlington		Denver		Oakland	
Grouping	N	%	N	%	N	%
Whole group						
Entire report	113	30	21	32	16	33
Part of report	196	53	30	45	19	39
Small group						
Entire report	24	6	3	4	4	8
Part of report	134	36	18	27	10	20
Individual work						
Entire report	14	3	8	12	8	16
Part of report	146	39	29	44	16	33
Teachers using mixed groupings		59		51		43
Teachers using a single type of grouping		41		49		57
Total reports	372		66		49	

Numbers in each column will not add to the total N because the grouping categories were not exclusive. For example, a teacher who used whole group, small group, and independent work in a lesson is counted once for whole group, once for small group, and once for individual work.

TABLE 9.5. Secondary Classroom Reports on Grouping for Instruction, 1993–2005

Grouping	Arlington		Denver		Oakland	
	N	%	N	%	N	%
Whole group						
Entire report	87	41	67	41	71	44
Part of report	82	39	10	6	31	19
Small group						
Entire report	16	8	27	16	31	19
Part of report	45	21	5	3	11	7
Individual work						
Entire report	15	7	59	36	25	15
Part of report	40	19	11	7	25	15
Teachers using mixed groupings*		44		7		20
Teachers using a single type of grouping*		56		93		80
Total reports	210		165		161	

Numbers in each column will not add to the total N because the grouping categories were not exclusive. For example, a teacher who used whole group, small group, and independent work in a lesson is counted once for whole group, once for small group, and once for individual work.

* In Denver and Oakland I collected far more yearbook photos than in Arlington. These snapshots showed only one form of grouping. The results, then, may overreport that grouping and be skewed against teachers who used mixed groupings within the same lesson.

These results for grouping again show variation among the three districts with the trend toward student-centered forms of grouping (small groups and independent work), noted in my earlier study as being more evident in elementary than secondary classrooms. I am most confident in the Arlington data for both levels because of the many diverse sources, but less confident in the Oakland and Denver secondary classroom grouping practices because the primary source for Oakland and Denver comprised student yearbook photos. Such data offer glimpses of only one flashlike moment in a classroom rather than an entire lesson.

Classroom Activities

If organizing space and grouping patterns revealing trends toward student-centered arrangements do not seem to fit the teacher reports and classroom anecdotes about what occurred in classrooms during the intense years (1990–present) of standards-based reform, testing, and accountability, then what patterns of teaching activities show up in over 1,000 classroom reports in the three districts?

TABLE 9.6. Elementary Classroom Reports on Instructional Activities in Three Districts, 1993–2005

	Arlington		Denver		Oakland	
Grouping	N	%	N	%	N	%
Whole group						
Entire report	100	27	38	58	15	31
Part of report	161	43	18	27	17	35
Small group						
Entire report	18	5	4	6	6	12
Part of report	107	29	11	17	4	8
Individual work						
Entire report	69	18	6	9	11	22
Part of report	137	37	7	11	16	33
Teachers using a mix of activities		50		27		35
Teachers using one type of instructional activity		50		73		65
Total	375		66		49	

Numbers in each column will not add to the total N because the activity categories were not exclusive. For example, a teacher who used teacher-directed, student-directed, and independent work in a report is counted once for each activity.

In the three districts' elementary schools but apparently less so in two districts' secondary schools (see caveat noted in above tables for secondary classrooms), a similar increase in student-centered teaching activities occurred as compared with earlier periods in each district. When teachers use a mix of teaching activities (see above table on typology of activities), more interactive tasks occur in classrooms with student talk consuming a larger chunk of air-time in speaking more to the teacher, with one another, and working together on tasks. In such classrooms, opportunities for student independence increase also.

Summation

Two statements distill the evidence I have gathered from the three districts between 1993 and 2005:

The social organization of elementary and secondary school classrooms continued to be informal. The pattern I noted occurring between 1890 and the 1980s in other districts across the nation had become dominant by 2005

TABLE 9.7. Secondary Reports on Instructional Activities, 1993–2005

Grouping	Arlington		Denver		Oakland	
	N	%	N	%	N	%
Whole group						
Entire report	44	20	114	69	80	49
Part of report	97	45	6	4	33	20
Small group						
Entire report	24	11	35	21	33	20
Part of report	53	25	5	3	4	8
Individual work						
Entire report	39	18	10	6	14	9
Part of report	86	40	4	2	31	19
Teachers using a mix of activities*		49		4		22
Teachers using one type of instructional activity*		51		96		78
Total	216		166		162	

Numbers in each column will not add to the total N because the activity categories were not exclusive. For example, a teacher who used teacher-directed, student-directed, and independent work in a report is counted once for each activity.
* In Denver and Oakland I collected far more yearbook photos than in Arlington. These snapshots showed only one form of instructional activity. The results, then, may over-report that activity and be skewed against teachers who used mixed activities within the same lesson. While such results could be viewed as strong evidence of teacher-directedness, the lack of other classroom data beyond photos leads me to raise this caveat. I am more confident of the results for classroom activities in Arlington where I drew from many different classroom sources.

in these three districts' elementary classrooms and more prevalent in secondary ones than in earlier decades. Classrooms filled with tables and movable desks, particularly in the early grades, placed students in situations where they could easily converse and work in groups. Students' work, colorful posters, and ceiling mobiles brightened elementary school classrooms. Teachers smiled often at their classes, used casual language, and used nonphysical warnings to preempt unacceptable behavior. In the upper grades, for example, a firm warning embedded in a teacher-told story about one of her students who used a cell phone in class was sufficient to remind students not to use them in class.

Pedagogical hybrids of teacher-centered progressivism flourished. Since first observed in the early 20th century, teachers exhibiting mixes of teacher-

and student-centered practices in arranging space, grouping for instruction, and in teaching activities had become widespread in three districts' elementary classrooms and more evident in secondary ones.

Recall that teacher surveys and stories from many teachers, administrators, and parents pointed to increased time being spent in meeting state curriculum standards and preparing for tests. From these reports, a reasonable person would have inferred that traditional teacher-directed methods—organizing space in rows of student desks; grouping for whole group instruction; and tasks for students such as seatwork, textbook recitation, lectures, and note-taking in secondary school classrooms—would have thoroughly dominated classroom teaching in these districts. That is not what I found.

Since none of the linked classroom features I concentrate on deal with the content of actual lessons it is, of course, possible, even likely, that many teachers, in varying degrees depending upon the school they were in, did focus their activities on test preparation and pursued specific state standards—after all, those many teacher reports in interviews and surveys were not contrived.

Moreover, consider that state and district administrators aligned curriculum-based standards to textbooks and tests. In addition, increased pressure from federal and state officials on district officials to raise reading and math scores to show sufficient gains to meet NCLB requirements in concert with text-based lessons, suggests that the survey and anecdotal evidence may well have reflected classroom practices. Yet even those test-prep lessons unfolded within distinctly informal settings where teachers used hybrids of teacher- and student-centered practices.

On the whole, then, the evidence I collected from reports on how teachers organized space, grouped for instruction, and the activities they designed for their students suggest that classroom informality and teacher-centered progressive hybrids I had noted throughout the 20th century in other districts have not lessened under district and state mandates but had even become more pervasive in these three districts by 2005.

MAKING SENSE OF CONFLICTING EVIDENCE

I understand that some readers may remain unpersuaded by the evidence I and a few other researchers (Coburn, 2004; Grant, 2003; Jacob, Stone, & Roderick, 2004; Joseph, 2005) have found in varied districts that informal practices and mixes of teaching approaches have, indeed, persisted and not shrunk even under pressures from state and federal standards-based curriculum, tests, and accountability measures. While these findings challenge the evidence reported by teachers and others about policy effects on teaching over the past few decades, I stop short of saying that the three classroom features I documented capture the complexities of teaching practice in these years. I do so because caution about overgeneralizing from my data also dictates that I not ignore opposite evidence but make sense of their apparent contradiction.

One explanation is that teachers, particularly in urban districts, have responded to administrator pressures to meet curriculum standards, testing, and accountability in their choice of content for their daily lessons and that the classroom indicators I used missed these responses. The constant refrain from teachers in surveys and myriad stories about more class time for test preparation of students and less time for nontest academic content, amply supported by principals' comments, journalist visits to schools, and researchers' studies, suggest strongly that the taught curriculum–the content and skills teachers choose to put in daily lessons–has, indeed, narrowed.

Furthermore, my classroom observations in many urban districts and listening to many elementary and secondary teachers in the past 5 years persuade me that teacher decisions about textbooks, worksheets, discussions, projects, field trips, and dozens of other activities have accommodated to state tests and accountability regulations. Thus, I cannot dismiss such evidence as either too subjective or anecdotal, especially when it challenges my findings.

If I cannot dismiss the evidence, then how can I explain the obvious expansion of student-centered practices in classrooms at a time when teacher-directed test preparation and a narrowing of lesson content to meet curricular requirements also expanded? What is possible is that both the patterns in observable features of teaching I found in three districts and teacher-reported curricular accommodations in content and lessons have occurred in classrooms.

The patterns I found in these three districts are evidence of the institutionalization of certain teacher-centered progressive practices begun decades earlier. Students working in small groups sitting at tables rather than in rows of desks, doing independent work in elementary school centers or in secondary school projects under the watchful eye of a teacher, and engaging in spirited discussions with a teacher are examples of practices that began over a century ago as progressive innovations and over time became routinized as "best practices" in "good" teaching without undercutting the teacher's authority to determine the classroom curriculum, pedagogy, and order (Tyack & Cuban, 1995).

Similar to the process of institutionalizing technological innovations in teaching over time such as the blackboard, the overhead projector, videocassettes, and the computer, this slow-motion incorporation of particular methods into teachers' repertoires as evidence of "good" teaching speaks to the practical ways that teachers in every generation have blended old and new practices to make their daily routines compatible with their beliefs about children and learning without diluting their authority (Cuban, 1986).

What has fueled this process of institutionalizing student-centered features I documented in classrooms is the pervasiveness of constructivist (or latter-day progressive) ideas and language over the past quarter-century in curriculum standards (see above), colleges of education, and textbooks. A few examples make this evident.

A 1997 survey of 900 randomly selected professors at schools of education who prepare teachers and administrators for schools found that 86% believe that it is more important for students to figure out the process of finding the right answer rather than knowing the right answer; that 82% believe that students should be active learners; 78% want less emphasis on multiple-choice exams; 64% believe that schools should drop honor rolls and other forms of competition; and that 60% want less emphasis on memorization in classrooms (Public Agenda, 1997). These beliefs, drawing heavily from progressive rhetoric and ideas about teaching and learning, dominate the thinking of 40,000 faculty spread among 1,300-plus institutions awarding degrees and licenses to teachers, administrators, and other educators (Labaree, 2004).

Finally, progressive ideas and language have penetrated not only curriculum standards but also textbooks in their teacher manuals. Consider Open Court texts mandated for all Oakland elementary schools, where I observed their use in two schools in 2005. Heavily scripted toward teacher-directed phonics instruction to the whole group, the teacher's manual recommends that teachers arrange the classroom furniture into a square where students face one another and organize reading, math, and writing workshop centers for small groups to follow up on earlier instruction—all indicators of student-centeredness.

Pervasive presence of progressive ideas and language among professors and textbook, plus the features that I documented in classrooms, may suggest to some readers that student-centered teaching practices have become widespread as some critics have claimed (Hirsch, 1996; Ravitch, 2000). But other evidence from teacher surveys, direct observations, and research studies point out the spread of teacher-centered activities responding to district, state, and federal pressures to meet curricular standards and raise test scores.

More to the point is that particular indicators of progressive pedagogy have given a student-centered patina to most classrooms where teachers focused on meeting state curriculum standards and preparing students for tests. Just as a teacher in jeans chats with her high school students conveying to an onlooker a relaxed, friendly presence in the classroom, the mood shifts with a clap of the teacher's hands and directions for students to take out their homework assignment and textbook to begin the day's lesson. Echoes of

John Dewey's comment on an earlier generation of progressive education in 1952 reverberate today: "There is a great deal of talk about education being a cooperative enterprise in which students and teachers participate democratically, but there is far more talk about it than the doing of it" (Dworkin, 1959, pp. 129–130).

The phrase *teacher-centered progressivism* points to the hybrid classroom practices and particular student-centered features that have been incorporated into most teachers' repertoires over the decades as they adapted their practices to regulatory policies. Thus, what initially appeared as conflicting data drawn from evidence I collected in three urban districts and teacher reports across the nation of accountability, standards, and testing policies reshaping the content of their lessons turns out to be another instance over the past century of teacher adaptiveness in melding progressive classroom practices to fit current policies that sustain teacher-centeredness.

NOTES

1. These teaching traditions are not dichotomous; hybrids of the two have always existed. I do not endorse either tradition as being better than the other or more worthy of implementation. My experience and research have made clear to me that neither tradition, however defined, is the best form of teaching for all students. I do believe that hybrids of the two pedagogies—meaning multiple approaches in a teacher's repertoire adapted to differences in setting, who the students are, subject matter, and other conditions—have the best chance of getting the most students to learn.

2. Determining that a mode of teaching causes student performance on tests to rise or fall has been claimed for decades but has yet to be proved because of the many variables that influence achievement (as measured by standardized tests) such as family background, teacher experience, peers, school safety and order, and dozens of other factors.

3. For recent writers who continue to use the language of progressives/conservatives or variations thereof, see Chall (2000), Hirsch (1996), Meier (2000), Nehring (2006), Spencer (2001), and Zoch (2004).

4. Also consider how students commonly work in pairs and small groups to dissect small animals in biology labs and do the same in chemistry labs when they use Bunsen burners, flasks, and chemicals to see reactions occur. These science labs differ in organization, grouping, and activities from most English, foreign language, social studies, and math classes.

5. In a study of socialization in 64 classrooms in four elementary schools, grades 2 and 5 in the late 1990s, Brint, Contreras, and Matthews (2001) found a blending of traditional and modern values in these classrooms. "The routine practices of classrooms similarly show a blending of the old and new" (p. 173).

6. "Hugging the Middle" is adapted from Stealers Wheel's, "Stuck in the Middle with You." Fiorina (2004) used these lyrics to characterize American public opinion during the "culture wars" of the 1990s.

7. This work was made possible by a small grant from the Spencer Foundation.

8. The vulnerability of self-reports among practitioners can be seen, for example, among medical personnel. In one study, a medical official in a pediatric intensive care unit in Melbourne, Australia, estimated that they hand-washed 73% of the time; observers found that they did 9% of the time (Tibballs, 1996).

REFERENCES

Arlington Public Schools. See http://www.arlington.k12.va.us

Barth, R. (1972). *Open education and the American school.* New York: Agathon.

Brint, S., Contreras, M., & Matthews, M. (2001). Socialization messages in primary schools: An organizational analysis. *Sociology of Education, 74,* 157–180.

Carlos, L., & Kirst, M. (1997). *California curriculum policy in the 1990s: We don't have to lead to be in front.* San Francisco: WestEd.

Cazden, C. (1988). *Classroom discourse: The language of teaching and learning.* Portsmouth, NH: Heinemann.

Chall, J. (2000). *The academic achievement challenge.* New York: Guilford Press.

Coburn, C. (2004). Beyond decoupling: Rethinking the relationship between the institutional environment and the classroom. *Sociology of Education, 77,* 211–244.

Cuban, L. (1986). *Teachers and machines.* New York: Teachers College Press.

Cuban, L. (1993). *How teachers taught.* New York: Teachers College Press.

Cuban, L. (2005). *The blackboard and the bottom line: Why schools can't be businesses.* Cambridge, MA: Harvard University Press.

Cutler, W. (1989). The cathedral of culture: The schoolhouse in American educational thought and practice since 1820. *History of Education Quarterly, 29*(1), 1–40.

Dillon, S. (2006, March 26). Schools cut back subjects to push reading and math. *The New York Times.* Retrieved January 18, 2007, from http://www.nytimes.com/2006/03/26/education/26child.html?ex=1301029200&en=0c 91b5bd32da be2a&ei=5088&partner=rssnyt&emc=rss

Dionne, E. J. Jr. (2006, January/February). Why the culture war is the wrong war. *The Atlantic Monthly,* pp. 130–135.

Doyle, W. (1986). Classroom organization and management. In M. Wittrock (Ed.), *Handbook of research on teaching* (3rd ed., pp. 392–431). New York: Macmillan.

Dworkin, M. (1959). *Dewey on education: Selections.* New York: Teachers College Press.

EdSource. (2001, January). *Aligning California's education reforms.* Mountain View, CA: Author. Retrieved January 18, 2007, from http://www.edsource.org/pdf/align0101.pdf

Fiorina, M. (2004). *Culture war? The myth of a polarized nation.* New York: Longman.

Fisher, C., Filby, N., Marliave, R., Cahen, L., Dishaw, M., Moore, J., & Berliner, D. (1978). *Teaching behaviors, academic learning time and student achievement.* Final report of phase III-B Beginning Teacher Evaluation Study. San Francisco: Far West Laboratory of Educational Research and Development.

Gallego, M., & Cole, M. (2001). Classroom cultures and cultures in the classroom. In V. Richardson (Ed.), *Handbook of research on teaching* (4th ed., pp. 951–997). Washington, DC: American Educational Research Association.

Garelick, B. (2005). An a-maze-ing approach to math. *Education Next, 5*(2). Retrieved January 18, 2007, from http://www.hoover.org/publications/ednext/3220616.html

Grant, S. G. (2003). *History lessons: Teaching, learning, and testing in U.S. high school classrooms.* Mahwah, NJ: Lawrence Erlbaum Associates.

Grossman, P., & Stodolsky, S. (1995). Content as context: The role of school subjects in secondary school teaching. *Educational Researcher, 24*(8), 5–11.

Gump, P. (1982). School settings and their keeping. In D. Duke (Ed.), *Helping teachers manage classrooms* (pp. 98–114). Alexandria, VA: Association for Supervision and Curriculum Development.

Hartocollis, A. (2000, April 27). The new, flexible math meets parental rebellion. *The New York Times,* pp. A1, B5

Hasiotis, D. (2006). *All in a day's work.* New York: Common Good.

Helderman, R. (2004, August 3). SOLs keep few from graduating in N.VA. *The Washington Post,* p. B1.

Herman, J. (2002). *Instructional effects in elementary schools.* Center for the Study of Evaluation, Graduate School of Education & Information Studies, University of California, Los Angeles.

Hirsch, E. D., Jr. (1996). *The schools we need.* New York: Doubleday.

Hook, C., & Rosenshine, B. (1979). Accuracy of teacher reports of their classroom behavior. *Review of Educational Research, 49*(1), 1–12.

Hunter, J. (1991). *Culture wars: The struggle to define America.* New York: Basic Books.

Hutchinson, D. (2004). *A natural history of place in education.* New York: Teachers College Press.

Jackson, P. (1986). *The practice of teaching.* New York: Teachers College Press.

Jacob, R. T., Stone, S., & Roderick, M., (2004). *Ending social promotion: The response of students and teachers.* Chicago: Consortium on Chicago School Research.

Jones, G., Jones, B., & Hargrove, T. (2003). *The unintended consequences of high-stakes testing.* Lanham, MD: Rowman & Littlefield Publishers.

Joseph, R. (2005, April). *No one curriculum is enough: Effective California teachers tailor literacy instruction to student needs despite federal, state, and local mandates to follow scripts.* Paper Presented at First International Congress of Qualitative Inquiry, University of Illinois, Champaign-Urbana, Illinois.

Katz, M. (1968). *The irony of early school reform.* Cambridge, MA: Harvard University Press.

Keyes vs. School District No. 1, 413 U.S. 189 (1973).

Kolker, R. (2006, May 1). A is for apple, B is for brawl. *The New York Times.* Retrieved January 18, 2007, from http://newyorkmetro.com/news/features/16775/

Labaree, D. (2004). *The trouble with ed schools.* New Haven, CT: Yale University Press.

Lakoff, G. (1996). *Moral politics.* Chicago: University of Chicago Press.

Lewin, T. (2006, September 13). Report urges changes in the teaching of math in U.S. schools. *The New York Times,* p. A18.

Mayer, D. (1999). Measuring instructional practice: Can policymakers trust survey data. *Educational Evaluation and Policy Analysis, 21*(1), 29–45.

McCorry, J. (1978). *Marcus Foster and the Oakland public schools.* Berkeley, CA: University of California Press.

Meier, D. (2000). Progressive education in the 21st century: A work in progress. In R. Brandt (Ed.), *Education in a new era* (pp. 211–228). Alexandria, VA: Association for Supervision and Curriculum Development.

Nehring, J. (2006, February 1). Progressive vs. traditional: Reframing an old debate. *Education Week*, pp. 32–33.

Oakland Unified School District. (2001). *Evaluation report: Implementation and outcomes of Open Court literacy program, year 1.* Oakland, CA: Author.

Owens, B. (2005, June 2). Veto message on S.B. 214 [press release]. Retrieved January 18, 2007, from http://www.colorado.gov/governor/press/june05/sb214.html

Pedulla, J. (2003). *Perceived effects of state-mandated testing programs on teaching and learning: Findings from a national survey of teachers.* Boston: National Board on Educational Testing and Public Policy, School of Education, Boston College. Retrieved January 18, 2007, from http://www.bc.edu/research/nbetpp/statements/nbr2.pdf

Perrone, V. (1972). *Open education: Promise and problem.* Bloomington, IN: Phi Delta Kappan Foundation.

Pressler, M. (2006, June 1). Schools, pressed to achieve, put the squeeze on recess. *The Washington Post*, p. A01.

Public Agenda. (1997). *Professors of education: It's how you learn, not what you learn that is most important.* New York: Author.

Ravitch, D. (2000). *Left back: A century of failed school reforms.* New York: Simon and Schuster.

Rothman, R. (1992, November 4). Performance-based assessment gains prominent place on research docket. *Education Week.* Retrieved January 18, 2007, from http://www.edweek.org/ew/articles/1992/11/04/09perfor.h12.html

Shuell, T. (1996). Teaching and learning in a classroom context. In D. Berliner & R. Calfee (Eds.), *Handbook of educational psychology* (pp. 726–764). New York: Macmillan.

Slavin, R. (1995). *Research on cooperative learning and achievement: What we know, what we need to know.* Baltimore: Center of Research on the Education of Students Placed at Risk, Johns Hopkins University.

Sloan, K. (2006). Teacher identity and agency in school worlds: Beyond the all-good/all-bad discourse on accountability-explicit curriculum policies. *Curriculum Inquiry, 36*(2), 119–152.

Spencer, L. (2001, February 28). Progressivism's hidden failure. *Education Week*, pp. 29, 32–33.

Stodolsky, S. (1988). *The subject matters: Classroom activity in math and social studies.* Chicago: University of Chicago Press.

Stodolsky, S., & Grossman, P. (1995). The impact of subject matter on curricular activity: An analysis of five academic subjects. *American Educational Research Journal, 32*(2), 227–249.

Taylor, M. (1990). *Leadership responses to desegregation in the Denver public schools, a historical study: 1959–1977.* Unpublished doctoral dissertation, University of Denver.

Tibballs, J. (1996, April 30). Teaching hospital medical staff to handwash. *The Medical Journal of Australia, 164*, 395–398.

Tyack, D., & Cuban, L. (1995). *Tinkering toward utopia.* Cambridge, MA: Harvard University Press.

University of Chicago School Mathematics Project. (2003). *Everyday Math.* Retrieved December 15, 2006, from http://everydaymath.uchicago.edu/index.shtml.

Viadero, D. (2005, November 16). Teacher logs reveal how class time is really spent. *Education Week,* p. 8.

Viadero, D. (2006, May 24). Survey finds majority of elementary schools still offer recess time. *Education Week,* p. 14.

Weinstein, C. (1991). The classroom as a social context for learning. *Annual Review of Psychology, 42,* 493–525.

Wilson, S. (2003). *California dreaming.* New Haven, CT: Yale University Press.

Yee, G. (1995). *Miracle workers wanted: Executive succession and organizational change in an urban district.* Unpublished doctoral dissertation, Stanford University.

Yee, G. (2004, April). *Who leads? The school board and governance change in the Oakland public schools, 1960–2004.* Paper presented at annual meeting of American Educational Research Association, San Diego.

Zimmerman, J. (2002). *Whose America? Culture wars in the public schools.* Cambridge, MA: Harvard University Press.

Zoch, P. (2004). *Doomed to fail: The built-in defects of American education.* Chicago: Ivan Dee, Inc.

CHAPTER 10

Reflections on Urban School Reform

For urban school reformers, good intentions, simple answers, and hoped-for miracles don't make a dent in the real world of urban schools and classrooms, except to heighten disappointment. Far more than a fairy-tale kiss is needed to transform a frog into a prince.

Consider the role of institutions beyond schools and money. Schools are embedded in communities. They reflect and sustain societal norms while working within socioeconomic structures that influence what occurs daily in school corridors and classrooms. Thus, schools alone cannot alter the conditions within which poverty, social injustice, and inequities exist in a democratic society. Partnerships with political and social institutions and active work within communities themselves are essential for students' lives to get better inside and outside of schools.

Take, for example, student demography—who goes to school with one another. The evidence of minority children going to school with White children drawn from years of research studies has shown repeatedly that low-income minority children benefit greatly in academic achievement and altering dominant social norms as both groups learn from one another and connect well with people very different from themselves. Yet de facto segregated schools a half-century after *Brown v. Board of Education* remains the norm in cities. Believing that society can erase poverty, racism, and other social ills through reforming schools has been a fairy tale passed down from one generation of policymakers and practitioners to another.

Money also matters. Sure, there is never enough money to go to schools and, sure, how the money that does go to schools gets spent is crucial. Yet any critic of schools who has not spent a week in big-city schools or rural schools enrolling largely poor children who says that money doesn't matter is missing neural networks.

These selections drawn from over 45 years of experience try to get beyond reform hype and address the much deeper (and currently unaddressed) issues of student access to equitable resources, the narrowness of current definitions of good schools, teacher quality, and whether schools alone can make a difference in the lives of students who have confronted (and still do) the inequities of poverty, class, and race.

Even with many stumbles and failures lightened occasionally by small victories over the past 5 decades, even after bouts of cynicism and despair over persistently low-performing schools darkened my hopes for the future, my optimism is battered, but intact. I still believe that urban schools can be better than they are—as long as policymakers and power elites avoid the arrogance of thinking that policies once adopted get easily put into practice, that schools alone can eliminate societal problems and ignore the tempting thought that they know better than teachers what works best in classrooms.

Although periodic outbursts of such arrogance and ignorance dampen teachers' and principals' enthusiasm to muster the energy to improve, I have seen, and continue to see firsthand, incredible practitioner expertise and determination to improve schooling through pragmatic problem solving and deep involvement with students and the community.

Yes, of course, there are too many schools that have become sinkholes of adult inaction and student neglect. In some of these broken-down schools, determined experienced staffs, often working closely with committed parents, stay long enough to turn them around sufficiently to see children learning. The facts remain clear that courageous teachers, administrators, and parents come to see that tension-filled dilemmas are deeply entangled in their communities and shaped constantly by socioeconomic structures in the larger culture, yet these determined practitioners, with the limited resources available to them, continue to frame and reframe the problem and dilemmas they face as they teach and lead schools each day. Inaction is not an option for them. Or me. What can be done to improve urban schools?

For nearly 5 decades I have either been involved in or studied reforms aimed at overhauling urban schools and classroom teaching. From these practitioner–scholar experiences, my once youthful unvarnished optimism has become tempered about what can be done in urban schools. Even as I have come to see that the problems of urban schools I defined at different stages of my career evolved into tougher dilemmas not easily solved by soaring rhetoric and goodwill, I have not yielded to corrosive doubt or paralyzing pessimism over what smart, determined leaders working closely with teachers can do in urban schools. In trying to be realistic about the frequent gap between school reform policies and classroom practice, I have blended an optimistic heart with a skeptical mind to cut through reformers' all too common pattern of overselling solutions and ignoring the devilish details of implementing policies while underestimating the influence of deeply embedded social, economic, political, and organizational structures. Reform-minded readers, allergic to charming peddlers of panaceas as I am, need to think smarter about the steady rollout of different policy strategies in the past quarter-century—each containing a problem defined subjectively and often negotiated among key players–aimed at bettering classroom practice. Yet without a clue about how to get an adapted policy to work successfully in schools and classrooms.

Four reform strategies aimed at raising students' academic achievement in urban schools have dominated national policy agendas in the past quarter-century. Whole School Reform began in the late 1970s with the Effective Schools movement's problem definition of low-performing schools focused on the solution of improving each school's academic achievement, one at a time, by sharply focusing on the principal, school climate, curriculum, instruction, and testing. The movement spun off dozens of different models to reform schools. Foundations continue this strategy in creating new small high schools.

Another strategy is parental choice. Since the early 1990s, reformers have pursued charter schools, theme schools, and vouchers on the theory that school choice will motivate individual parents and students to do well in school while marketplace competition between district schools will turn low-performing ones into high-achievers.

Standards-based accountability is a third approach that shifted into high gear in the 1990s when U.S. presidents, governors, and mayors embraced it wholeheartedly. The theory behind this solution is that when a district's goals, curriculum, textbooks, tests, and instruction are tightly coupled, teachers will get students to become high performers on tests, graduate high school, and go to college.

The fourth reform strategy is to concentrate authority and accountability in elected federal, state, and local officials who can do something about bad schools rather than weak school boards and district educators who too often block reform. The theory behind this solution is that changing school governance–including state takeovers of low-performing districts and mayoral control–will place elected officials in positions where they can raise school achievement.

Based on my school and district experiences and research into these four reform strategies over the past quarter-century to improve schools, I have concluded the following:

- Most urban districts, either with or without mayoral control, have combined standards-based accountability and parental choice to enact whole school reform. Many big cities, for example, focus on state standards while offering parents a portfolio of choices in elementary and secondary schools.
- While some national leaders call for overhauling the existing system–think of the 2007 report from CEOs and civic leaders, *Tough Choices or Tough Times*, or state voucher plans–these four reform

strategies have sought incremental changes in existing structures, not fundamental changes in the relationship between schools and larger communities. In fact, acclaimed entrepreneurial ventures such as Teach for America, New Leaders for New Schools, Knowledge Is Power Program (KIPP), and Edison Schools use the rhetoric of fundamental reform but choose to work within districts and press for small but important policy changes.[1]

• The good news is that some strategies have worked in some districts for a while. Many urban districts, using standards-based accountability strategies, for example, have raised the percentages of students testing proficient in reading and math in the elementary grades. The Broad Prize for Urban Education, leaning heavily upon test scores, has awarded each year since 2002 one million dollars for improving academic achievement to Houston, Long Beach, Garden Grove, Norfolk, and Boston.[2]

There is bad news, however. None of these district reform strategies, alone or in combination, has yet overcome persistent challenges in raising test scores, closing the achievement gap between minorities and Whites, and raising graduation rates. Let me review these challenges because anyone marketing a solution to low-achieving urban schools has to not only make the case for the success of the particular strategy but also show how it can triumph over unrelenting socioeconomic and political structures and persistent human obstacles to make it past the classroom door and help students earn better grades, score higher on tests, and graduate from high school.

Too often district reforms are implemented partially. To convert existing high schools into many small ones, for example, is complicated work. It requires time, redirected resources, sensitivity to different school settings, and extensive logistics. Because of insufficient knowledge, limited time and staffing, skimpy funding of teacher support, leaders lacking political will, or negligible community aid (or some mix of these)—putting larger reform strategies into practice often omits key components. And half-done implementation means that it is impossible to determine whether the strategy is a good idea that can be copied in classrooms everywhere. Partially baked breads seldom rise sufficiently to taste good. And half-done policy implementation means that the question of whether the reform-driven policy works seldom gets answered. Which policies work depends, first, on whether they were put into practice completely in schools and, second, whether they came to fit the place and the people. In education, think of Head Start and computers in schools as examples of partial implementation. There are, of course, notorious non-educational examples of half-done implementation in post-invasion Iraq and New Orleans in the wake of Katrina.[3]

When a new strategy is fully put into place across a district, it still may not alter classroom practice. Even after school boards adopted curriculum standards, mandated tests, created small high schools, and established structures for parents to choose their schools—these fully implemented district strategies often stumbled in getting teachers to translate these structural changes into changed classroom practice. To overcome this challenge, many districts hire coaches to help teachers convert broad curriculum standards into daily lessons. This sensible tactic provides expert help to teachers in their classrooms.

Yet in many districts aching to do well on the state tests and avoid the penalties that rain down from both state regulations and No Child Left Behind, reform-minded district officials ask teachers to use classroom techniques that get students to plunge deeper into academic content to understand the concepts and to think independently. Inevitably, tensions arise for teachers committed to these goals and the goals of scoring well on state tests to earn the label of proficient in a subject or skill.

When these seemingly similar state and district reform policies hit schools insofar as requiring teacher time for collaborative planning and execution, then conflicts arise over which time slots during the day and which professional development times and days will get primary attention and which ones recede to the background. All of these conflicts raise doubts about whether policies aimed at altering what teachers do in their lessons enter classrooms as intended. Again, however, this sort of professional help, sensible as it is, requires sustained funding, staffing, and district leaders who can buffer the reform from the inevitable criticism that occurs when test scores fail to rise high enough, plateau, or even fall.[4]

No one yet has demonstrated how to improve achievement for the lowest quartile of students. When I say the "lowest quartile" I mean those students, often minority and poor, who year after year receive grades of "D" or "F" in their subjects and perform below proficiency levels on tests. Many of these students are neither troublesome nor delinquent but they are years behind in grade.

They struggle with basic reading and math. They need early identification, even before they arrive in kindergarten, and far more instructional and personal intervention than offered by the mainstream reform strategies I have described.[5] They need the benefits derived from close cooperation with other social and community institutions that bring essential city and state services to children and youth.

Sustainability of school reforms remains out of reach of most districts. Without 7–10 years of steady attention to district improvement, early victories will slip away and that lowest quartile of students will remain forsaken. For example, in the 1980s and 1990s, cities touted as national models of what

urban systems could do to improve schools, eventually faded into medioc-
rity. Sustainability of school reform means continuity in school board and
superintendent tenure. Broad Foundation awards went to urban districts
that had superintendents who served at least 5 years and two who had
served 10 years. Continuity in reform also means providing stable funding;
it means building leadership within the district to adapt reforms; it means
unflagging political support from business and civic leaders, community
groups, and state officials.

Good schools do more than have high academic achievement. Because reformers
in the past quarter-century have focused so sharply on preparing youth for
a highly competitive, knowledge-based workplace, the definition of a good
school has narrowed to high test scores, increased high school graduation
rates, and college admissions as evidence of goodness. There is, of course,
nothing wrong with these benchmarks. But these are constricted measures
when one considers the multiple goals of public schools and many versions
of good schools across the nation.

Requiring parents to send their children to public schools historically has
gone far beyond literacy benchmarks. Taxpayers and parents expect that
schools will graduate youth who can think independently and are equally
as literate in the arts, sciences, and humanities as in reading and math. They
expect graduates to understand that a democracy requires them to be active
in their communities and interact with others different than themselves in
school, work, and church. In affluent districts these expectations of a good
school exist. Rarely, however, are such views broadcast for schools enrolling
largely poor and minority students.[6]

Given these persistent challenges to reformers for the past quarter-
century, being realistic about urban school reform demands candor. The
historical record is clear that in some districts and individual schools, for
a few years, the stars are aligned. Civic and business leadership, political mobilization of resources and people, and educator expertise come
together to convert academic disasters into successes. Such turnarounds
have occurred and will occur again.

But there is the downside to these important victories. Most of the turnaround schools are elementary; success with middle and high schools occurs
far less often and when it does, it has a short shelf life. Moreover, students
who do least well academically—that bottom quartile—particularly by the
time they reach middle and high school, remain largely unserved.

If these are the challenges, what must be done? Here I offer a tempered optimistic voice and argue for changes that can be achieved by
experienced leaders who are informed about past efforts to improve
urban schools and understand that small increments of change can be significant inside and outside schools. In short, they think smarter about district

reform. But I give no specific advice. My years as a practitioner–scholar have convinced me that five- or seven-step recipes for reform may be satisfying to readers but drop dead when confronting a particular district, school, or classroom. Instead, I propose seven essential questions that must be asked (and answered) by change-driven civic and business leaders, policymakers, administrators, teachers, and parents when decisionmakers seek school improvement:

1. *Are the goals for improved schools restricted to only what schools can do?* Current reformers believe that better schools will produce economic growth while reducing significant inequalities between the poor and wealthy, minorities and Whites. If so, then reducing inequalities as an aim of schooling demands that policymakers recognize that schools cannot do the job alone. Reducing inequalities requires community collaboration and substantial changes in societal norms and structures. If the vision of what schools can achieve includes economic growth and reducing inequalities, then far more players from the community have to be recruited to play that important game and be reflected in the stated goals for school action in improving the life chances of children and youth.

2. *What assumptions about the connections between schools and their communities, change, school organization, leadership, teaching, and learning are built into the reform strategy?* Every reform strategy makes key assumptions about how organizations change, what happens in schools, and how things go from point A to point B. Making explicit these assumptions helps educate those who do the implementing of the strategy and aids considerably any assessment of the effects of the reform.

3. *Did the reform strategy's new structures and processes (standards-based accountability, choice, governance, whole school reform, etc.) get fully implemented as intended?* Partially implemented reform means you never know whether what was invested ever touched classroom practice.

4. *When implemented, did the reforms change the content and practice of teaching?* Putting parental choice structures and curriculum standards in place, for example, occurs frequently. But if policymakers intend these structures to alter classroom content and practices and hardly cause a ripple of change in what teachers and students do daily, then the reform has failed.

5. *Did altered classroom content and teaching practice lead to desired student learning?* If the answer is yes, determining exactly what

students learned from the changes teachers instituted in content and methods must be assessed. If the answer is no, then dumping the reform is the best policy.

6. *Was student learning captured by state tests?* Much of what students learn in classrooms changed by reform policies can be assessed by standardized tests, and much cannot. If the state tests miss, say, the desired outcomes of critical thinking skills or civic engagement, then state tests should be changed or other assessments used.

7. *Did students who have achieved proficiency on state tests go to college, graduate, enter jobs, and contribute to their communities?* This question puts the fundamental belief that education is linked to the economy and the community to the test and asks that evidence be collected and judgments be made on whether the assumption is accurate. Few districts and evaluators do this.

How to end? Yes, recognizing the above challenges that remain and demanding answers to these questions from those in authority go part of the way to getting better schools. But there is no guarantee that even meeting the difficult challenges and answering these questions will, indeed, make the difference in urban schools. It is possible, of course, that the larger socioeconomic structures that govern a market-based society and account for a persistent level of poverty and large inequalities in the distribution of income, and substantial political resistance to deal directly with those structures and inequalities—the constant background hum in our ears that few hear and most take for granted—will remain unexamined and untouched, quietly continuing to shape public school funding and teacher quality for urban and rural poor children and youth.

Although much still angers me about squashed hopes of children and youth in urban schools, the minority of time-serving mediocre teachers and administrators, and ill-informed policymakers eager to make their mark, I remain hopeful, not despairing, about improvement. While the years have softened my anger and battered my enthusiasm, hope still remains an ingredient in my belief that urban schools can become better places for children and youth to thrive and learn. Sure, while I can gussy up my hope by drawing quotes from Reinhold Niebuhr, *Don Quixote,* and even steal a lyric or two from *Man of La Mancha* about a never-ending quest, I do not need to do so since my practitioner experience and research have led me slowly but steadily to the conclusion that working for better schools is worthwhile labor even in the face of a sad history of superheated hype and so many failed reforms. Some tasks are worthwhile to work on even though the hope for success may remain slim. And so it is for urban school reform.

NOTES

1. See Larry Cuban, "Educational Entrepreneurs Redux," in F. Hess (Ed.), *Educational Entrepreneurship: Realities, Changes, Possibilities* (Cambridge, MA: Harvard Education Press, 2006), pp. 223–242.

2. See the Broad Foundation website: http://www.broadprize.org. For a recent and astute survey of the complexity of policy, place, and people in implementation, see Meredith Honig (Ed.), *New Directions in Education Policy Implementation* (Albany: State University of New York, 2006).

3. In the past 4 years, articles and books about the reasons the United States invaded Iraq, the assumptions driving the war and subsequent occupation, and responses to the religious and political civil war have revealed all too clearly the abject failure of U.S. elected leaders in invading Iraq and staggering from one ad hoc strategy and hastily designed plan to another as the occupation and resulting insurgency evolved. By 2007, what was supposed to be a good idea had turned out to be a foreign policy disaster for the nation, a tragedy for American military families in casualties, and severe losses and dislocation for the Iraqi people during the civil war and insurgency. Whether it was a bad idea to begin with or a good idea that was badly implemented or a good idea that uninformed leaders failed to examine too closely for flaws or some mix of these (and other) explanations, I cannot say. Although George W. Bush was re-elected in 2004, by November 2006 when the Republicans lost both houses of Congress, the American people had registered their dismay with the president and their elected representatives in a clear display of opposition to the Iraq War. See, for example, Bob Woodward, *State of Denial, Bush at War, Part I* (New York: Simon and Schuster, 2006); and Thomas Ricks, *Fiasco: The American Military Adventure in Iraq* (New York: Penguin Press, 2006). Also see James Fallows, "Getting Out of Iraq: What's the Right Idea When All Ideas Are Bad?" *Atlantic Online,* November 30, 2006 at http://www.theatlantic.com/doc/200611u/fallows-iraq-withdrawal

4. See, for example, the experience of San Diego city schools between 1998 and 2005 in Amy Hightower and Milbrey McLaughlin, "Building and Sustaining an Infrastructure for Learning" in F. Hess (Ed.), *Urban School Reform: Lessons from San Diego* (Cambridge, MA: Harvard Education Press, 2005), pp. 71–92.

5. Meredith Phillips, James Crouse, and John Ralph, "Does the Black-White Test Score Gap Widen after Children Enter School?" in C. Jencks and M. Phillips (Eds.), *The Black-White Test Score Gap* (Washington, DC: The Brookings Institution Press, 1998), pp. 229–272; Ronald Ferguson, "Can Schools Narrow the Black-White Test Score Gap?" in C. Jencks and M. Phillips (Eds.), *The Black-White Test Score Gap* (Washington, DC: The Brookings Institution Press, 1998), pp. 273–317.

6. David Labaree, "Public Goods, Private Goods: The American Struggle over Educational Goals," *American Educational Research Journal, 34*(1), 1997, pp. 39–81; Larry Cuban, *Why Is It So Hard To Get Good Schools?* (New York: Teachers College Press, 2003); Jeannie Oakes and John Rogers, *Learning Power: Organizing for Education and Justice* (New York: Teachers College Press, 2006); John Rogers and Jeannie Oakes, "John Dewey Speaks to *Brown*: Research, Democratic Social Movement Strategies, and the Struggle for Education on Equal Terms," *Teachers College Record, 107*(9), 2005, pp. 2178–2203.

Index

Academic achievement
  computers in classrooms and, 155–156
  effectiveness of school reform and, 14–15,
    80–81, 190–195
Accountability movement, 159–184
  assessment focus and, 104, 112
  conflicting evidence on impact of, 180–183
  historical perspective on, 164–165
  impact on classroom instruction methods,
    164–165, 174–183
  instruction methods of past and, 160–164,
    165–174
  No Child Left Behind in, 112, 165, 171, 180,
    192
  target districts for comparative study of, 165,
    170–174
Addison Junior High School (Cleveland, Ohio),
  14–15
Ahlbrand, W., 86
Amphrey, Walter, 120
Anderson, Jill, 158 n. 14
Anderson, Robert, 79, 84 n. 11, 84 n. 14
Apple, M., 101
Applebee, A. N., 86
Apple Classroom of Tomorrow (ACOT),
  154–155
Arlington, Virginia schools, 3–4, 42–69
  computers in classrooms and, 151–153
  demographics and profile, 171–172
  district policies, 45–50
  impact of accountability movement in, 165,
    170–183
  implementation of school improvement
    strategies, 50–61
  unanticipated consequences and, 61–65
Armstrong, Betty Ann, 68 n. 17
Assessment. *See also* Accountability movement
  No Child Left Behind and, 112, 165, 171,
    180, 192
  role of, 104
Atkin, J. M., 146 n. 4
At-risk students, 70–84
  compulsory attendance laws, 71, 72–74
  framing problem of, 72–74
  graded schools and, 73–79
  historical perspective on, 70–71, 76–77

  incremental change process and, 79–83
  nature of, 71
  redesign of schools and, 76–79
  what works with, 80–81
Au, Kathryn, 84 n. 22

Bacharach, Samuel, 65–66 n. 3
Banks, C. A. M., vii
Banks, James A., vii–x, 84 n. 22
Barth, R., 167
Bauchner, Joyce E., 67 n. 12
Benjamin, Robert, 66 n. 5
Bennett, Bill, 65 n. 1, 66 n. 5
Bentzen, Mary, 68 n. 16
Berlak, Ann, 9 n. 6
Berlak, Harold, 9 n. 6
Berliner, D., 169
Berman, Paul, 66–67 n. 10
Bernanos, Georges, 70, 83 n. 1
Bernstein, B., 101
Berra, Yogi, 87
Bestor, A., 88
Bickel, William, 84 n. 23
Bidwell, Charles, 65–66 n. 3, 104
Billig, Michael, 9 n. 6
Bobbitt, Franklin, 146 n. 9
Borja, Rhea, 157 n. 1, 158 n. 8
Bossert, Steven, 65–66 n. 3, 68 n. 18
Bottom-up reform, 51–52
Bowles, S., 98
Boyd, W., 92
Bridges, Edwin, 66 n. 9
Brint, S., 183 n. 5
Brophy, Jere, 84 n. 20
Brown v. Board of Education, 113, 188
Bush, George W., 111, 117, 165, 196 n. 3
Bussom, Robert S., 68 n. 20

Cahen, L., 169
California. *See also* Oakland, California schools
  curriculum mandates in, 89
Callahan, Raymond, 68 n. 19, 92, 99
Campbell, Ernest Q., 65 n. 2
Cardozo Project/Urban Teacher Corps, 1–2, 8 n.
  2, 26, 27–32
Carlos, L., 173

Carnegie, Andrew, 98
Carnegie Forum on Education and the Economy, 97
Carnoy, M., 96, 101
Cazden, C., 168
Centralizing authority, 89–90, 190
Cesari, J., vii–viii
Chall, J., 160, 183 n. 3
Charles Kettering Foundation, 63–64
Chicago schools
  centralization of authority in, 90
  compulsory attendance laws, 71
Child-centered practice. *See* Student-centered instruction
Civil rights movement, 113–114, 161
Clark, Kenneth, 84 n. 12
Clark, Richard, 156, 158 n. 15
Clark, Terry A., 66 n. 8, 68 n. 17
Classroom activities
  before accountability mandates, 168–170
  historical perspective on, 163
  impact of accountability mandates on, 177–178
Classroom communities, 81
Classroom practice. *See* Instruction methods
Cleveland Board of Education
  Addison Junior High, 14–15
  Glenville High School, 1, 13–19
  Great Cities Improvement Project (GCIP), 14–15
  Higher Horizons Program, 17
Coburn, C., 180
Cohen, D., 89, 146 n. 6
Cohen, Michael, 65–66 n. 3
Cole, M., 168
Coleman, James S., 65 n. 2
Coleman Report, 41–42, 47
Collins, Marva, 41
Comer, James, 84 n. 19
Committee for Economic Development, 92, 97
Committee of Ten, 88
Community involvement
  in proposed training model for teachers, 35–38
  as role of teachers, 22–23, 27, 32–35
Compulsory attendance laws, 71, 72–74, 100–101, 193
Computers in classrooms, 148–157
  academic achievement and, 155–156
  changes in pedagogy and, 154–155
  common patterns of use, 150, 151–153
  historical perspective on, 151
  moving toward 1:1 ratio, 149–150
  productivity and, 150–151
Conant, James B., 17, 71, 83 n. 4, 88
Condor, Susan, 9 n. 6
Contreras, M., 183 n. 5

Coolidge, Calvin, 95
Crandall, David, 67 n. 12, 68 n. 17
Cremin, L., 87, 88, 90, 94, 98, 102
Crim, Alonzo, 66 n. 5, 66 n. 7
Cromwell, Sharon, 157 n. 4
Cronin, J., 90, 113
Crouse, James, 196 n. 5
Crowson, Robert L., 67–68 n. 15
Cuban, Larry, ix–x, 68 n. 19, 86, 87, 99, 104, 120, 146 n. 1, 146 n. 2, 146 n. 7, 157 n. 3, 158 n. 6, 162, 165, 170, 181, 182, 196 n. 1, 196 n. 6
Cubberly, Ellwood, 146 n. 9
Cultural deprivation, as label, 13–14
Curriculum
  curriculum theory and, 128
  decisions concerning, 22
  in graded schools, 73
  historical perspective on, 88–89, 93–94, 130
  impact of students and teachers on, 101–102
  transition from academic to practical, 87–89
Curtis, Diane, 158 n. 14
Cutler, W., 166
Cycle metaphor for reform, 94–97

Dakin, E., 94, 96
Daniels, L. A., 90
David, Jane L., 67 n. 11, 68 n. 17
Dearborn, N., 87
Decentralizing authority, 89–90
Demirtas, Hakan, 158 n. 17
Denscombe, M., 101
Denver, Colorado schools
  computers in classrooms and, 151–153
  demographics and profile, 172–173
  impact of accountability movement in, 165, 170–183
Dewey, E., 94, 96
Dewey, John, 182–183
Dilemmas
  nature of, 5–6
  problems versus, 6
Dillon, S., vii, 165, 174
DiMaggio, P. J., 103
Dinkins, David, 117
Dionne, E. J., Jr., 161
Dishaw, M., 169
Doris, John, 83 n. 8
Dornbusch, S. M., 104
Dougherty, Van, 65 n. 1
Downs, A., 99
Doyle, W., 167–169
Dreeben, R., 104
Dropouts, 17. *See also* At-risk students
Duke, D. L., 104
Dworkin, M., 183
Dwyer, David, 65–66 n. 3, 68 n. 18, 102, 158 n. 9, 158 n. 11

Easley, J., 86, 146 n. 4
Eastland, Terry, 65 n. 1, 66 n. 5
Eck, Diane L., vii
Edmonds, Ronald, 53, 55–56, 65 n. 1, 67 n. 13,
    84 n. 12
EdSource, 173
Educational reform. *See* School reform
Education Commission of the States, 41
Education Professions Development Act, 24
Edwards, Derek, 9 n. 6
Effective schools, 41–69, 190
    in Arlington, Virginia, 3–4, 42–69
    Coleman Report and, 41–42, 47
    district policies and, 45–50
    financial issues for, 47–48
    implementation of policies, 50–61
    incentives and sanctions for, 56–57
    in-service training for teachers, 54–56
    leadership of, 57–61
    in Milwaukee, Wisconsin, 53
    in New York City, 47, 53, 55–56
    personnel issues for, 48–50, 54–56
    problems with research on, 43–44, 63–65
    unanticipated consequences of, 61–65
Effective teachers, for at-risk students, 81–83
Eisenhower, Dwight, 95
Elbow, Peter, 9 n. 6
Eliade, M., 94
Eliot, Charles, 88
Elmore, Richard F., 66–67 n. 10, 91, 92,
    102–105
Eubanks, Eugene, 66 n. 6, 66 n. 7, 67 n. 13
Expectations
    for impact of accountability movement on
        schools, 174–175
    of public for school systems, 103, 122–123
    of public for superintendents, 116–118
    of public for teachers, 102–103
    of teachers for students, 15–16, 120–122

Fallows, James, 196 n. 3
Farber, Peggy, 84 n. 19
Farrar, E., 89, 146 n. 6
Ferguson, Ronald, 196 n. 5
Filby, N., 169
Fine, Michelle, 83–84 n. 10
Fiorina, M., 161, 164, 183 n. 6
Fisch, R., 146 n. 3
Fischer, David, 140
Fisher, C., 169
Ford Foundation, 14–15
Fullan, Michael, 67 n. 12

Gall, Meredith, 67 n. 12
Gallego, M., 168
Gane, Mike, 9 n. 6
Garelick, B., 161

Gide, Andre, 85
Gintis, H., 98
Gittell, M., 90
Gleick, J., 93
Glenville High School (Cleveland, Ohio), 1,
    13–19
    influences on teachers, 18–19
    labeling students and, 13–17
    new social studies instruction and, 18,
        136–138
Good, Thomas, 84 n. 20
Goodlad, John, 79, 84 n. 11, 84 n. 14, 86, 87
Gould, S. J., 98
Governance
    centralized versus decentralized, 89–90,
        104–105, 190
    changing systems of, 118
Graded schools, 73–79
    case against, 75–76
    curriculum requirements, 73
    efforts to redesign, 76–79
    historical perspective on, 93–94
    incremental change process and, 79–83
    problems for at-risk students, 74, 75–76
Grant, S. G., 180
Great Cities Improvement Project (GCIP),
    14–15
Grim, Alonzo, 48
Grossman, P., 163
Grouping of students, 82
    before accountability mandates, 167–168
    historical perspective on, 163
    impact of accountability mandates on,
        176–177
Grubb, N., 99
Grubb, W. N., 98
Gulek, James, 158 n. 17
Gump, P., 168
Guthrie, J. W., 98, 99

Hallinger, Philip, 65–66 n. 3, 68 n. 18, 68–69
    n. 21
Hammond, Jay, 41
Hansot, Elisabeth, 68 n. 20, 102
Harding, Warren G., 95
Hargrove, T., 174
Harris, William T., 83 n. 6
Hartocollis, A., 161
Hasiotis, D., 174–175
Health programs for students, 15
Heath, Shirley Brice, 84 n. 17
Helderman, R., 172
Herman, J., 174–175
Herodotus, 18
Hess, F., 196 n. 1, 196 n. 4
Hightower, Amy, 196 n. 4
Hirsch, E. D., Jr., 182, 183 n. 3

Hobson, Carol J., 65 n. 2
Hoetker, J., 86
Home visitor program, 14
Honig, Bill, 85, 89, 91
Honig, Meredith, 196 n. 2
Hook, C., 166
Hoover, Herbert, 95
Hornbeck, David, 120
Hough Project, 14
House, E., 146 n. 4
House, Gerry, 120
How Teachers Taught (Cuban)
  follow-up on, 165–183
  introduction to, 127–146, 162–164
Hunter, J., 161
Hurwitz, Emanuel, Jr., 67–68 n. 15
Hutchinson, D., 166

Imber, M., 104
Incremental reform, 79–83, 129, 130–140
Instruction methods, 127–146, 159–184. *See
  also* Computers in classrooms
  before accountability movement, 160–164,
    165–174
  for at-risk students, 81–83
  curriculum decisions and, 22
  explanations for constancy and change in,
    140–146
  fundamental reforms, 129–130
  impact of accountability movement on, 164–
    165, 174–183
  incremental reforms, 129, 130–140
  metaphors for schooling, 138–139
  nature of, 133
  in new social studies, 18, 136–138
  objective analysis of, 135–140
  resistance to changing, 131–132
  student-centered. *See* Student-centered
    instruction
  teacher-centered. *See* Teacher-centered
    instruction
  teacher role in shaping, 145–146
  transforming fundamental changes to
    incremental changes, 130–140
  types of teaching tasks, 169
Irwin, Elisabeth, 83 n. 7

Jackson, Philip, 86, 146 n. 8, 160, 164,
  168
Jacob, R. T., 180
James, T., 96
James, W., 86, 146 n. 8
Jencks, C., 196 n. 5
Johnson, Lyndon B., 34, 95, 98
Jones, B., 174
Jones, G., 174
Joseph, R., 180

Kaestle, C., 94, 96, 99
Kane, Michael, 66–67 n. 10
Kasarda, John, 65–66 n. 3
Katz, Michael, 65–66 n. 3, 86, 87, 93, 96, 98,
  146 n. 8, 160
Katznelson, I., 90
Kay, Alan, 156, 158 n. 16
Kearns, D., 90, 99
Kennedy, John F., 95
Kerchner, C. T., 92
Keyes v. School District No. 1, Denver, 172–173
Kirp, D. L., 91
Kirst, M., 96, 102, 173
Klein, Joel, 161
Kleine, P., 102
Kliebard, H. M., 89, 91, 96
Kolker, R., 161
Krug, E., 88

Labaree, David, 182, 196 n. 6
Labeling students. *See also* At-risk students
  academically talented, 17
  culturally deprived, 13–14
  educationally disadvantaged, 13–17, 120–122
Lakoff, G., 161
Lampert, Magdalene, 9 n. 6
Lane, Dawn, 157 n. 2, 158 n. 7
Langer, J., 86
Lansner, K., 88
Larson, Lars, 68 n. 20
Lazerson, M., 98, 99
Lehming, Rolf, 66–67 n. 10
Leinhardt, Gaea, 84 n. 23
Levin, H., 90, 96, 101
Levine, Daniel U., 66 n. 6, 66 n. 7, 67 n. 13
Lewin, T., 162
Lieberman, Ann, 68 n. 16
Little, Judith Warren, 54, 67 n. 14, 67–68 n. 15,
  68 n. 16
Loucks, Susan F., 67 n. 12, 68 n. 17
Lynd, A., 88

Macrorie, Ken, 84 n. 15
March, J. G., 102
Marks, Louis, 83 n. 7
Marliave, R., 169
Martin, P., vii
Mason, Richard, 9 n. 5
Master teachers, 1–2
Matthews, M., 183 n. 5
Mayer, D., 166
McCarthy, Dennis, 66 n. 8, 68 n. 17
McCorry, J., 169
McLaughlin, Milbrey W., 66–67 n. 10, 91,
  102–105, 196 n. 4
McPartland, James, 65 n. 2
Meier, D., 183 n. 3

Meister, G. R., 96, 102
Mercer, Jane, 75, 83 n. 9
Meyer, J., 98, 99, 102–105, 146 n. 7
Middleton, David, 9 n. 6
Midgley, E., vii
Miller, Lynne, 68 n. 16
Milwaukee, Wisconsin schools, 53, 79
Mitroff, Ian, 9 n. 5
Mood, Alexander M., 65 n. 2
Moore, J., 169
Morris, Van Cleve, 67–68 n. 15
Mullis, I., 86

National Commission on Excellence in
    Education, 97, 99
National Council of Teachers of Mathematics
    (NCTM), 161–162
National Defense Education Act, Title XI, 24
National Teachers Corps, 8 n. 2
Nation at Risk, A, 114
Natriello, Gary, 83–84 n. 10
Negroponte, Nicolas, 157 n. 1
Nehring, J., 183 n. 3
New York City schools
    Balanced Literacy mandate, 161
    decentralization of authority in, 90
    Free School Society, 70–71
    myths concerning, 119, 120
    School Improvement Program, 47, 53, 55–56
Niebuhr, Reinhold, 195
No Child Left Behind, 112, 165, 171, 180, 192

Oakes, Jeannie, 196 n. 6
Oakland, California schools
    computers in classrooms and, 151–153
    demographics and profile, 173–174
    impact of accountability movement in, 165,
        170–183
Odden, Allan, 65 n. 1, 65–66 n. 3
Ogawa, Rodney, 68 n. 20
Olsen, J. P., 102
Organizational structure, impact on instruction
    methods, 143–144
Organization of classroom
    before accountability mandates, 166–167
    historical perspective on, 162–163
    impact of accountability mandates on, 175–
        176, 178–179
Osborne, A., 146 n. 4
Owens, B., 173

Paige, R., 112
Palmer, Emerson, 83 n. 2
Parental choice, 190
Parents
    attitudes toward schools, 20
    professionalism of teachers and, 20–21

relationships with teachers, 22–23, 27, 32–35
Payzant, Tom, 120
Peace Corps, 1–2, 19
Pedulla, J., 165, 174–175
Pendulum metaphor for reform, 91–94
Perkinson, H. J., 98
Perpich, Rudy, 92
Perrone, V., 167
Phillips, Meredith, 196 n. 5
Pincus, J., 102, 103
Pitner, Nancy, 68 n. 20
Plato, 18
Plutarch, 18
Pollock, Jackson, 140
Pomfret, Alan, 67 n. 12
Popkewitz, T. S., 101
Porter-Gehrie, Cynthia, 67–68 n. 15
Powell, A., 89, 146 n. 6
Powell, W. W., 103
Presseisen, B. Z., 96
Pressler, M., 174–175
Principals
    conflict with teachers, 62–63
    isolation of teachers from, 104–105
    as leaders of effective schools, 57–58
    selection and reassignment of, 49–50
Problems
    dilemmas versus, 6
    importance of framing, 5, 72–74
    kinds of, 5–6
Professional development, effective schools
    and, 54–56
Professionalism of teachers, 20–21
    community involvement and, 22–23, 27,
        32–35
    curriculum decisions and, 22
    instructional decisions and. *See* Instruction
        methods
    teacher education and, 23–32
Prunty, John, 65–66 n. 3, 102
Purkey, Stewart, 65 n. 2, 65–66 n. 3, 90

Radley, Alan, 9 n. 6
Ralph, John, 196 n. 5
Ravitch, D., 85, 89, 90, 97, 182
Raywid, Mary Anne, 84 n. 17, 92
Reagan, Ronald, 8 n. 2, 95
Reese, W., 90
Reform. *See* School reform
Remedial programs, 15
Resnick, D., 104
Resnick, L., 104
Ress, David, 157 n. 2
Ricks, Thomas, 196 n. 3
Ringstaff, Cathy, 158 n. 9, 158 n. 11
Rockman, Saul, 158 n. 7
Rockwell, Norman, 41

Roderick, M., 180
Rogers, John, 196 n. 6
Roosevelt High School (Washington, D.C.), 2
Rosenshine, B., 166
Roth, D., 85
Rowan, Brian, 65–66 n. 3, 68 n. 18, 102–105, 103, 146 n. 7
Rumberger, Russell W., 83–84 n. 10
Rutter, Robert, 83–84 n. 10

Samuelson, Robert, 157–158 n. 5
Sandholtz, Judith, 154, 158 n. 9, 158 n. 11
Sarason, Seymour, 9 n. 6, 83 n. 8
Schlesinger, Arthur, Jr., 94–96, 105
Schmidt, William H., 67 n. 12
School reform
    assessment focus, 104
    bottom-up approaches to, 51–52
    as choice versus mandate, 53–54
    criticism of schools, 112
    curriculum change, 87–89
    decentralization, 89–90, 104–105
    effectiveness of, 14–15, 80–81, 190–195
    for effective schools. *See* Effective schools
    efficiency in schooling, 99, 103, 114
    fundamental, 129–140
    historical perspective on, 76–79, 91–97, 99–102
    incremental, 79–83, 129, 130–140
    institutional perspective on, 102–105
    instruction methods in. *See* Instruction methods
    nationalizing, 111–112
    partial, 191
    recurring reform, 91–97, 99–102
    shift from teacher-centered instruction, 18, 86–87, 103–105, 129–140
    strategies for, 190
    sustainable, 192–193
    top-down approaches to, 51, 52, 56–57
    in urban schools. *See* Urban schools
    value conflicts in, 97–102, 103
School-within-a-school program, 14–15
Schorr, Lisbeth, 84 n. 19
Schramm, Wilbur, 158 n. 15
Scott, W. R., 104
Self-fulfilling prophecy, 15–16
Shapiro, M. S., 87
Shuell, T., 168, 169
Siegel, F., 117
Silberman, Charles, 84 n. 14, 88, 93
Silvernail, David, 157 n. 2, 158 n. 7
Simon, Herbert, 9 n. 7
Slavin, Robert, 84 n. 23, 91, 93, 96, 167
Smith, Louis, 65–66 n. 3, 102
Smith, Marshall, 65 n. 2, 65–66 n. 3, 90
Socialization role of schools, 141–142

Socrates, 18
Spencer, L., 183 n. 3
Spindler, George, 131, 146 n. 5
Spindler, Louise, 131, 146 n. 5
Stake, R., 86, 146 n. 4
Standards
    No Child Left Behind and, 112, 165, 171, 180, 192
    school reform based on, 190
    standardization versus, 115
Steele, Donald, 48
Stephens, J. M., 138, 146 n. 9
Stereotypes
    self-fulfilling prophecy and, 15–16
    for urban schools and students, 13–17, 118–122
Stiles, Lindley, 26 n.
Stodolsky, S., 163, 168
Stone, S., 180
Student-centered instruction
    classroom indicators of, 135, 166–170, 175–180
    impact of accountability movement on, 165, 170–183
    move toward, 18, 86–87, 103–105, 129–140
    nature of, 133, 160
    objective analysis of, 135–140
    teacher-centered instruction versus, 132–134, 161–162
Students. *See* At-risk students; Labeling students
Superintendents
    of Arlington, Virginia schools, 3–4, 42–69
    of Atlanta, Georgia schools, 48
    conflict with teachers, 62–63
    district policies and, 45–65
    expectations for, 116–118
    isolation of teachers from, 104–105
    lack of research on, 44
    as leaders of effective schools, 58–61
    in national offices, 111, 117
    of New York City schools, 47, 53, 55–56
    turnover of, 120
Suydam, M., 86, 146 n. 4
Swerdlick, Steve, 65

Taylor, M., 172
Teacher-centered instruction
    classroom indicators of, 135, 166–170, 175–180
    hybrids of teacher-centered progressivism, 163, 179–180
    impact of accountability movement on, 165, 170–183
    move away from, 18, 86–87, 103–105, 129–140
    nature of, 132–133, 160
    objective analysis of, 135–140

student-centered instruction versus, 132–134, 161–162
Teacher education, 23–38
  in-service programs, 54–56
  need for change in, 23–32, 35–38
  proposed training model, 35–38
  reports of teacher interns, 28–32
  teacher versus social worker role and, 32–35
Teachers
  of academically talented students, 17
  of at-risk students, 81–83
  certification of, 102–103
  community involvement of, 22–23, 27, 32–35
  computer use and. *See* Computers in classrooms
  conflict with administrators, 62–63
  of educationally disadvantaged students, 13–17, 81–83, 120–122
  education of. *See* Teacher education
  helplessness and frustration of, 20–21
  influences on, 18–19
  in-service training for, 54–56
  instructional decisions of, 18–19, 145–146. *See also* Instruction methods
  isolation from administrators, 104–105
  professionalism of. *See* Professionalism of teachers
  quality of, 15
  relationships with students and parents, 22–23, 27, 32–35
  roles of, 22–23, 27, 32–35
  shift from teacher-centered instruction, 18, 86–87, 103–105, 129–140
  technical assistance programs for, 55–56
  types of, 15–17
  in Urban Teacher Corps, 1–2, 8 n. 2, 26, 27–32
Teaching cultures, 144–145
Technical assistance programs, 55–56
Testing. *See* Assessment
Thucydides, 18
Tibballs, J., 166, 184 n. 8
Timar, T. B., 91
Toch, Thomas, 65 n. 1
Top-down reform, 51, 52, 56–57
Trotter, Andrew, 157–158 n. 5
Tyack, David, 68 n. 20, 88, 90, 94, 96, 102, 146 n. 9, 181

U.S. Department of Education
  effective schools and, 63–64
  recurring waves of school reform and, 100–101
Urban schools, 111–123. *See also* Glenville High School (Cleveland, Ohio); *names of specific cities*

  agenda for 2000s, 115–118, 122–123
  at-risk students and. *See* At-risk students
  Great Cities Improvement Project (GCIP), 14–15
  historical perspective on, 113–115
  ideal size of, 15–16, 17
  myths concerning, 118–122
  nationalizing education reform, 111–112
  in popular culture, 111–112
  reflections on reform in, 188–196
  research on computers in classrooms, 151–153
  stereotypes of, 15–17, 118–122
  unique problems of, 112
  variations among, 115, 116–117
Urban Teacher Corps, 1–2, 8 n. 2, 26, 27–32

Vallas, Paul, 120
Value conflicts, 97–102, 103
  capitalist system and, 101
  elite classes and, 98, 101–102
  recurring waves of school reform and, 99–102
Viadero, D., 166, 174–175
Vicars, William, 68 n. 20

Washington, D.C. schools
  Cardozo Project/Urban Teacher Corps, 1–2, 8 n. 2, 26, 27–32
  Roosevelt High School, 2
Watzlawick, P., 146 n. 3
Weakland, J., 146 n. 3
Webb, L. Dean, 65–66 n. 3
Wehlage, Gary, 83–84 n. 10
Weick, K., 104, 105
Weinfeld, Frederic D., 65 n. 2
Weinstein, C., 166
Weir, M., 90
Westbury, I., 86
White, E. E., 83 n. 6
White, Michael, 117
Whole school reform, 190
Willis, P., 101
Willower, Donald, 67–68 n. 15
Wilson, Cynthia, 65 n. 1, 66 n. 5, 66 n. 7
Wilson, S., 173
Wittrock, Merlin, 84 n. 20
Wolcott, Harry, 67–68 n. 15, 146 n. 4
Woodward, Bob, 196 n. 3

Yee, G., 120, 174
York, Robert L., 65 n. 2

Zehm, Stanley, 83 n. 5
Zimmerman, J., 161
Zoch, P., 183 n. 3

About the Author

Larry Cuban is professor emeritus of education at Stanford University. He has taught courses in the history of school reform, curriculum, instruction, and leadership. He has been faculty sponsor of the Stanford/Schools Collaborative and Stanford's Teacher Education Program. His background in the field of education prior to becoming a professor included 14 years of teaching high school social studies in ghetto schools, directing a teacher education program that prepared returning Peace Corps volunteers to teach in inner-city schools, and serving 7 years as a district superintendent. Trained as a historian, he received a B.A degree from the University of Pittsburgh in 1955 and an M.A from Cleveland's Case Western Reserve University 3 years later. On completing his Ph.D. work at Stanford University in 1974, he assumed the superintendency of the Arlington, Virginia, Public Schools, a position he held until returning to Stanford in 1981. Since 1988, he has taught three times in local high school semester-long courses in U.S. History and Economics. Between 1981 and 2001, students in the School of Education selected Cuban for an award in excellence in teaching seven times.

His major research interests focus on the history of curriculum and instruction, educational leadership, school reform, and the uses of technology in classrooms. His most recent books are: *Cutting Through the Hype: A Taxpayer's Guide to School Reform* (2006, with Jane David), *The Blackboard and the Bottom Line: Why Schools Can't Be Businesses* (2004), *Powerful Reforms with Shallow Roots: Improving Urban Schools* (2003, edited with Michael Usdan), *Why Is It So Hard to Get Good Schools?* (2003), and *Oversold and Underused: Computers in the Classroom* (2001).